Three Men in a Raft

Three Men in a Raft

An improbable journey down the Amazon

BEN KOZEL

Pan Macmillan Australia

First published 2002 in Macmillan by Pan Macmillan Australia Pty Limited
This Pan edition published 2003 by Pan Macmillan Australia Pty Limited
St Martins Tower, 31 Market Street, Sydney

Reprinted 2003

National Library of Australia
Cataloguing-in-Publication Data:

Kozel, Ben.
Three men in a raft : an improbable journey down the Amazon.

ISBN 0 330 36460 X.

1. Kozel, Ben - Journeys - Amazon River Region. 2. Borthwick, Scott - Journeys - Amazon River Region. 3. Angus, Colin - Journeys - Amazon River Region. 4. Rafting (Sports) - Amazon River. 5. Amazon River Region - Description and travel. I. Title.

918.110464

Typeset in Galliard by Midland Typesetters
Printed in Australia by McPherson's Printing Group
Text design by Deborah Parry Graphics
Cartographic art by Laurie Whiddon, Map Illustrations

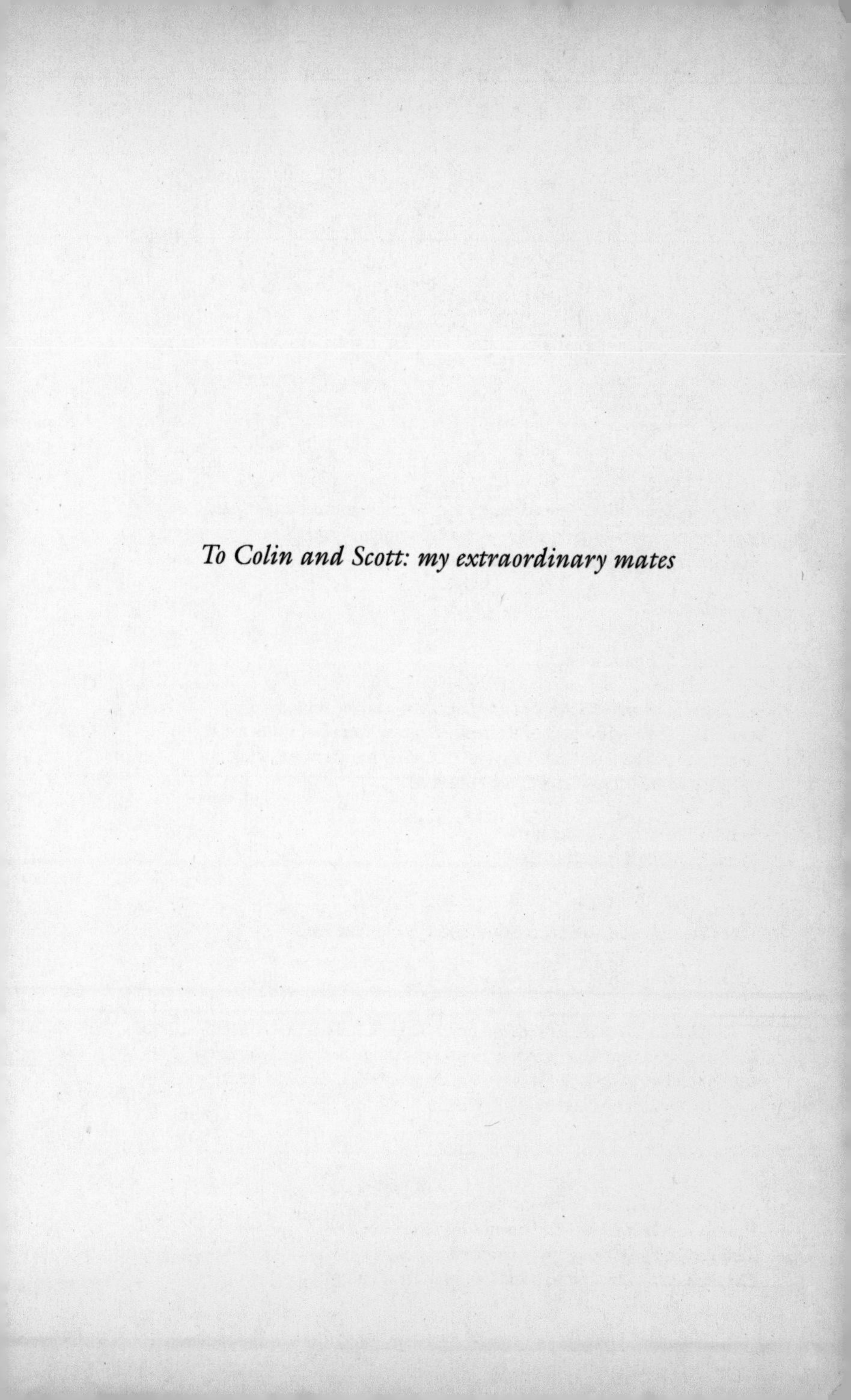

To Colin and Scott: my extraordinary mates

Contents

The Amazon		viii–ix
The Headwaters of the Amazon		xi
Prologue		xiii
1.	Peru	1
2.	From the Pacific Ocean	13
3.	The Coastal Desert	32
4.	Colca Canyon	46
5.	The Source of the Amazon	56
6.	The Apurimac	82
7.	Instinct	110
8.	The Portage	122
9.	Trial by Whitewater	134
10.	The Guerrillas	164
11.	The Militias	185
12.	The Ucayali	197
13.	Iquitos	220
14.	Heading for Brazil	236
15.	The Race for the New Millennium	252
16.	Manaus	266
17.	The True Amazon	275
18.	The Delta	291
19.	The Atlantic	308
Epilogue		313

PANAMA CITY
PANAMA
VENEZU
Medellin
BOGOTÁ
Cali
COLOMBIA
QUITO
Rio
ECUADOR
Rio
Rio
Japurá
Napo
Amazon
Guayaquil
Içá
Pebas
San Pablo de Loreto
Santo Antônio do Içá
Amatura
Iquitos
Tabatinga
Ucayali
Requena
Juruá
Piura
PERU
searched by drug police
Rio
Orellana
near collision with lancha
Pu
Rio
Trujillo
Pucallpa
Rio
Pacific
Rio Branco
Cerro de Pasco
Huancayo
LIMA
Rio
Machu Picchu
Ayacucho
Cuzco
Apurimac
Ica
Ocean
BOI
Mt Mismi
Lake Titicaca
Arequipa
LA PAZ
Camaná
ANDES

The Amazon

SCALE 1:14,000,000
0
500
Kilometres
Atlantic Ocean
GEORGETOWN
PARAMARIBO
CAYENNE
GUYANA
SURINAME
FRENCH GUIANA
LA
Boa Vista
Macapá
Ponte Taipu
start of the delta
Marajó Island
Vigia
Vigia Canal
Belém
Porto de Moz
Gurupá Canal
Negro
Amazon
Manaus
Parintins
Santarém
Itacoatiara
Manacapuru
Codajás
Coari
Madeira
Rio Tapajós
Rio Iriri
Rio
Imperatriz
Rio Xingu
BRAZIL
Porto Velho
Rio Araguaia
Tocantins
VIA
Cuiabá
BRASÍLIA

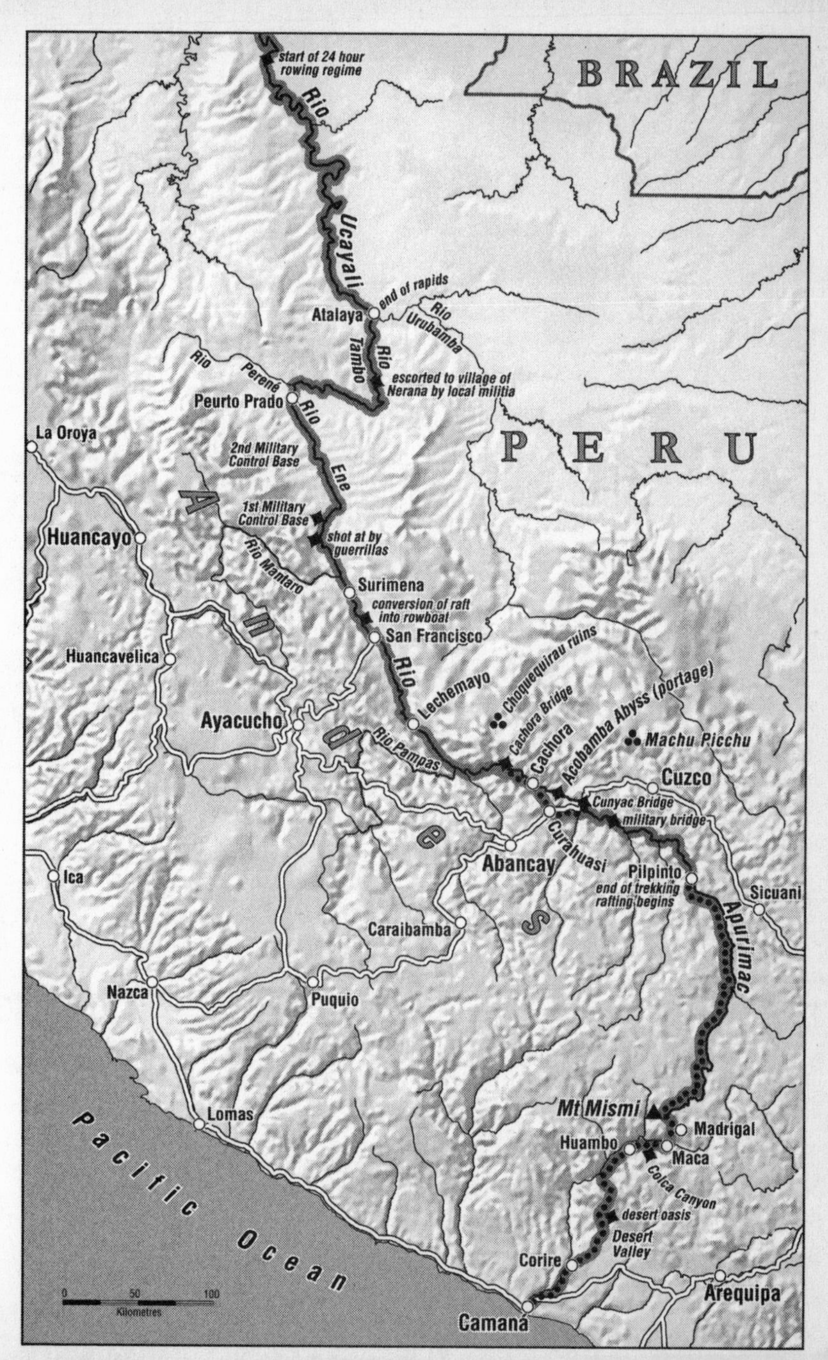

The Headwaters of the Amazon

PROLOGUE

24 August 1999: Kicking Horse River, British Columbia, Canada

The world turned black, deafeningly loud and ice-cold. In the space of a few seconds, my chest constricted and relaxed a dozen times. I wanted air, lots of it, but those first few gasps brought in nothing but liquid.

More than air, I craved light. For in that frozen moment, when the inflatable raft had propped on its edge before finally tipping over, I was certain I'd looked down into oblivion.

My helmet butted up against taut rubber. Neck ligaments crunched. I was still beneath the boat, running out of oxygen, and yet, strangely, I felt sure the thick, wet darkness would squeeze the life out of me before I drowned. Into my ears, the thunderous roar of the river pounded. It was as though I'd been thrown into a stampede of terrified animals. 'Kicking Horse' had seemed an odd name for a river, up to now.

I made another grab for light and air. This time my head punched through the surface – but even then, it was by no means a permanent arrangement. My eyes felt numbed, vision blurred by the cold water splashed across my corneas.

I watched my friend (and only companion that afternoon), Colin Angus, haul himself onto the upturned boat. Quickly, he unravelled a length of strapping from his waist and hooked one end onto the raft's perimeter rope. Then, holding the other end of the strapping to his stomach, he leant back and over the edge, using his weight to make the boat's edge a pivot point. As Colin deliberately toppled backwards into the river, the four-metre inflatable flipped upright. He'd worked the summer as a commercial raft guide, and his experience showed.

The boat looked healthier, but my own situation was now worse. While I'd been marvelling at the Canadian's smoothly executed response, diverging currents had pulled us well away from each other. Getting back to the raft wouldn't be a quick exercise, and it wouldn't be easy.

I suddenly remembered something Colin had mentioned earlier that day, when I'd picked his brains on the topic of flipping: 'Keep your legs up. Don't try standing.' People had been known to get their feet caught in a gap between the riverbed rocks. The force of the current had then pushed them over and they'd drowned. As easy as that. I made sure I flapped about as close to the surface as I could.

To my own great shame, I'd never been at home in the water. Perhaps it was genetics. No one in my family could play a musical instrument, and similarly, none of us rated ourselves as much of a swimmer. In truth, though, keeping your head above water is a big ask for anyone in rapids. Sloppy waves came from all directions, bobbing me up and down like the float on a fishing line – a fair analogy, except that I wasn't floating too well in the first place. The water in my belly had taken on the role of a lead weight, and I felt the walls of my stomach stretching as more of the silty brown stuff cascaded down my throat.

This wasn't my first time shooting rapids – it was my second. The first had been three years before, a tourist rafting trip on the Tully River in far north Queensland. I could hardly label it a *whitewater* experience, however. Someone had forgotten to open the dam that morning, meaning the volume of flow below it was much less than usual. The resultant sleepy rapids had managed to coax little more than a few subdued 'yee-ha's from the punters on board.

There was no such dud performance from the Kicking Horse today. Her rapids were in full bloom. Late August heat was biting hard into the Rocky Mountains' reserves of snow and ice, which, mixed with the chalky soil gathered up by the countless glacial trickles, had made rivers of iced coffee (in temperature as well as colour). Water levels were high. It was a good time of year to be on the hunt for big whitewater.

This time, I wasn't the tourist punter looking for a rush of blood to spice up his weekend; today was the beginning of active training. In two weeks I would be in South America, one of three men with their sights set on travelling the Amazon River from source to sea. Among many other things, it meant getting familiar with the idea of being tossed around for a month on one of the river's longest and most tormented tributaries – the Apurimac.

In effect, today's practice run was no different from the hepatitis, tetanus and yellow fever vaccinations that had already been pumped into my veins: an inoculative dose of adrenalin, a shot in the arm against the mighty Amazon itself. Yet as I struggled to reach the relative safety of the raft, the term 'practice run' seemed woefully inadequate. 'Baptism of fire' or 'prelude to disaster' sounded more appropriate.

The feeling was going from my hands and feet, and my confidence was fast dissolving. I was stunned by the water's power, shocked by how defenceless I was in it. Compared with what was promised to us in the Apurimac, running this section of 'the Horse' was meant to be a lazy cruise, a gentle breaking-in. Half choking on another involuntary mouthful, I began to rethink just how much I'd chosen to bite off – more to the point, what exactly I was about to start chewing on.

Colin's proposition had arrived by post four months earlier, on 17 April, at the end of a particularly rotten day at work. I was supervisor of a rainforest planting project near Mackay, a sugar-cane town on Queensland's central coast. Not a bad job, except for the unruly antics of my team of teenage trainees, and the apathetic local council who'd commissioned the project in the first place. On the day that letter arrived, both parties had driven me to the point of breakdown. In that sort of mood, I was liable to make a split-second decision, and agreeing to a six-month paddling trip down the world's second-longest river brought instant relief.

More than a long river voyage, it would be a journey from one side of South America to the other. I always knew the Amazon spilt into the Atlantic Ocean, not far from the Equator, on the continent's east coast; what had surprised me was the fact that the river started in the Andes of southern Peru, a mere 250 kilometres from the Pacific Ocean. The plan was to trek this distance before putting our boat in the river.

Working back from the Atlantic, the Amazon's most

distant source was an obscure peak named Mount Mismi. At 5650 metres, it wasn't exceptionally high by Andean standards, nor was it meant to be a technically difficult mountain to climb, although at those altitudes, the air promised to be thin. Slotting this initial trek into the bigger picture, our goal was to cover 7000 kilometres completely under our own power. No vehicles, motors or sails would be involved at any stage. Crew-wise, there'd be just Colin, myself and a 23-year-old South African named Scott Borthwick, whom I'd never met. Three blokes who had never done anything like this before . . .

It shocked me to discover that not until quite recently had the first team traced the Amazon successfully from source to sea. In 1986, a team led by a Pole and an American reached the mouth in kayaks. Only one other person had made it since then. This was a South African, Mike Horn, who had succeeded using a peculiar craft known as a 'hydrospeed', with which you have to trail your legs in the water and kick for propulsion. It seemed totally bizarre to me. More than 1000 people had climbed Everest, the highest peak in the world, yet, only *three* people could say they'd travelled the entire Amazon, the mightiest river in the world. If we got there, we'd be numbers four, five and six. On top of this, we'd also become the first team to do it by raft.

The opportunity to appear so high up on the list had drawbacks in so far as finding out what we could expect on the journey. My local library had no shortage of books discussing the wildlife and indigenous peoples of Amazonia. There were even several prominent accounts of explorers and naturalists who'd spent time living there, tucked away in some remote pocket of rainforest. Pickings proved slim, though, when I wanted something more specific to our plans.

For instance, an account was available of Spaniard

Francisco de Orellana's 1542 journey from the Napo River in Ecuador down the Amazon to the Atlantic. But more than 450 years had passed since then and he'd had a crew of 50, so his log held little relevance. (Incidentally, it was Orellana who'd given the river its name, after his men mistook long-haired, spear-wielding Indian men for a race of female warriors from Greek mythology called the Amazons.) More recently, a few people had either kayaked, sailed or motored down various lengths of the flat portion of the river, recording their experiences as they went. Fewer still had tackled the Apurimac and lived to document their experience.

The most accessible was Joe Kane's account of the 1986 expedition. *Running the Amazon* (published in 1989 by Vintage Books, New York) is widely regarded as a classic of modern adventure. For us, it would assume the role of guidebook and Bible, although at times it seemed a story more of the seamier side of group politics than of adventure. A second book from that expedition, written by Francois Odendaal and entitled *Rafting the Amazon* (1992, BBC Consumer Publishing, London) contradicts several of Kane's claims. Theirs was a big team (ten altogether, including a doctor and a film crew) with a big budget and a fair whack of expertise and experience among its members. In almost every respect, the structure of their expedition seemed light years away from ours; the only elements we appeared to share were a spread of nationalities and English as a common language. As far as the nature of the river went, of course, what they encountered was destined for us as well.

The essence of the journey had been brewing in Colin's mind for half a year. 'Chopping wood when it's minus forty gets you thinking about the tropics,' he'd said, recalling the moment when the initial spark of a plan had ignited. Twice daily throughout the bitter winter just gone, he'd driven into the forest, cut up fallen dead pine and spruce trees, then delivered them to the fireplaces of homes and businesses. The job had been ideal for him. Colin was a one-man show in many ways, and a habitual daydreamer. 'Any job where I have to use my head means I don't have my ideas and imagination to myself,' he insisted.

Menial tasks that would drive most deep thinkers to the verge of madness instead allowed Colin to formulate plans, to test his ideas mentally, and to devise inexpensive means of carrying them out. The Amazon represented more than a yearning for somewhere warmer than Canada: it was part of a world that beckoned to him through his imagination. The thing that separated Colin from the majority of daydreamers was his habit of making imaginings reality.

I met Colin Angus in 1997, at one of London's seediest backpacker hostels. We'd shared the fetid air of a basement common room, and chatted for hours among the pot-smoking Brits and a hoard of job-hungry Eastern Europeans. Our motives were the same: make some fast money, live cheaply and get out of gloomy London as soon as possible. For several weeks we had laboured together at a garden nursery near Heathrow Airport and lived with a neurotic Polish family who illegally sublet the rooms of their welfare apartment. In the spring of that year we pooled our savings to nurse a clapped-out Volkswagen campervan down the western side of France and across the high roads of the Pyrenees. We had driven across many a mountain river together; now, it appeared, we would raft along them together.

I knew Colin well. Scott, the South African, remained only a voice with a funny accent at the other end of the phone line. Colin had met him after returning to London from the campervan trip. They'd worked for a company that converted coal cellars into added living space. Scott had been committed to the Amazon project for almost as long as Colin.

On top of the rough journey outline supplied with his proposal, Colin had included for me a short bio that Scott had written about himself. It didn't reveal much except that he was an avid watersports athlete, worked at a university in England, and in his spare time studied Amazon botany. On paper he seemed the star recruit.

Up until April 1999, there had been an Englishman involved as well. He'd pulled out, citing his reasons as a serious romance, a new house, and its associated mortgage. A replacement was needed. 'I'm a little hurt you didn't think of me when you first came up with the plan,' I jibed Colin, semi-seriously. Of course, it was understandable. A couple of years had passed since our last meeting, a year since our last communication. 'I thought you'd be studying,' Colin had shrugged. 'I never really expected to hear back from you.'

Whether he thought there was a slim chance of me being available or a slim chance of me making it to the Atlantic, I don't know. His reply had made me grimace all the same. Every year for the past three years, I'd claimed I was going back to university to finish my science degree. I'd been happy to put it off yet again and, after the possibility of a free passage on a Vancouver-bound freighter had come to nothing, I bought the cheapest one-way flight I could find. Within a couple of months of receiving the letter, I found myself on Colin's homeground, in the province of Alberta, south-western Canada.

Colin's base for the last two years had been Canmore, an hour's drive west of Calgary, and the same distance east from the Kicking Horse River, which is in the neighbouring province of British Columbia. The town had also doubled as our Amazon launch pad for the past couple of months.

Throughout that time, I had slept on the couch in Colin's tiny apartment and worked as a labourer on a construction site while he worked as a raft guide on the highly tamed Kananaskis River. In the evenings, we played chess and talked river strategy. We also typed out sponsorship proposals, although we knew deep down it was unlikely there would be any favourable replies for a bunch of rogue amateurs like ourselves.

In terms of finances, we were all (the absent Scott included) doing things by the skin of our teeth. The money I'd set aside for going back to study covered most of my initial bare-bones costs. To make ends meet, I'd sold everything on my short list of assets (which didn't include a car, unfortunately). Luckily, a lot of my old backpacking gear was still in acceptable condition, including my sleeping bag. Colin had picked up a new one in Calgary for $30 (Canadian) and had spent the same amount on new hiking boots.

The raft was the only piece of equipment on which we all insisted on spending enough money to ensure good quality. Colin's boss had offered to get one in for us at the discounted price available to operators in the rafting industry. It was a saving we couldn't pass up. Unfortunately, the boss's sense of urgency hadn't mirrored our own and the boat had only just arrived from the manufacturer in Idaho. Had we simply driven down south over the border to pick it up ourselves, we would have been in training six weeks earlier.

Only the weekends were free for us to take the raft out for a spin. Ideally, we would have loved to focus on nothing but our preparations, but the weekdays were chewed up trying to earn enough money before we left for South America. It was a horrible dilemma. However, it was one in which certainty beat mere probability. Spending more time in the raft *might* save our lives on the Apurimac; scraping together a few more bucks now *definitely* meant we'd be able to feed ourselves for a few more weeks while we were there.

Scarceness of funds was also the reason why I would meet Scott for the first time only five days before we boarded the plane to Lima in Peru. Colin was annoyed about it. Apparently, just three months before, Scott had flown home to South Africa to visit friends, and while there, he had blown most of the cash he'd set aside for the Amazon. He got back to London sporting a good tan but not much left in the bank. Time that had seemed critical for building team skills and cooperation, and for simply getting to know each other, had become time Scott needed for making enough money to cover his share of the costs.

Time was no less critical on this day on the Kicking Horse. The cold had penetrated deep into my muscles. My legs – from the start, stiff from the previous day's hike up Canmore's Mount Rundle – were starting to lose their kick. Still, I'd managed to flap my way back to the raft.

Bobbing alongside it now, it was all I could do to grip stiff, unfeeling fingers around the perimeter rope. My arms, jelly-like, and burning despite the cold, didn't stand a chance of pulling me from the Horse's gluey embrace. Colin reached down and grabbed the shoulder straps of my life jacket. I was hoisted into the boat, convulsing, wide-eyed and babbling nonsense, as though I'd just cheated death. I looked up at him and saw his face cast in the unmistakable gape of exhilaration.

I couldn't believe it! He had *revelled* in the whole thing! And it was this reaction, conflicting so strongly with my own, that stunned me as much as anything. More so than before, hardening truths needed to be faced up to: no experience, no money, and two team members who didn't know each other from a bar of soap. Just a fortnight from the start of the journey, they seemed like the only three certainties. And they seemed overwhelming.

So why was I going?

I was going precisely because the Amazon for me was an unknown, illuminated by the odd flickering fact. Whatever scant knowledge I did have drove my curiosity. For instance, before it reaches the Atlantic, the Amazon collects water from 15,000 tributaries and drains a basin the size of Australia. And there was more – much more. The mouth of the river is 276 kilometres wide. Each day, some 1,500,000 tonnes of sediment dye the ocean in a fan spreading 250 kilometres out from shore.

As a young boy, I had thumbed through atlases, always pausing longest on the maps of South America. I recalled being mesmerised by macabre TV documentaries in which swimming cows were gobbled up by piranhas and the odd human corpse got cut from the belly of a six-metre-long anaconda.

I was going because what would happen to us there was something I could only guess at. And even then I knew my guess would be far from the mark. That in itself, was a force I couldn't fight. For months my thoughts had raced, trying to imagine what the land would feel like and what it meant to travel down a river so mindbogglingly huge that it carried 20 per cent of all the freshwater on earth.

Jagged cliffs? Smoking volcanoes? Natives blowing poison darts? Guerrilla warfare? Unrecorded jungle diseases? Man-eating fish? Cascading waterfalls? The unknown was seductive, and it ate at me.

One proverb had always struck a chord in me. Put nice

and simply, it goes: 'It is better to regret something you have done than to regret something you haven't done.' If going to the Amazon meant a one-way trip to oblivion, then so be it.

ONE PERU

9 September 1999: approaching the city of Cuzco

The plane dipped suddenly in the turbulence as if it were an insect being swatted by an enormous hand. My stomach sank as much from a sense of foreboding as from the dip itself – were we out of control and about to crash? I tried to block out images of severed body parts spread out over hillside wreckage. In their place, I pictured a diligent ground crew-mechanic, whistling through a comprehensive pre-flight safety check. Conjuring up such a fantasy in a poor Latin American country like Peru required supreme effort.

I was calmed by the knowledge that, along with the likes of myself, this aircraft also shuttled wealthy jet-setters. They too were on their way to the old Inca capital of Cuzco, Peru's centrepiece of international tourism. Among other notable attributes, Cuzco is the oldest inhabited settlement in the Americas. Bearing this in mind, I was most likely aboard the pride of the Aero Continente fleet. Nevertheless, right down to the dour uniforms of the flight attendants and the paisley-trimmed vinyl upholstery, it was obvious that little had changed since this aircraft's inaugural flight.

In wake of the dip, every passenger jiggled to an aftershock of wobbles, bumps and tremors. Then, the smooth ride returned. Dubiously bolted-down cabin furniture ceased rattling. I had just settled my nerves when the cabin began tilting forward. My fingernails dug into the armrest and a fearful shudder passed through me. Several seconds passed. The air remained free of panicked screams, and I realised that nothing more sinister than the descent into Cuzco had begun.

This nervous edge surprised me. I'd flown with second-rate airlines before and it had felt positively indulgent. My time as a poor backpacker taught me long ago to gratefully accept the needling seat springs and dodgy toilets of poorly cared-for passenger hulks. They were cheap, and fell out of the sky only slightly more regularly than those of the expensive airlines.

Perhaps my mood stemmed from fatigue. The last week had been a flurry of tying up loose ends, packing gear, making a sequence of flights and a mad dash around Lima for last-minute arrangements and purchases. Fittingly, the end of our first day in South America had been topped off with all-night salsa dancing with three beautiful Lima girls. We'd arrived at the airport for our 4 a.m. flight to Cuzco with hips still gyrating and heads full of sangria and tequila.

Blinking away sleep, I peered out of the scratched window onto a brown, treeless landscape of rolling hills, especially dull-looking in the pre-dawn light. A middle-aged Peruvian man sitting next to me leant across and said proudly, in heavily accented English, 'Is the Pampa.' I recognised the word. It was the name for the plateau grasslands lying in the rain shadow of the high Andes. The terrain here looked like a rumpled carpet, without a hint of the true immensity of the mountains that stretch like a spine down the western edge of South America.

Abruptly, the weary heads of Colin and Scott appeared above the seat backs in front of me. 'Maaaate! How do you feel?' Colin's tongue-in-cheek imitation of the classic Australianism sounded very hoarse.

'Knackered,' I replied mechanically. 'I need to get off this plane and into bed.' Scott yawned in agreement but knew as well as I did that there would be little chance of such luxury. He turned to the smiling Peruvian alongside me and asked him if he was from Cuzco. I only half listened as the man happily began his spiel about the old city's tourist attractions. Instead, my attention centred on the faces of the two men in front of me – the two faces, the two personalities, I would be around every day for the next six months.

Colin looked even younger than he had in England. Clean-shaven and with hair neatly parted, his complexion still radiated a strangely boyish glow that belied his 27 years. In a strange way, the gap between his two front teeth masked any evidence of the hard, rugged lifestyle he'd maintained for almost a decade. At age nineteen, he'd sailed from the shores of his native Vancouver Island, crossing the Pacific Ocean in an eight-metre boat. It said something about the size of the man's testicles that he had regarded a weekend sailing course and digesting several technical manuals as adequate preparation for this.

Scott was a native of South Africa's administrative capital, Pretoria, but had settled himself in the UK for several years as he had the luxury of dual citizenship. He worked as a procurement officer in the Finance Department of London's prestigious King's College. When the professors and other resident academics begged the institution for the latest research equipment, it was Scott they went to with their wish lists. He would then track down and buy their microscopes, solar panels or particle accelerators.

He was very fair, with the sort of hair colour and bright blue eyes known to make young children in remote jungle villages flee in terror. At first he had appeared subdued, almost shy. Amid all the final chaotic preparations and the whirl of anticipation created by the Amazon vortex, there hadn't been much chance for me to get to know this reserved 23 year old. Our first conversation had delved into the mechanics of kite flying, a hobby that he appeared to enjoy. I was more keen to find out about his interest in tropical flora.

'I heard you've been studying plants.'

'I'm sorry, what?'

'Amazon botany,' I reminded him.

'Oh, that . . . Well, no. It just sounded like a good way to get sponsors' attention.' Fair enough.

At first glance, there was nothing extraordinary about his manner to make me form any early opinion of him. Instead, I'd borrowed Colin's opinion and trusted my friend's judgment of the quiet South African. One thing about Scott was apparent from the moment I met him, however, and it explained why he'd been included in this project from the start. Like Colin, he was the sort of guy who would have a crack at anything. In the course of eleventh-hour rafting practice, I'd found myself both envious of and impressed by his eagerness to tackle rapids, and his obvious confidence – especially praiseworthy given the fact that, like me, he had barely even set foot in a whitewater raft. Unlike me, though, he seemed to have a thirst for adrenalin that somehow overrode his sense of risk, dulled any urge to hold back. It was the type of gung-ho mettle that to me did not make good sense, and yet at the same time seemed something to aspire to. Was this a trait inherent to all successful adventurers?

As I continued to regard the South African through bloodshot eyes, a familiar line of thinking burnt across my mind. A wildfire of self-doubt, unopposed by my tired brain, fed on tinder-dry notions. Here I was, just days away from embarking on this journey, and the sheer enormity of it all struck me: from west coast to east coast across an entire continent, along the length of the world's mightiest river, and with nothing more than our legs and a four-metre-long inflatable raft.

Naturally, I realised the importance of careful calculations and problem-solving skills for any expedition that went off the beaten trail. Clear, rational thinking was a must – I felt I was capable of that. But how important was it to play by the rules of 'do first, think later'? Without a doubt, such an approach had been the driving force behind many renowned feats of exploration and endurance. I swallowed hard. Was I too cautious? Was my mind geared in such a way that it would resist and agonise over every step into this type of unknown? Would I end up a nervous wreck because of what lay ahead? Where would I draw the line on risk versus reward? All these questions had been circling around my head since that afternoon in Queensland almost five months earlier when Colin's letter had arrived. They infused my sleep as much as my waking hours, and still the answers remained fuzzy at best or else lacked form entirely.

Not surprisingly, it was still the whitewater leg that concerned me most. Joe Kane's book painted a grim picture of the Apurimac, and our grand total of five afternoons of rafting practice sounded tragically comical as preparation for a solid month of running big rapids. Those Rocky Mountain whitewater runs had taught me to see death in even the most benign-looking rapid. Sure, veteran rafters and kayakers might very well spout on about how wise it was to have respect for the moods of a river. A reserve of fear was 'healthy', it would hold one in great stead. But in my life up until then, ignorance had definitely been bliss.

A burst of rapid, crackling Spanish from the pilot buzzed through the cabin. The language student in me stirred, harked intently, then sighed. I could pick a couple of words out of the barrage, but could only guess that it was all something to do with our imminent landing. Nevertheless, I was thankful for the distraction and the chance to shelve my worries about the Apurimac for now. There was little to be gained by dwelling on what sort of wickedness was promised by that river. Besides, on our time-line of activity, it was still a few weeks away. It was time to focus on the immediate battle – a long overland trek to reach the summit of Mount Mismi, the ultimate source of the Amazon.

'Si, si,' nodded the old woman as I made a motion of bringing the bunch of dried leaves to my mouth. Her cracked and shrivelled lips framed just half-a-dozen teeth. Like almost all of the vendors in the Cuzco central market, she wore a convoluted layering of bright fabrics, the traditional outfit of Quechua women.

The leaves I inspected were from the infamous coca plant, the source of cocaine. While the intense narcotic derives illegally from an intensive refining process, medicinal benefits were available to the humblest of Peruvians by simply munching on the dried leaves. Chewed with a small wad of charcoal from the quinoa bush (the catalyst which orchestrates the release of active compounds), they were known to be especially handy in staving off *soroche* – altitude sickness. As a result, the coca leaf took prominent place in Andean travel lore. References to it littered the guidebooks. Perhaps as much out of an attraction for 'tasting the forbidden fruit' as from its promised impunity against *soroche*, we were quickly on its trail.

The air in Cuzco was thin. At 3300 metres, it was already more than half a kilometre higher than the Pyrenees mountain passes I'd hiked through some years before. After five minutes of wandering the cobbled streets, Colin, Scott and myself had each felt a shortness of breath, a vague giddiness, and the ache of excess lactic acid in our calves. But despite our lightheadedness, we were acutely aware of the fact that Cuzco squatted well below the dizzying heights of Mount Mismi.

'I read somewhere that people have been known to drop dead from altitude sickness at just 3000 metres,' Scott had said on our way to the market. Colin had thrown him a dark look, signalling this was far more than he needed to know – then he'd quickened his step. Scott spoke the truth. While pulmonary and cerebral oedemas weren't normally a threat until above 5000 metres, some folk were extra-sensitive. An oedema could strike fast, was very painful, and might inflict permanent damage to the brain and lungs.

The Quechua woman produced a golf-ball-sized aggregate of charcoal powder from some hidden pouch in her costume. With a dirty fingernail she dislodged three small pieces, deftly rolled them in several leaves, then handed me the final product. Alone, coca leaves might have tasted palatable enough. But the sharp bitterness of charcoal cast the whole experience of coca chewing in an unpleasant light.

Cuzco was not our starting point. Yet, just as it had been the chief staging point for conquests by the mighty Inca Empire, so now Cuzco became a crucial springboard from which to throw ourselves onto the Amazon. While we trekked to the summit of Mount Mismi then followed the Amazon's first trickles on foot as far as the upper Apurimac, the raft and other river equipment needed to be stored. Initially this had been a worry since we had no support crew. In a poor provincial city, gripped by corruption at the highest levels, and prone to almost ritualistic theft against travellers, where did one leave $4000 worth of gear for a month?

The South American Explorers Club solved our dilemma. This renowned institution, source of facts, figures and first-world respite for intrepid westerners, was our best bet for the secure storage of all the items we wouldn't need during the Mismi ascent. The live-in volunteer who answered the doorbell was a slim New Zealander named Mark. We explained our situation, but he made it clear there was no charity option – if we wanted to store some equipment we first needed to become members. I tried talking him into accepting a single membership, but he would have none of it. All three of us had to sign up.

I was caretaker of the 'kitty', the well-worn beige-coloured money belt into which equal sums were to be deposited by each of us when required. Although it guaranteed peace of mind, membership of the club was an unexpected expense, and a hefty one at that. I fumbled for the scrap piece of paper on which I had earlier scrawled under distinct headings a breakdown of our budget. The tip of my pen danced above the paper for a few seconds before coming down to hover menacingly above one particular total. I glanced up at Scott and Colin. Their nods silently ratified my decision: I shaved $120 from the generous total set aside for bribing the police and other officials.

Despite our last-ditch efforts to boost finances, the money situation still loomed potentially as party-pooping as any marauding crocodile or terminal jungle disease. Our shoestring was already fraying badly. We each had a similar amount of savings, and Scott and I had credit cards we could use as back-up. Still, our total operating budget of $16,000 (Australian) had to account for everything, and the equipment and flights had already chewed up over two-thirds of it. A total of $5000 to get all three of us through 7000 kilometres over six months – that worked out to be about 70 cents per kilometre. It was peanuts.

Our attempts at gaining sponsorship had been belated, and then made only half-heartedly. We did not regard ourselves that highly. A few ordinary blokes off the street, no pedigree, doubtful planning, no real experience in adventuring, out to simply have a go – that best described us. Our intentions were vague, usually based on little more than the crude maps and highly subjective quotes found in budget travel guides. People who did not even appreciate the enormity of such an undertaking gave us small chance of returning. For others, we had all but signed our death certificates by daring to venture into South America, full stop.

One week before we left, a journalist at the Canadian Press Office in Calgary got wind of our plans, interviewed us, and released a story. (Later she admitted to being sure that we wouldn't come back. It had been easy enough then to read between the lines: by running that initial story she had set herself up for the scoop when word of our deaths broke.) Had it not been for this media interest and for the semi-intoxicated urging of several drinking companions, we might not have bothered looking for sponsorship at all. As it turned out, the majority of our letters failed to generate even a reply confirming the anticipated 'thanks, but no thanks'.

The bus ride from Cuzco to Camaná proved to be strangely soothing. I'd suffered through my fair share of long coach trips between Australian cities and towns (the seating on board is never designed for we 'tall and graceful' types). But although my kneecaps wedged tighter than ever, and my head snapped back and forth to an endless sequence of bone-jarring potholes, I managed to sleep.

I awoke in the very early hours of morning. The bus snaked its way around a series of steep switchbacks and tight bends. The engine groaned with the struggle of the climb but was finally rewarded with a crest. In fact, this was the continental divide. The act of breathing had degenerated into the task of trying to suck enough air into my lungs. All that was left at this altitude was chill. We were much higher than Cuzco. The Andes rise sharply and unbroken for thousands of kilometres, like a high wall with no door, daring the inhabitants of either side to find an easy way over. There is a spectacular train journey from Lima to Huancavelica. Rising to nearly 6000 metres, the rail tracks are the world's highest. The conductor does his rounds with an oxygen tank and mask.

The narrow dirt road squiggled its way downwards to the Pacific coast. I could see little more than a diffuse blackness through the streaked window but the G-forces at work on my body provided me with a clear impression of the rugged terrain. True to form, the driver displayed all the classic third-world disrespect for it and the lives of everybody on board. At one point, as we skirted the outside edge of a bend, the left-hand side of the bus abruptly slumped. There was a grinding crunch of chassis metal on loose rock, then the tyre clawed its way back onto the unstable lip of road and away from the threshold of oblivion. Exasperated cries of '*Despacio! Despacio!*' came from a dozen passengers – 'Slow down! Slow down, you bloody maniac!' And this was the response from locals who quite possibly knew no standard of driving different from the bus driver's. I shuddered at the significance. It seemed even the most bread-and-butter travel experience in South America translated into adventure.

Nearing the sea, we sped through a murky dawn light. The view was a stark one. On the roadside, old and new political slogans were splashed across the smooth, flat faces of boulders. It wasn't frivolous graffiti; in Peru, democracy and freedom of speech have never been taken for granted.

The landscape was also marked in more obscure ways. Not far to the north stretched the dust-bowl plains of Nazca, home to the famous array of alienesque figures and straight lines whose origins have archaeologists stumped. They are the ancient equivalent of 'crop circles'. Only when aeroplanes started flying in the area were the figures revealed for the first time. Many experts believe that the lines marked out landing areas for spacecraft – indeed, the precision with which the shapes were drawn suggests that the designers had a view from the sky above.

The countryside felt tinged by the supernatural. Through the window of the bus, it seemed to murmur with secrets, whisperings of ghosts from all ages. And these could not be muffled by the thin coating of vegetation. I was surprised by what I was seeing. Cuzco had appeared barren, but against this landscape it now seemed abundant. What a bizarre place to begin an Amazon journey. It's a fact that more water rushes through the mouth of the Amazon in one day than out of the Murray River mouth in one year. From what was unfolding here on the opposite side of the world, a few of Australia's harshest deserts would be given a run for their money. In fact, the driest desert on the planet – the Atacama – lay just 300 kilometres to the south. In parts of the Atacama, rainfall has never been recorded. The contrast between here and the point for which we ultimately strove looked to be absolute.

For all of its desolation, the landscape beckoned. The low morning sun did its best to slice through the vapour haze, managing to coax a dull glitter from the Pacific Ocean, while plastic wrappers and junk lacked grass, shrubs or other foliage in which to remain discreet. Soon enough, rusting car hulks and assorted auto-part fragments adorned the road edge like some diabolically abstract piece of artwork commissioned by a mayor for the entrance to his town. The city of Camaná came next.

TWO
FROM THE PACIFIC OCEAN

13 September 1999 (day 1): Camaná

The beach was deserted, and filthy. The guidebook mentioned that La Punta was likely to be unclean but it said nothing about it looking almost post-apocalyptic. Several people in Camaná had proclaimed the charm of their coastal getaway. Camaná itself, set back five kilometres from the sea, with its belching cars, box-like buildings and seedy cafes, had struck me as the height of charmlessness.

'Many people come here from Arequipa,' the taxi driver had boasted, referring to Peru's second-largest city. He had quickly hauled the last of our backpacks from his car boot, then sped off in a pall of dust, back to Camaná, as if he thought he was at risk of catching something. And yet, colourfully festive posters, flapping against crumbled walls, conspired to press home the message that La Punta was a desirable seaside location. As I kicked at another pile of rubbish on the drab grey sand, I was struggling hard with that concept.

It was only early spring. The residents of Arequipa would swarm over this place in summer; however, this so-called 'resort' town had the feel of having been all but abandoned years earlier. Every building seemed to be in disrepair or half-ruined. Even the ocean looked haphazard. The water was a silted brown, and far from redeemed by the low-hanging overcast sky. There was even a certain ugliness to the way in which the waves broke against the shore.

Scott came and stood next to me, hands in his pockets. At the sight of the mess at my feet, he screwed up his nose in distaste. 'I don't fancy hanging around here for long,' he said. 'This place is quite a hole.'

I agreed entirely. 'Yeah, I kind of imagined having a dip in the surf then getting a nice send-off from a bunch of sexy local girls in bikinis.'

Colin walked towards us, filming Scott and me with a video camera, the prized component of our small electronic arsenal. 'Don't worry, mate. All's not lost. Maybe they'll go home and get their bikinis on.' He inclined his head towards a couple of figures on the esplanade.

Two elderly women hobbled along – the first people we'd seen in half an hour – each carrying live chickens by the feet. They stared as they walked. We waved. Two bewildered chickens were promptly hoisted in acknowledgment, like shots of tequila. That was as good a send-off as we were likely to get.

We bypassed Camaná township, and were instead funnelled towards the valley of the Camaná River. A succession of quiet hamlets littered the roadside. The houses became more crooked and earthier as they trickled down dusty lanes, soon dwindling altogether into fields. To the left stretched the fertile Camaná flood plain. On the right, the terrain rose steadily until it reached the base of a chain of uplands, sculpted from pale sands.

From the outset, my fully loaded backpack felt too heavy. I had more or less lived out of the thing for three years. First, it had been with me on a string of short conservation projects all over Queensland. Then it had accompanied me on a twelve-month backpacking pilgrimage through Europe. On the way back from there, it had suffered attacks of mould in South-East Asia. Following that, I had used it for the first four months of my work stint in Mackay, snubbing the spacious built-in wardrobe in my flat. Perhaps all this suggested a subconscious aversion to being settled. Whatever the case, I was accustomed to my peacock blue-and-black backpack always being somewhere nearby. I loved what it stood for.

Now, it was fit to burst. Whatever didn't fit inside was strapped onto the outside. I had never carried so much before. The main items of communal gear – maps, stove, pots and pans, tent, food and water filter – were divided between us. The final weight, tallied up with all my personal gear, neared 30 kilograms. It was immediately apparent in my hips and lower spine that this was more than the pack's waist harness and lumbar support were designed for. The shoulder straps pressed on me hard and creaked ominously. My trusty day-pack was brimming equally full and draped back to front over my chest. Although my shoulders protested more angrily than ever, this pack helped to balance my centre of gravity. It also supplied a comfortable resting spot for my arms.

For the first couple of hours, the simple act of walking drew heavily on my reserves of concentration. At the slightest change of direction, the load on my back would shift, gaining a momentum to tip me over and send me sprawling. Muscles and ligaments yelped as I tried to regain equilibrium. Much to the chagrin of chiropractors worldwide, I'm sure, my hopes centred on the belief that I'd soon be moulded into a posture that was immune to the strain. We reckoned on the trek to Mount Mismi lasting about ten days. If I was to get through the next 250 kilometres without being crippled, something needed to click into place fast.

We'd set forth from La Punta at a unified three abreast. But while I slowly came to grips with my heavy burden, Colin and Scott gained more and more ground on me. I struggled to find a rhythm. Compared with their smooth unhampered strides, I seemed to be plodding along. I could faintly hear them talking and see their hand gestures. It made me fume. There were things I wanted to chat about. This far back, though, I could only mutter to myself.

My face contorted into a grimace, and my eyes coldly returned the bewildered stares of villagers. I was annoyed – partly by the fact that my physical suffering had already begun, but more than this, it irked me that already there appeared to be chinks showing in the armour of our solidarity. Here at the back of the pack, I was left to endure alone.

We passed through the town of San Grigorio and rested on its outskirts, overlooking where the flood plain of the Camaná River abruptly and impressively bottlenecked. Haze obscured the details of the low, yet very rugged, mountains, lending the valley entrance an almost fairy-tale air. For several seconds, I imagined myself on a quest in a Tolkien novel.

Immediately to our right, the road bordered on a steep slope of earth. A breeze scattered swarms of dust particles across the face of the slope. I took another swig of water and noticed Scott peering at something protruding from the loose dirt. It took a few moments for me to focus properly on what it was. When I did, my mouth instantly went dry. Bones.

The unease in Scott's announcement left little room for doubt: 'Holy shit, boys! There's half a fucking human skeleton here.' There was a jawbone, several ribs and part of what must have been the pelvis. They were clearly old: bleached white and fissured. Erosion had exposed them.

'Could be an old cemetery up top,' I ventured, pointing to where the slope flattened out several metres above our heads. I had seen news reports of hillside cemeteries plagued by unruly coffins that migrated down the slope. Gravity had a habit of subverting the claim of 'final resting place'.

'Or maybe this lot know something about it,' stammered Scott. Colin and I followed his gaze up the road leading back to San Grigorio. Three short middle-aged men and a stooped woman stood by a ramshackle dwelling, watching silently. Any casual movement on their part might have relaxed us. Instead they were utterly still, hands by their sides, almost zombie-like in expression.

'Time to go, I think,' Colin murmured.

The warm afternoon breeze caressed my face but only gave me goosebumps. 'Good idea,' I agreed. Despite the aching all over my torso, I gladly re-shouldered the packs.

The shape of the valley was unlike any I had seen before and had a hypnotic effect. The Camaná River meandered from side to side across the level valley floor. The plain granted us an easy path through the already rugged foothills of the Andes. It varied between one and two kilometres wide. On either side, the plain ended at a steep face of barren rock. My knowledge of basic geology told me it could only be the carving power of a river that had created such a perpendicular landscape. My imagination, on the other hand, leant more towards the fancy of these crags having been conjured from the bowels of the earth by arcane magic. The rock walls fended off the late afternoon sun, casting shadows across everything below. They meant that the only way in or out of this valley was via each end. Their towering presence turned the Camaná Valley into a claustrophobiac's nightmare.

Almost every square centimetre of the plain was used as farmland. Water from distant snowy peaks burbled along irrigation channels that sustained a patchwork of fields. Donkeys stood idly by. The occasional rusting ute chugged along a dirt track. And scattered in their family groups, bending over the crops, were the field workers.

The responses to our passing by were mixed. Some groups broke into an excited chatter among themselves; one or two would muster the courage to wave, while our shouts of '*Hola!*' and '*Buenos dias!*' put smiles on the faces of even the most seasoned matriarchs. But as we pressed deeper into the valley and the light of day retreated, the level of wariness increased. Our passage began to be met with deadpan expressions and the now familiar but chilling pose of arms hanging limply by sides. For all we knew, this region might be the Peruvian equivalent of the US's Appalachian hillbilly country, where even the residents of nearby Camaná were despised.

As leaden twilight began to fail, the road bent close to three mud-walled huts. They were built on two levels that had been cut like enormous steps up from the road. Backing onto the steep slope of the valley, the rickety structures obviously clambered for high ground against the threat of flood. At road level, an attractive woman in her mid-thirties was emptying a bucket of rotten fruit in front of two pigs. She greeted us with a faint smile and a nod. Up on the first level, an old, shrivelled, yet sprightly, woman regarded us with barely concealed suspicion.

'It will be dark soon,' said the younger woman. 'Where are you going?' She spoke slowly and simply, making a rarely offered allowance for the fact that our Spanish might be rudimentary. At this early stage, she was correct.

'We're heading for Corire.' From our topographic maps, Corire was the nearest village of a size worth printing. It lay another two days' trekking to the north-east.

'Soon it will be night,' she repeated. We had been keeping an eye out for a campsite, but nowhere as yet had offered seclusion from the road and the apparently xenophobic attitude of the locals.

'Do you know a good place for us to camp?' Even in wobbly Spanish, my tone implied that we'd be very grateful for a show of hospitality. The question was deflected with a shrug. '*Muchillas grande*,' she noted. From the way we stood, the weight of our packs was obvious.

'We're hiking to Cuzco,' I proclaimed dumbly.

From her perch above, the old woman cackled. The younger woman snorted. 'It's not possible. There is no way through the mountains,' she stated with certainty. We knew from the maps, and from the recent account of the Amazon adventurer Mike Horn, that this was not true.

'Our maps say that it is possible,' Colin asserted. This was ignored.

'*Y muchos banditos!*' she continued, her tone more serious than before. 'These are very bad people. And you gringos have much that they want!'

Despite our westerners' reservations about travel in South America, this news came as something of a reality check. All of a sudden, the image of pistol-toting desperados pouring out from behind a rock to rob us of everything, then guaranteeing our silence with a bullet, became easy enough to visualise. I was reminded of a hard truth – that in a place like Peru there were many people who regarded human life as having less worth than I was used to giving it. We pressed for more information about the *banditos.*

'They are mostly in the higher mountains, but here, there are also a few.'

'Ben, ask her straight out if we can stay here tonight,' Scott appealed.

I gathered the best Spanish I could lay claim to and did so. The young woman responded with an almost apologetic downcast gaze. Then in an unintelligible dialect, she relayed our request to the figure above. The old woman mumbled something, shook her head slowly, and turned away from us. There was no mistaking the answer.

In the last flickers of daylight, we found a suitable spot, at a point where the valley narrowed to just 100 metres wide. Stony infertile soil prevented any agriculture. The river braided around a series of bars. We picked our way gingerly across an overshot of loose stones and onto one such bar, where we set up the tent. Cool sand made the ideal moated campsite.

As the evening progressed, we spoke about mundane topics like camping equipment, but we didn't really listen to each other. Instead our attention was focused on scanning the approaches to our makeshift island fort.

The air was crystal-clear and chilly. Gone was the haziness that afflicted the coast. Scott prepared a meal of boiled rice and vegetables, which we supplemented with hunks of dried meat and cuts from a wheel of goat's cheese. Beyond the reach of our firelight, the valley floor was veiled in blackness. It seemed unlikely that anybody, friendly or otherwise, could stumble into camp. Anyone coming across to our island must have an agenda with these three gringos. No one came.

In the middle of the night I woke up, my bladder bursting in sympathy with the sound of the babbling rivulets outside. The fire had died. As I stood alone, pissing on the sand, the distant howling of stray dogs got me shivering while the walls of the valley glowed eerily in the light cast by a crescent moon. From further up the valley came human shouts. Echoes made it impossible to know how far away they might be. I squeezed back into the crowded tent and lay down again. Sleep was some time returning.

The power-line poles looked more and more random, then disappeared altogether. The electricity stopped. It was as loud a statement as any that called attention to the fact we were entering a remote, forgotten realm. The road had already degenerated into a dusty lane. Now it ended altogether, at a point where the fast-flowing river cut the plain from one edge of the valley to the other. The only bridge, made from tree branches lashed together, allowed foot travellers to cross. For each of us, crossing it produced some heart-fluttering moments. Creaks sounded from under foot. My fully laden bulk was squeezing every last ounce of flex from the knobbly timbers. No doubt the bridge was meant only for the diminutive frames of local Peruvians, who crossed with their sacks of farm produce. I felt like a vandal, an irresponsible adult on kids' playground equipment.

A walking track snaked further into the valley. According to our map, the river at this point lost the title of 'Camaná' and was now referred to as the Majes (pronounced *Mahees*). The desiccated scrub hinted of the Australian interior. Hard-edged grasses and spiked thickets signalled the margins of the coastal desert and signs of farming all but ceased. The air smelt of dry, hot earth. The only people we saw were those who shuffled along the trail. As it had been until now, the gradient was barely perceptible. From the Pacific, the source of the Amazon sits less than 250 kilometres away. Somewhere up ahead, the steeper climbs were waiting.

A man on horseback pulled up alongside us and offered to carry one of our backpacks. Each of us politely declined. We didn't refuse out of any suspicion of his motives; it was rather that in the eyes of the other two, accepting the offer might be mistaken for an admission of struggle. It was an unspoken paranoia among us – at this early stage, struggling just wasn't on.

'I am Roberto,' the rider told us. 'And this is my horse, Maria.' He slapped the beast's neck and laughed a genuinely cheerful laugh. The brim of a straw hat shadowed his face, while a grubby waistcoat covered his torso and a pair of old suit trousers ended in frayed tatters at his ankles. His feet were bare, but the soles looked as tough as leather. '*Americano?*' he asked.

'No.' We explained our origins.

'Ah, yes,' he nodded. 'Those are good countries.' I sensed, though, that one or two of the names were new to him. 'And where are you going?' he continued.

'Mount Mismi.'

'El Misti?' El Misti was a cone-shaped volcano near Arequipa, popular with climbers from around the globe.

'No, no. *Montaña Mismi.* Where the Amazon River begins.' It was Colin who quickly corrected him, proud to confirm the uniqueness of our trek.

The look Roberto gave was a blank one, which soon

transformed into a puzzled expression. As with almost all Peruvian folk we had met, the word 'Mismi' meant nothing. 'But who is looking after your farms back home?' he queried.

'Err . . . we have no farms,' I said, chuckling.

At this, Roberto raised his eyebrows, pouted, and stuck his head out in a show of complete perplexity. Then his face split into a humorous smile. 'Ah, you gringos are crazy people!'

Here, the source of the Amazon had no meaning. Why on earth would anyone lug a backbreaking pile of gear around to find it? Roberto bid us farewell. '*Buen suerte*,' he added, reaching down to shake our hands. 'Good luck, you crazy gringos.'

And with that he trotted off.

On the morning of day 3, during breakfast, the stove got sick. A saucepan full of porridge sat half boiled, but appetites fled as we digested instead an unpalatable reality – the future looked grim for our only cooker.

We retreated into the tent to perform emergency surgery. Hoards of bloodthirsty insects, known locally as moskies, had awoken to begin another day of hellraising. They pattered like raindrops against the tent fabric. The sun quickly heated the tent's interior, capping off an all-round feeling of discomfort. Dissection of the stove confirmed our worst fears. Somewhere in the complex fuel-flow mechanism there was a blockage. Several attempts at resuscitation, using a pair of pliers and a Swiss Army knife, proved futile. With no specialised tools to hand, and with little prospect of finding an 'authorised repairer' in the next 5000 kilometres, its condition was finally deemed terminal.

Amid free-flowing obscenities, I dug a burial hole just as I would have for any other piece of campsite garbage. Colin took the death badly. He, the most out of the three of us, felt betrayed at the hands of the stove's manufacturer. I knew him as a man fixated on the 'value for money' ethic whenever he bought anything. Brand names and fashion trends meant little to him. It was a refreshing attitude and very sensible. As long as the product performed as claimed and was sturdily built, what else mattered? In this case, the stove had certainly not performed, and therefore had failed to supply value for money.

When the hole was deep enough, Scott handed me the now worthless hunk of metal. 'Well, I suppose that's that,' he sighed. He took a few steps back and slid his hands into his pockets.

'Yep. Time to get bloody good at starting fires,' I observed. As Colin looked on, stony-faced, I interred the first casualty of our journey.

In truth, the loss did not come as any great surprise. The stove had been designed to run best on 'white fuel', a form of highly refined petroleum, which, we discovered, is impossible to come by in a country like Peru. The only alternative had been unleaded petrol: the stove could burn it, but the impurities in 'Peruvian grade' fuel would always threaten to cause havoc. Unfortunately, the havoc had come much sooner than hoped. And now, suddenly our low-tech, shoestring approach was looking more backyard amateur than ever.

The day advanced with the sun again blazing in a cloudless sky. So far, we had not seen a drop of rain in Peru. This, together with the aridness around us, nurtured my confidence that being able to start a fire was guaranteed.

We came to a forsaken-looking hamlet. On its outskirts,

a shepherd boy slept in the shade granted by a spindly tree while his half-a-dozen goats tore at tussocks of brown grass. The landscape offered only fragments of greenery. Gone was the fertility and productivity we'd seen in the lower valley. Now the soil was stony, shallow and dry. If it had ever possessed nutrients for crops, millennia of flooding had long carried them away.

I wondered what was sustaining the people of this hamlet. Was there any source of livelihood beyond a few hungry herds of goats? By all appearances, the community had never flourished. My gut feeling was that nothing had changed in the 400-odd years since Spanish settlement. Time had disregarded this place.

Every house in the settlement was made of cane poles perched on a foundation of sun-baked dirt. Windows were nothing more than a cut-out in the wall. Each had a single shutter, hinged at the top, designed to shield the interior from the sand-laden winds that cut through the Majes Valley.

'Coca-Cola!' screeched a voice from one of the open doorways. A sheet of metal, inscribed with a faded Coke logo, leant against the wall next to the opening.

We stopped. A small shopkeeper appeared in the doorway. With one hand, he shaded his eyes from the bright sun. The other he stretched outwards and flapped in a shooing motion. Anywhere else, such a wave meant only one thing – 'Go away' – here in Peru, however, it was the gesture used to beckon someone. It had taken us a while to figure out the ambiguity of otherwise friendly citizens who seemed to be telling us to get lost.

'Coca-Cola!' repeated the shopkeeper. His statement and the waving were supplemented by a grin that cleaved his face in two. 'You have Coca-Cola?' we asked.

'Si.'

The thought of sipping an ice-cold fizzy drink in the cool shade led us towards him. I had to stoop to enter the store. The sleeping bag on top of my backpack snagged the top of the door frame. The result was a graceless movement, similar to the lurch of a weightlifter as he attempts to hoist the bar skyward. Both of my knees let forth protesting cries, but held firm. Scott gave me a welcome shove and I burst through into the store's dim interior.

My eyes needed several seconds to adjust to the gloom. The delightful fragrance of roasting corn quickly numbed the ache in my knees. A young girl clung to the shadows behind a low counter. Three sacks squatted in the centre of the hard dirt floor, lips rolled down neatly to expose their contents. The first contained rice, the second held small red beans, and the third offered kernels of Andean corn.

The shopkeeper had found my clumsy entrance highly entertaining. 'You need a drink,' he chuckled. 'I have no tequila. But Coca-Cola is good, yes?'

'Sure. Three Cokes, please.'

He nodded and began rummaging through a crate at his feet. Gratefully, we dropped our packs and sat on a bench. Seconds later, we each had a bottle of warm soft drink in our hands. The bottles were slender, chipped from years of re-cycling, and coated in dust.

As we drank in silence, the shopkeeper propped himself on a stool and looked at us with bright eyes. He seemed to view us as prizes, not just as oddities. That's when I felt a pang of guilt. Here we were, reinforcing a widespread belief that westerners let nothing but fizzy drinks pass their lips. Probably in his mind, we'd stood no hope of resisting; at the mere mention of the name of the giant multinational, a sort of hypnosis would surely come over us. To some extent, he was right. In a land so foreign to us, Coke supplied a familiar frame of reference. Peruvians themselves embraced the cola obsession, and even this hamlet, which lacked allegiance to the modern world in every other respect, had the stuff for sale. Here, as in many other parts of the western and third worlds, the belief had been instilled that Coke cured thirst, then went to work purifying one's body from within. It was a symbol of health and progress.

Near sundown, a bicycle clattered towards us from the trail behind. Despite being decades old, it was the most modern form of transportation I'd seen in two days. The rider held up his hand in greeting, almost losing his balance when the front wheel deflected off a rock. '*Hola!* Wait, amigos.'

He came to a halt alongside us then vigorously shook our hands. 'Amigos, where are you from?' he asked, without originality.

In practised tones, we told him.

'Ah, yes, yes. I know of these places.'

'And where do you live, señor?' queried Colin. Each one of us already knew the answer but we gave polite nods of surprise as he waved a hand in the direction we had walked from.

'It's a nice bike you have,' I noted, with even more remote interest. At this stage of the day, I was too footsore and weary to probe more deeply. He seemed to be just another curious local, with the same list of questions. The conversation was surely doomed to banal pleasantries.

'I have cocaine for sale,' the bike rider declared.

The injection of intrigue was absolute. Even Scott, who understood the least amount of Spanish, caught the gist of what had just been said and let forth a low whistle. The bike rider smirked, but it was the sly expression of a businessman.

Another South American reality was staring us in the face. Thoughts of *banditos* returned and I noticed the rider's attire for the first time. He wore a felt hat with a narrow brim. His clothes, despite the dust stains, were not those of a typical rural peasant. In place of sandals he wore a pair of finely crafted leather shoes.

'So . . . how much are you selling?'

'One kilogram for one thousand dollars.'

I didn't know much about the street value of the drug in the western world, but I did know the price he quoted was a bargain. It was no wonder that dozens of people got nabbed at airports every day returning home from business or pleasure in South America.

'Sorry, we're not interested,' I said.

'It is a very cheap price I give you,' insisted the rider.

'Yes, but we don't want to buy.' There seemed little point citing moral reasons, so I added simply: 'We have no money.' This was close enough to the truth, anyway.

This last statement had the same effect as saying goodbye. Without another word, the cocaine merchant turned his bicycle around and rode back the way he'd come. I hoped that news of our poverty would spread through the local *bandito* community.

An hour later, the wind was howling; a campfire was impossible. Instead, we ended the day as we had begun it, huddled in the tent. This time it was not the biting insects but the blowing sand from which we hid. By the time our shelter had been erected, sand grains had penetrated our hair to the scalp, bored into eye sockets, and generally snuck into every bodily orifice.

'Cold camp' was miserable. Colin and Scott both complained of stomach pains and nausea. For dinner, I divided the remaining portion of goat's cheese, a can of sardines, raw onion, stale bread and some dried beef. We crunched sand with every mouthful.

'Mind where you put your feet,' Colin muttered from his sleeping bag.

It was a timely warning. Outside the tent in the diffuse pre-dawn light, I was about to step through a minefield of diarrhoea. During the night, the bowels of my companions had given out to illness. Their groans followed me as I picked my way to the riverbank. The doleful noises entwined with a squalid stench that hung in the air. My belly lurched. The urge to vomit passed, but it left behind a dim unease.

Yesterday's road dust, sand and sweat had become a crust of grime over my skin. I stripped naked and waded into the cold, fast-flowing Majes. The current and the slippery rocks made scrubbing difficult. As I washed, the stirrings of discontent in my stomach gradually spread through the rest of my body. I knew that whatever illness Colin and Scott had was also coming my way.

Although it sat right in the heart of the tropical latitudes, this region saw little rainfall. Virtually all of the water in the Majes came from snow that topped the peaks located further into the Andes. Despite the parched surrounds here, the river flowed plentiful and clear. But this clarity did not fool us. We had filtered every last drop of the water used for drinking and cooking. We didn't doubt that the villages and towns upriver dumped their wastes directly into the Majes; after all, it still happened even in the world's most developed countries. When one factored in the dung of livestock, it became even easier to imagine this water as a cocktail of microscopic nasties.

The question was: had the bug managed to get through our water-filtering process? Or had it infiltrated our bodies through our food? I'd regarded our shank of dried beef as dodgy from the outset and hygiene standards in the Camaná market had not inspired much confidence. But what did it matter now? I was neither surprised, nor overly worried by the sickness on its way. I knew from experience that it came with the territory. In some perversely comforting way, I viewed it as the one certainty of travel in the third world.

By lunch I was in bad shape. I could eat nothing. Although my gut had not yet yielded to the diarrhoea, alternating hot and cold flushes washed over me and my breathing became a rapid pant. My only strength came from the thought of collapsing onto a hotel bed in Corire. At rest stops, I sprawled like a lizard in the hot sun, soaking in the warmth, oblivious to the sharp stones, prickles and biting insects. No one spoke. We each sank into our own world of feverish torment.

Things continued to get worse. My neck muscles were very sore because of the backpack. There was exposed flesh on the boniest part of my hips, where the belt harness had rubbed for almost four days. Every step gave stinging confirmation that the pack and my body were operating beyond what they had been designed for.

As the day wore on settlements became more frequent. The trail became a road once more and the power lines returned. The occasional scooter buzzed by and pedestrian traffic became a steady flow.

'Can you tell us how much further to Corire?' we asked one passer-by.

'Only one hour, señors.'

'Oh, good. Thank you.'

We checked this with the very next person. 'Four hours' was the reply this time. It was said without hesitation.

We tried another approach: 'How many more kilometres?'

This brought on a thoughtful expression, then a response made with the usual certainty: 'Five kilometres.' That sounded better. We shuffled onwards for another hour before asking the same question of a man leading his donkey.

'It is eight kilometres. You will be there in half a day,' he said matter-of-factly.

I had never come across anything like it. How could wild guesses be given with so much conviction? Was the concept of distance and time so undefined here? In a state of semi-delirium and an almost childlike yearning for bed, I felt all but broken, as if subjected to a type of psychological abuse. Colin seethed. Scott's eyes rolled back into his head.

'Do you know what you're fucking talking about?' he spat out in English. The man shrugged, uncomprehending. I smiled wryly at his admission. Finally, here was some truth.

Corire sprawled across a wide expanse of the Majes Valley. The mountains temporarily lost their severity, allowing a bitumen road to slink off in the direction of Arequipa. Two smaller valleys, one on each side, cut in at near right angles. Each was host to an ephemeral tributary of the Majes. Our route continued up the valley that headed east. But it could wait. Now it was time for us to bow to infirmity – and to bow low, at that.

Our room at the *hostal* smelt dank and musty. I slumped onto one of the beds as a cockroach scurried out from under the stained pillow. Mattress springs jabbed into my spine. It was the most luxurious bed in the entire world. I let the wave of heavy blackness break.

THREE
THE COASTAL DESERT

20 September 1999 (day 8):
five kilometres from Corire,
75 kilometres from the
Pacific Ocean

We made our way through the valley, through shimmering waves of heat. I puffed away the dust that had collected at the corners of my mouth. My backpack was the consistency of a lead weight. The outlines of Colin and Scott smudged the landscape several hundred metres up ahead as moisture continued to seep from my already dehydrated flesh. Four days of diarrhoea, fever and vomiting had left me drained. Memories of sickness occupied my mind. Never had I known such a chronic form of diarrhoea, which the three of us predictably (but no less appropriately) soon termed 'squirting'.

I will never forget the rancid image of that tiny ill-lit space that served as both shower and lavatory for three sick men during our stay in Corire. The tiles were cracked, chipped and yellowed. A waste-paper basket for used toilet paper and the fact that the toilet itself rarely flushed ensured that the smell of excrement was never less than appalling. There was no seat, and fecal remnants encrusted the bowl. For each of us, in our fragile states, those bathroom dashes were the stuff of nightmares.

As we headed east towards Mismi in the stifling heat, the only thing giving me anything close to amusement was the recollection of a scene from the previous evening – our last one in Corire. It had involved the *hostal*'s caretaker, who'd been the poor fellow with the task of cleaning the toilet at the end of the hall during those terrible days. Up until the night before our departure, I had passed him in the hallway or on the staircase several times, receiving little more than a quick smile, a shy nod or perhaps a timid '*Hola*'. Given our repeated assaults on his bathroom, it surprised me that he could muster any sort of pleasantries at all.

The caretaker had beckoned me over to his desk as I returned from a late-night mission for bottled water. He flashed a shy grin, then took a deep breath as if calming his nerves. 'How do men like you satisfy a woman?' he asked, struggling to conceal his embarrassment.

The question caught me off guard, but I managed to return a wide smile. The caretaker relaxed instantly. His eyes brightened and, after he'd peered over my shoulder to make sure that no one was eavesdropping, his mouth curled into a mischievous smirk.

'Umm . . . there are many ways to do it,' I answered, wondering where this was leading.

'Please tell me what you know,' he said excitedly.

I felt too drained to be self-conscious or embarrassed. I described several techniques, which in my bad Spanish must have sounded especially perverted. He nodded eagerly after each description and insisted on sketches when my language skills totally failed me.

'Will you show me a little?' he whispered keenly, after again craning his neck to peek down the corridor.

'What?'

'My wife, she would also like it. I only want to watch.'

'Er . . . I don't really feel up to it,' I admitted. Certainly it would normally be an offer worthy of some thought, but I felt too weak. Illness stifles libido. And besides, on several occasions I had passed a very stout woman in the *hostal* foyer with a devilish glint in her eye – she was quite possibly the unsatisfied wife in question.

Colin, Scott and I had been unified in sickness. We had all succumbed to it within a day of each other, each of us slipping into the pit of intestinal hell. Some had it worse than others. I remembered surfacing from a fitful slumber several times to a loud, reverberating boom. At first I would be gripped by panic as I recalled what I'd read about the high frequency of Andean earthquakes. But then a long groan, wailing down the corridor like some aural aftershock, would reveal the truth – Colin's bowels had again exploded.

I had been the last one to get sick and I was the last to recover enough even to think about hitting the trail once more. There was such a long way to the summit of Mount Mismi and each of us knew the importance of keeping to our schedule. More than the illness itself, I had a feverish desire to see the back of that stinking loo.

Only a few hours out of Corire, however, the sun's intensity made me wish I'd indulged in a couple more days of rehydrating convalescence. As I mechanically dragged one foot in front of the other, thoughts of home and its easier lifestyle were with me constantly. Why was I subjecting myself to these living conditions? Why was I forgoing the company of old friends and an interesting life back at university? Again the notion that this journey across South

America was physically and mentally beyond me crept into my throbbing head. Right now, six months couldn't go fast enough.

The map suggested a 50-kilometre trek up this bone-dry riverbed to reach a road that would then lead us to the village of Huambo. It looked like a short cut, more direct than if we continued following the Majes.

The hottest part of the year was coming. Every day the high-altitude snow packs further melted, swelling the upper tributaries of the Amazon, breeding more and more strength into the rapids that we would tackle on the other side of the mountains. The longer it took us to reach the source of the river, the tougher it would be for us later. None of us had argued against making a charge through this nameless desert valley, and we were all now doubled over by the addition of six litres of water – the agreed minimum for a two-day crossing of the valley.

I'd never been in a setting that at first glance looked so devoid of life. I was sure that no place on earth could be more barren. The valley epitomised the South American coastal desert – a strip of parched land sweeping down more than half the western edge of the continent.

Across the Pacific, people on the east coast of Australia know the opposite: a green, fertile coastal strip with a dry interior stretching west of the Great Dividing Range. Indirectly, the Peruvian coast is withered by ice-cold seawater, upwelling from the abyssal ocean depths. Instead of rising to form rain clouds, cold, moist air wafts landwards, where it cloaks the thirsty communities in a useless haze of water vapour. I'd once seen a documentary about a kind-hearted and innovative Swiss engineer who'd gone to one particular Andean village with a contraption that condensed the mist and fog. This machine provided a reliable water supply. In our nameless desert valley, there was no moisture in the air to harness.

Occasionally the rains come, and when they do, they are powerful and devastating. At the same time, the sea warms slightly, decreases in nutrients, and collapses the Peruvian fishing industry. The rotting carcasses of hundreds of thousands of starved birds stain the coast. The people in the flooded villages and the poor anchovy fishermen sigh and once more blame 'El Niño'. Simultaneously, in Australia the drought-stricken farmers murmur the same name.

I lugged three bottles of water in the day-pack on my chest. Soon the water was hot enough to lightly scald my tongue. But all I cared about was that those swigs from the bottle were wet. They lubricated my throat for several moments and went some way to replenishing the sweat being sucked out of me. Unfortunately, the imbalance was a severe one; the movement of fluids was essentially a one-way street. The heat and lingering symptoms of illness meant that our trek through the desert valley was a race against time, handicapped by the frail state of our bodies.

On the map, the point where we'd aimed to intersect the road was marked by a natural spring and a church. On paper, it looked like the only source of water for perhaps 50 kilometres in every direction. The threat of relapsing into chronic diarrhoea hovered. And something else bothered us: the reliability of our maps.

At the Geographical Institute in Lima, we had spent good money to get our hands on the best topographic charts available. They had seemed so formidable as a thick, heavy roll, and conjured up a vague sense of professionalism in us as we laid them end to end across the width of the bare concrete floor in our hotel room. Since then, however, we had noticed that they were 50 years old! As I trudged through the dust, it was hard not to think that the lonely church might well be in ruins, and the spring long since dried up.

When I caught up with my companions, they were taking refuge in the sliver of shade offered by a sheer rock wall. Scott, hands on his knees and head bowed, spat out the last chunks from a mouthful of vomit. Colin wiped a dirty forearm across his brow, then slumped against the rock wall. None of us spoke. We just sat in our corner, lightheaded and puffy-eyed. Round one went to the desert.

My eyes snapped open next day in the crisp coolness of early dawn. I did a quick calculation. My bowels had held firm for twelve hours, an impressive feat given my recent form. It was the first night of decent sleep I had been able to boast in almost a week.

Crawling from the tent, a different world greeted me from the one that I had bid an exhausted goodnight to at 6 p.m. the evening before. I was captivated instantly by the stark loveliness of the desert valley. It was much narrower than the Majes Valley. Ochre, sepia, copper and cobalt hues oozed from the earth. The land was utterly still. Shadows and the clear morning air accentuated the outline of rock formations. It took a grubby-looking Scott, stirring porridge over a smoky fire, to spoil the purity on display. My soul was at last finding a reason to perk up. The misery of Corire had made me feel so vulnerable, so mortal. I knew that disease would always be lurking nearby as we made our way across South America. It was not that the Amazon jungle harboured an infinite range of bizarre afflictions on top of the usual dysentery, malaria and hepatitis; it was more that in the event of a health crisis, I had my doubts whether we would find anything out there that resembled medical help.

By midday, the heat was again brutal. I was down to my last half-litre of water. And still the valley trailed off into the shimmering distance. A scampering desert fox broke the stillness. It was the first life form we'd seen in more than a day.

We crouched in the shade of a large boulder and our dry, tired eyes scrutinised the map. As we compared the terrain to the contours, one of our greatest fears became reality. I pointed the compass at a prominent rise, looked back at the squiggles, and then shook my head. A coldness washed over me. Colin snatched the compass from my hand and took a bearing off a conical-shaped hill that fringed the valley. 'Fucking hell,' he murmured. 'She's out.'

Scott's squinting eyes betrayed little, but I thought I saw his throat constrict in a premature swallow. We all knew what these discrepancies in compass readings meant. The dirt road, the church and the spring, together representing our only salvation, might not be where they were supposed to be.

'Well, let's keep chugging along,' Colin encouraged. It came out of his mouth a little too loudly to lift the anxious mood.

We pushed on. As if to drive home our situation, tall cacti began to dot the landscape. Their slim, vertical trunks punched through the hard-baked earth.

At the head of the valley, a steep ridge cut across our route. From this point, the map promised it would be no more than two kilometres to the church. It should be visible from the top of the ridge, but here again, the compass pointed out a discrepancy that dried out my throat beyond anything the desert conditions could do. Our ascent coincided with the hottest part of the day. I sipped the dregs of hot fluid in my remaining water bottle. Less than halfway to the crest of the ridge, it was all gone. Leg muscles ached. Low clumps of cactus gouged holes in our ankles and shins. My boots slipped on loose ground. As the top of the ridge neared, blood thumped in my sunburnt ears. I craved sight of the church.

Nothing! It wasn't there.

How had it happened? Was it only a matter of inaccurate maps? I felt betrayed. The trek wasn't supposed to be like this. The memory of that last mouthful of water flashed through my mind. As it faded, I knew the final buffer between me and a thirsty death was gone.

The alarm was plain to see on Scott and Colin's haggard faces. Their water was gone too and their reserves of strength also fast running out. We had to keep our nerve.

'Backpacks,' croaked Colin. 'We've got to keep going without them.'

He unshackled himself. Scott shrugged off his own pack and sat on it like it was a stool. 'Go where?' he asked.

Colin nodded in the direction we'd already been heading. Something in me didn't like it.

'It'd be more *that* way, don't you reckon?' I argued, waving a wobbly finger towards the north-east.

But Colin was adamant. 'Trust me, mate. It's this way.'

My face screwed up. I was not convinced, although I couldn't give reasons for my own suggestion. I guess it was that, given the whole map scenario, I was willing to trust only my instincts.

'Look over there.' Scott was pointing to a groove in the dust, winding off through the cactus clumps. It was a well-worn trail, probably made by goats and other livestock plodding single-file over the ridge. It headed in the same direction that Colin claimed was the escape route. The voice in my head insisted that the church must lie to the north-east but I had to concede that the stock trail would at least take us somewhere.

Dropping the backpacks bought us time. Machine-like, we trudged down the first ridge then up a second, running parallel to the first. Half an hour later we crested this one too. Again, our hearts broke. There was nothing but another cactus-speckled ridge spanning the horizon. By my foot, a scorpion the size of my fist scuttled away in terror.

'We could drink our own piss,' Scott offered hoarsely. I raised my eyebrows in economic response. 'It's a common British Army technique,' he added.

Remembering how the fumes from my last toilet stop had almost burnt my nostrils, I was still far from enthused.

'This ain't your standard urine,' I pointed out. Mine was brown, so concentrated and acidic that I suspected it might be lethal.

Scott emptied his bladder into a water bottle then held it up for inspection. The stuff was the colour of dark ale. Now that it was before his eyes, Scott, too, was having doubts. He brought the bottle slowly towards his mouth. As he closed quivering lips around the opening, the fumes struck home. He gagged and dropped the bottle. I chuckled, but regretted it instantly as my bottom lip split.

Meanwhile, Colin had his pocketknife out and was jabbing at the skin of a cactus. The liquid oozing from the cuts ignited a blaze of hope in his eyes. 'Who's game to try a bit of this instead?' he asked, holding aloft a dripping piece of the plant.

I knew enough about the evils of cactus juice to baulk at this option too. It may have looked sweet and refreshing but there was a good chance that devilish hallucinations and excruciating muscle cramps would bring about a more horrible end than dehydration ever could. In my mind, such a tease was no different from the poor shipwrecked soul on a desert island, dying of thirst while surrounded by an ocean of water: the cacti were *everywhere*.

Colin knew all this himself, but he was insanely thirsty.

More importantly, he was the sort who would never die wondering. Had the world expert on that species of cactus materialised to wag a finger and say, 'No, no, no!', it would have made no difference. Colin always insisted on discovering the truth for himself – and so he did.

Through all my discomfort and the seriousness of the situation, the sight of Colin's face contorting into an expression of pure repulsion made me smirk. My bottom lip split again and I winced in agony. Clearly, none of this was meant to be a laughing matter.

All I wanted to do was stop and lie down. The dysentery had taken so much out of me, leaving virtually no resources to cope with a crisis like this. And yet, from somewhere within, the energy came to drive my body onwards. Unlike dropping out of a football training session and risking a severe earbashing from the coach, here, the penalty would be much greater. I realised then that all through my life, regardless of the task at hand, there had always been the option of calling it quits. My dad had always complained that I never stuck things out. I had retaliated with 'Well, if I try it and don't like it, I'll try something else'.

But deep in the unforgiving coastal desert of Peru, I was quickly finding out that the escape clause had been deleted. In short, either I gritted my teeth and endured, or I died. This was a world with different rules.

The sun flayed my shoulders as I slogged it up the third ridge. My knees bent only enough to drag one foot in front of the other. My mind was willing – it wanted to survive, to not give in – but I wondered when my body would start to disobey my commands to push on. How long would it be before the limits of human physiology came into play and made me crumple in a heap? I had no idea, but I knew that in this respect, too, I was in barely charted territory.

Nearer the third ridge-top, a wooden cross came into view. My heart rate quickened. There seemed no doubt that it watched over the church beyond the ridge. It was certain at least that we would make it there. Now there remained one last desperate question: did the spring still flow?

The two cross timbers were like old bones, drained completely of the life they had once known. We prayed the spring had shown more resilience against the desert. I leant on the cross, the answer in sight below. I felt giddy; my hands trembled with relief. Tucked into a crook of a valley below was the oasis, a fortress of greenery that beat back the savage hills and their prickly henchmen.

We sat there for half an hour, enjoying the view. Happiness came just from knowing that we'd be able to live beyond that day – we forgot about the need to actually get something wet down our throats.

Scott had the most appropriate response to this moment: 'Who brought the beers? This needs a bit of celebrating.' For me, a great irony was suddenly plain. While searching for the source of a river so vast it carries a fifth of all the fresh water on the planet, we had come face to face with the real prospect of dying from thirst.

The desert softened. A road dribbled northwards over rounded hills. In the gullies, hard-leaved shrubs crouched. Wispy grasses tickled my legs from the road edge. A chinchilla (something like a cross between a cat and a rabbit) fled to its burrow. The creature had every right to be timid. Too many of its finely furred cousins had already relinquished their skins to clothe the world's rich and 'fashionable'. This land supported more life, although it still had no intention of making things easy for three mammals more used to turning on a tap when they needed water.

We carried twice the amount of water this time. At the church, spring water had been channelled into a concrete pool. There it stagnated, providing a home for yellow-green algae. We had stumbled from the ridge-top and guzzled it down, ignoring the slimy fronds as readily as we had the dogs that had rushed at us with bared fangs. Thoughts of possible contamination had taken a back seat to the need to drink as much water as our bellies could hold.

Thinking more clearly in the morning, we filtered our water rations for the hike to the next settlement. For total peace of mind, we had added a couple of drops of regular household bleach to each bottle.

As I walked up the road's switchbacks, my gut seemed content enough. At the same time, I would have welcomed a couple of days spent under a tree beside that slimy pool of spring water. Ravaged bodies or not, we needed to keep going. Too bad about my sore back. Too bad about Colin's splitting headache. Too bad about a blistered right heel that screamed with every step and looked more fleshy every time I peeled off my sock. Distance markers helped to improve our mood. I counted off each kilometre as proof of another tiny dent made in the long haul to Mount Mismi. We passed four markers per hour.

No vehicle came from either direction the entire day, which made me wonder if the next settlement marked on the map would amount to much. Few people lived in this region. Back at the spring, we had seen no one other than an old woman. We didn't get the chance to speak with her. She had appeared long enough to call off the dogs and then retreated back into a mudbrick hovel. I doubted she had much to do with the world beyond her desert oasis. Contact with her fellow Peruvians was probably as rare as the arrival of a half-dead band of westerners.

As we approached the next settlement in the stillness of dusk, it became clear that the residents were long gone. There had certainly been at least a handful of people around in 1951 – the year our map was drawn – but now it was deserted. Like most of the tiny hamlets we'd seen in the Majes Valley, every structure here was built in simple style, from materials found locally. Roofs were thatched and the walls assembled from rough-fitted stones. Animal yards had perhaps known alpacas or llamas once upon a time. Inside, the dirt floors were littered with broken jars, scraps of newspaper and the odd iron bed frame. The reddening sun cast each empty hovel in an eerie light. What had driven these folk away?

While Scott made a campfire, Colin and I hunted for more water. Our remaining supply would not last the expected two-day hike to Huambo, and the map offered no other possible sources en route. As with the church oasis, we'd banked on being able to refill our plastic bottles at this place.

We followed a dozen small birds darting in seductive formation towards the chasm that split a nearby cliff of rock and opened into a natural amphitheatre over 20 metres across. The amphitheatre was filled with plant life I'd seen nowhere else in this harsh, arid zone. Overhangs shielded a collage of delicate shrubs and flowers from the blazing heat.

The scene revitalised a couple of weary travellers. The icing on the cake would have been a crystal-clear spring. Instead, the twittering of the birds led us to water that wasn't quite so tantalising.

'Not exactly what I was hoping for,' lamented Colin as I stirred the thick broth with a stick.

The pool was about three metres across and choked by

blooms of algae. Judging from the layers of guano forming a halo around its edge, the pool probably represented the only source of water for many kilometres. It gave off the kind of stench that triggers a voice in the head saying: 'Don't drink! Don't drink!'

'We'll have to put this stuff through the wringer,' an exasperated Colin said.

'Might be a meal in it too,' I offered with faint optimism. The algae reminded me of cooked spinach.

Scott was unimpressed by the olive-coloured liquid we returned with. 'I'm not drinking bird shit!'

'Don't worry, everything's under control,' Colin insisted. 'We'll give it a strain, a filter, boil the hell out of it, then slosh in a good dose of bleach.'

I drew the short straw and was asked to supply a T-shirt for the straining. We preferred not to think about the mixture of road dust, sweat and bodily grime that would dissolve in place of the slime and bird muck.

The results of the T-shirt straining were disappointing. The bulk of suspended gunk simply washed straight through the fabric. It was asking too much of the water filter to do much better. The murky substance seemed to mock the idea of anyone attempting to make it drinkable, and after two pumps, the filter was clogged. The boiling stage yielded greater success. We let the water roll and bubble away for half an hour. Gunge collected on top as a layer of frothy scum, and was easily skimmed off. Finally, in went the bleach. This was our substitute for expensive chlorine tablets.

The end result was a potion the colour of chicken soup. It smelt of boiled socks, tasted like foul medicine, and left a hint of bleach lingering on the tongue. But it would keep us going to Huambo and hopefully without inflicting more gut-twisting illness, or perhaps something even worse.

FOUR
COLCA CANYON

23 September 1999 (day 11):
140 kilometres from the Pacific

Thirty kilometres before Huambo, the road we followed struck the crest of a range and began its slow descent towards the almighty Colca Canyon. At the 3700-metre crest, the vegetation became an expanse of rugged grassland, known as the Puna. Over these high natural pastures, llamas, alpacas and the dainty vicunas roamed in their herds. From this vantage point, we got our first glimpse of the high summits at the heart of the Andes. They looked like the teeth of the world – the home of dragons. Somewhere among them, the Amazon was born.

While my mind soared, my heart fluttered. The emergence of those peaks defined our goal in much clearer terms for me. I'd never before seen land higher than 4000 metres, and in some respects, it was only now that I could start to prepare myself for the challenge of climbing a 5650-metre mountain. Only now was I able to brace myself for heading into very thin air. Bearing in mind my nonexistent mountaineering experience, it might as well have been Everest.

As far as I could tell, I had no symptoms of *soroche* here at 3700 metres. I'd at least progressed from the lightheadedness of Cuzco. Nothing to get too excited about, but it was encouraging. We had enough reason to feel frail without a lack of oxygen in the blood. Right now, it was from the hunger and malnourishment of recent days. We needed to eat *big*. And we needed to eat something that wasn't straight from a can or boiled out of a packet.

Huambo clawed at the sides of a valley that plunged quickly into the Colca. Eucalypt trees surrounded the village. At almost 3000 metres above sea level, these plantations grew much higher than their cousins in the loftiest regions of Australia. And yet, against the backdrop of snow-dusted peaks and the world's deepest canyon, they did not seem out of place. Introduced as a fast-growing source of hardwood, gum trees thrived in the middle altitudes of the Andes. It felt good to see their peeling bark and droopy leaves, especially after passing through so much countryside dominated by cacti.

We beelined for the central square, the plaza, the most likely place to find a shop selling food. The plaza is a fixture of Latin American settlements. As the British sought to mould Australia in the image of the motherland, the Spanish planned the towns of 'the New World' in true Iberian style. In most towns, the plaza remains the hub for conducting business, meeting people and for protests.

Against its stunning backdrop, the plaza was a picture of beauty. One side was dominated by an old church; a baroque structure used by the police and local government graced another side. But tucked into a corner was a rough plastered cottage with a buckled tin roof. This was the only structure we were ready to pay homage to.

The store bulged full of groceries. It also doubled as a cheap eatery, and a lone table and three chairs fought with sacks of rice and beans for floor space. We pounced on them. For the next two hours, the growling of our stomachs warded off other would-be diners as surely as our alien look.

The sole menu option was the standard rural meal: chicken soup (usually with a couple of chooks' feet floating around for good measure) and rice topped by a thin meaty gruel. We devoured one helping, made short work of another, waited a respectable fifteen minutes so as not to look like complete gluttons, then called for thirds. We also knocked back a string of sodas, tore through several packets of cream biscuits, and freed the shelves of half their burden of chocolate bars. I leant back, rubbed my belly and belched. Just sitting in a chair was an extravagance that would help me put all the strain and struggle of recent days aside.

Returning to the plaza, we lay under a gum tree and tried our best to blend in for an inconspicuous siesta. It didn't happen. A flood of children poured out of a neighbouring schoolyard and into the plaza; a sea of exotic faces and brightly coloured clothes quickly surrounded us. Their cardigans and jumpers were made from alpaca wool, and every one was a gush of reds, yellows, purples and blues. After all the sombre, earthy hues of the Majes Valley and emptiness of the desert valley, it came as a bit of a shock.

The children were different from the ones we'd met in the lower lands. In their eyes I saw more vividly the shimmer of wonder and innocence. These children were mountain-bred. Here, colonial Spanish culture had merged with the native Quechuan. The people of Huambo drew their heritage from the Incas and their once vast highland empire – the Inca live on as the Quechua folk.

More than a full belly and lie-down could ever do,

making an impression on a society of such historical richness renewed my strength. I felt that perhaps the ancient gods of the sun, moon and earth were now watching over us as we journeyed through this extraordinary land.

Our trek from Huambo to the larger settlement of Cabanaconde was a field trip of living archaeology. The road wound through terraced farmland, carved from the mountain slopes even before Inca times. Each year, for the past 600 years or more, crops had been sown then harvested from these same terraces.

For kilometre after kilometre we walked through a sculpted landscape. People were scattered near and far, usually working in small groups. I watched a typical scene of farmer and bull tilling the soil with a simple wooden plough.

We tramped past men, women and children of all ages. Many lugged heavy hessian bags. Others carried hoes or pitchforks over their shoulders. All were dressed in hand-stitched work clothes or traditional outfits. The expressions on careworn, dirt-streaked faces suggested that they knew very little beyond the toil of their existence. Probably the only significant change seen here in half a millennium was the swapping of llamas for donkeys and cattle as preferred beasts of burden.

Cabanaconde sprawled over a rare flat expanse of land. The Colca Canyon's southern flank dropped away at the edge of town. A staggering two kilometres below, the Colca River raged and thundered.

We checked into the Valle de Volcane *hostal*, ate alpaca steaks and met two American students. The girls informed us that Cabanaconde was prime condor-spotting territory, a claim supported by the presence of a giant concrete statue in the middle of the plaza. A condor spread its wings in a frozen display of power, forming the centrepiece of an otherwise garish fountain.

Our maps suggested two options for reaching Madrigal, the village closest to the foot of Mount Mismi. The more clearly defined route continued to skirt the Colca's southern rim, taking in several small settlements until a squiggled side road dared to cross the gentler slopes upriver. A shorter, more direct route plunged straight from Cabanaconde into the Colca's depths. On the other side of the canyon, the trail of black dots became disjointed and vague. We considered there was no guarantee that it wouldn't end abruptly at a vertical rock wall or gaping fissure. Memories of our last short-cut experience still left a dry taste in the mouth. The longer path was a safer bet.

As we neared the place where the trail forked, a now familiar kind of procession plodded towards us. Two donkeys were led by a small Quechua boy and a woman who might have been the boy's mother. The donkeys kept their heads bowed in glum obedience. While the boy wore drab, torn clothing that seemed a magnet for trail dust, the woman was dressed in the traditional array of bright fabrics, the sort of outfit most Quechua women wore. Her felt hat was something straight out of a Sunday afternoon lawn-bowls tournament. The layers and loose folds of her clothes shrouded her, making it hard to guess her age as she ambled along. Looking at the woman's face up close, I could see a softness of youth that belied her squat stature. In fact, she was most likely the boy's older sister.

'Are you going to see the condors?' the boy asked, his tone self-assured, almost cocky. Although no older than ten, the boy was clearly the spokesperson.

I remembered the American girls had talked of a point

on the valley bottom that was the best place to see them. 'We can carry your bags,' the boy continued. He patted one of the unconsulted 'we' on its bushy mane.

'This kid's had a sniff of tourist money,' Scott noted.

'It depends,' I said to the boy. 'Does the trail keep going on to Madrigal?'

'Yes, it does,' came the confident reply.

Colin, Scott and I looked at each other and nodded. These were the sort of people who'd know. Then before we'd even negotiated a price, the little businessman was making room on the *buros* for our backpacks. Trade of this nature begged prudence. Our fingers had been burnt, Peruvian style, more than once since arriving in the country. A fair price was set before we let anything else happen.

It seemed like the ideal arrangement. The two Quechuas lived on the other side of the Colca. Their donkeys would make our crossing a much easier one. Two thousand metres down, across a bridge, then 2000 metres back up again. As the condor flew, it was less than a kilometre to the far side. The world's deepest canyon appeared as a moat, guarding the fortress stronghold of Mount Mismi.

The grade of the trail proved as steep as we'd imagined. At least once on every switchback, my feet rolled over loose rubble, as though it were a spill of marbles. Each time I did so, my spine would momentarily dissolve in ice-cold twinges – the ones that come when the body believes that its grip on earth is about to be exchanged for a slide into oblivion. Conversely, the donkey's surefootedness never wavered. Their hooves seemed more effective than a pair of space-age suction boots.

After an hour of rhythmical zigzagging, I felt like we'd been caught in a brutal time loop. The bottom of the canyon looked no closer. The Colca River was still just a silvery thread trickling through its gloom. My eyes searched the far side for the mirror zigzag trail. It seemed to be cut into an even steeper slope. Further right, in the direction of Madrigal, a tangible aura of defiance seemed to emanate from the terrain, as though daring any living thing to try passing. Colin made the same observation.

'So how long will it take us to reach Madrigal?' he queried, taking in the rugged vista with a sweep of his arm.

'Madrigal?' repeated the boy, as though it was the first time the name had come up. 'This way does not go to there.'

'What do you mean?' asked Colin.

'It is impossible to get through.'

My throat tightened. I came to a halt as fast as I could without shattering both my knee joints.

'Eh?'

'Whoa!'

'You bloody what?'

Simultaneously, three cries of outrage boomed out through the silent canyon.

'Stop the donkeys!' I growled.

Colin began pulling at the ropes that held our back-packs in place.

'What are you doing?' the boy spluttered. 'The condor oasis is this way.' He was genuinely puzzled by our reaction. His quiet companion nodded and also pointed to the base of the canyon.

I glanced up. The canyon's rim had long since vanished behind a curve of dirt, rock and prickly scrub. All that wasted effort made my gut churn. If choosing to climb a mountain meant entering into a war of bodily attrition, then a company of my best troops had just been wiped out without firing a shot.

The boy began to squawk, 'The condors are down there.' He retightened the rope just loosened by the Canadian.

'No!' Colin thundered, ripping it from his hands. 'We go to Madrigal, not to see condors.' I'm not sure which one of the three of us was angriest.

It was painfully obvious now that beyond Cabanaconde, with its guesthouses and tacky souvenir stores, the pedestrian tourist had only one destination in mind – the condor oasis.

We shouldered packs once again, muttering obscenities and groaning at the prospect of an arduous backtrack. Boy and woman regarded us with continued confusion and fast-growing dislike.

From the kitty I pulled half the agreed sum and dangled the notes in begrudging fashion between thumb and forefinger. The little businessman rushed up and snatched them away. He flicked through them with the aplomb of a city gangster. Then his head jerked up and a pair of dark, vicious eyes fixed on me.

'More!' he snarled, reaching for the kitty. 'It is not enough!'

'No! It is too much!' I roared. I swatted his hand away and countered his evil expression with my own look of disgust.

Unfazed by my towering frame, the boy spat a volley of incomprehensible abuse. The woman forgot her bashfulness and levied a barrage of high-pitched curses herself. Soon, everyone was putting forth their opinion in no uncertain terms. Amid threats of revenge, we started the hike back up, stomping with an energetic fury that stemmed as much from the gall of these two Quechuas as from what their stereotyping had cost us in the first place.

We reached Maca. A huge bird landed on top of the church's only belfry. For a long while, the bird drew my attention away from a pile of rubble that had once been the second belfry, before the ruins again transfixed me.

An ancient-faced villager shuffled past the street corner where we sat resting. Folds of brown, leathery skin parted to reveal a welcoming smile.

'Is that a condor?' I asked him.

The old man's head slowly creaked around to look where I pointed. Then his tongue clacked in the negative: 'I have never seen a condor that small.'

'That's one of the biggest birds I've ever seen.' My response was tinged with more than a hint of scepticism. The fearsome-looking bird of prey stood roughly a metre from beak to claw.

'If perhaps you get to see a condor so close one day, you will understand what I am saying.'

Then the devastated church recaptured my imagination. A gaping fracture line split the remainder of the facade in two. The right-hand side was crooked and sunken. It looked like an earthquake ruin.

This time my speculations were right. The old man took off his hat as a mark of respect while he spoke of that tragic night in Maca five years earlier. A dozen houses had collapsed, claiming 20 lives. He'd slept through the whole thing, after spending the evening drinking pisco with his mates.

In the overall scheme of things, Maca's earthquake hardly rated as catastrophic. The Andes seemed to regularly test the faith of its residents on a more dramatic scale. The worst involved the Huascaran Massif in central Peru. In 1962, an avalanche of rock, ice and snow roared into the Santa River valley, wiped out several villages and killed over

3000 people. But this was just a warning from the mountain about what it would do next. On 31 May 1970 a severe earthquake (magnitude 8 on the Richter scale) rocked the same valley. The trembling earth broke loose a massive amount of rock and ice. The size of the chunk of mountain involved is staggering: estimates are that it was over 1000 metres wide and 1.5 kilometres long. It steamrolled towards the hapless town of Yungay at an average speed of over 200 kilometres an hour. About 20,000 people were killed instantly. Elsewhere, another 50,000 died in the same earthquake.

From Maca, we planned to cut across to the other side of the Colca Canyon. Madrigal was only a few hours' trekking away. Before leaving town, I bought an alpaca wool jumper for $10. Within days we'd be in the snow-swept passes, and I couldn't shake the fear that I didn't have enough clothing to ward off the cold. Without exception, every sheep-wool jumper I'd ever worn had made my skin itch. Alpaca wool offered one absolute miracle quality: no itching. It was also regarded as warmer than sheep's wool. This was the feature most important to anyone worrying that he would freeze to death halfway up a mountain.

FIVE
THE SOURCE OF THE AMAZON

25 September 1999 (day 13):
Madrigal, 210 kilometres from the Pacific

The policeman stood sober-faced as we deposited our backpacks on a bench outside the station house. He was tall, broad-shouldered and had the chiselled features of an eau de cologne model. He cut a commanding presence in his neatly pressed dark green and beige uniform and knee-high leather boots. The officer may have had us worried about a possible interrogation but for the pink beanie on his head with its fluffy white pom-pom.

His face split into a broad smile and he shook our hands vigorously. He ushered us through a low doorway, and into an atrium with high ceilings. The spacious room contained little except for a desk, a wooden chair and a bench against one wall. The desk snuggled into one corner. Above it hung two portraits – one of a famous military general (long dead), the other a chief of police from the turbulent 1930s.

From what I had seen so far, the difference between the army and the police force in Peru was hard to spot. Both men looked cruel. In many circles, they were considered to have been national heroes. To me, their expressions revealed the kind of merciless attitudes from which the Peruvian people have suffered for decades at a time throughout the nation's history.

Peru's tumultuous past stretches right back to its bloody founding. In 1533, Spanish Conquistadores obliterated the Incan Empire. From that point on, uprisings by the mistreated indigenous peoples were interspersed with civil wars and the struggle for independence from Spain. In modern times, military juntas, violent communist movements and a continuing territorial conflict with its northern neighbour – Ecuador – have made Peru notorious for civil unrest.

I knew all this. I also knew that tourists and travellers were sometimes caught in the crossfire or kidnapped and held for ransom. The current word on the travellers' grapevine was promising. For the past few years, travel in Peru had been a relatively safe affair. Even the *Sendero Luminoso*, a rebel movement that terrorised the country throughout the 1980s and early '90s, had at last been quelled. In the eyes of my mother, though, I was putting my life on the line by heading to South America. Then again, in her eyes, simply going anywhere beyond Australia's shores meant I was asking for trouble.

The policeman's name was Alvarez. He gave a low whistle as we each handed him a passport from a different country.

'I have never seen a passport that is not Peruvian!' he exclaimed delightedly. Alvarez rummaged in a drawer for his own. He showed us his picture and a wad of empty pages. 'I don't know if I will ever use it. Perhaps one day I can go to Bolivia. I am told the people there are very interesting.'

'What about Ecuador?' I ventured.

The deputy sucked in his breath. 'It is not easy to go there,' he said. 'My country and Ecuador, they hate each other.'

'Why?'

'They claim half of Loreto is theirs!'

He was obviously outraged by the thought of this. Loreto was Peru's largest, most untamed and resource-rich province – the perfect staging point for a frontier battle.

His tone softened. 'I don't know much about it. Madrigal is so far away from everything.'

There was a hint of regret in this last statement. It was clear that Deputy Alvarez regarded the soaring mountains and spectacular valleys in his patch as something of a prison. For him, the world beyond the Andes must have seemed pretty much out of reach.

'What are you doing here?' he asked, almost as an afterthought.

We filled in the blanks for him. As usual, the significance of Mismi, apart from being just another local mountain, had escaped everyone.

'We need donkeys,' I told him.

The deputy smiled, as if to say 'You've come to the right place.' 'Come with me,' he said.

Outside, the light was fading fast; a chill wind hurried down from the mountains to whip our faces. Alvarez led us through empty lanes fringed by rows of whitewashed hovels. No light glowed from within any of them. It would have seemed a far gloomier scene but for the pom-pom bobbing so comically with each step Alavrez took.

The pom-pom came to rest outside a plain door. The deputy knocked. As with all the other houses, not even a candle flame shone through the front windows. Something shuffled behind the door. Then came the grinding of metal as a peephole slid open. Until now, I had not envisioned the donkey trade as a cutthroat one. After a brief exchange between the policeman and a pair of eyes, the door creaked inwards to reveal a stooped man. Satisfied, the deputy bid us goodnight and strode off.

For several uncomfortably silent seconds, the old Peruvian looked at us, his wariness mirroring our own. Then he turned and melted into a dim hallway. Apparently, this was equivalent to 'Welcome, please come in.' We entered and shut the door, plunging ourselves into thick, musty darkness. The hallway ended at a rectangular halo of light. This door eased open, delivering us into a brightly lit room and the stares of ten or more men.

Four crowded around a table, interrupted in the strange type of backgammon they were playing. Several others were in standing conference at the far end of the room. The rest slouched on benches and nursed pipes. Highland folk certainly weren't renowned for ageing well, but no one looked less than 50 years old. I wondered if this gathering might be the Andean version of the Freemasons.

All talking ceased. I didn't know where to look. Voicing a 'hello' seemed feeble. Our sheepish smiles were met with nothing more than curious grins. Here was the proverbial collision of cultures, leaving both sides temporarily stunned.

Just inside the entrance we'd come through, a man was seated at an empty desk. To him the doorman mumbled the reason for our presence. Two-dozen ears strained to overhear.

'We need to rent donkeys,' I confirmed.

'To where?' quizzed our host.

'*Montaña Mismi*.'

He waved at us to stay put, then left the room through an archway. We waited, feeling like intruders but pleased to be closing in on some beasts of burden.

I took in more of the surroundings. There were no windows. As with the police station, this room boasted the bare minimum in furniture and wall decoration. Two naked light bulbs dangled from a cracked plaster ceiling. A map was glued to the back of the door. Considering the clothing and headwear on show, we could have been in a French Resistance bunker during World War II.

The fellow who entered next dissolved my illusion. He wore a llama-wool poncho and high-cut boots. Half of his face hid in the shadow cast by a wide-brimmed felt hat. I saw only a Cheshire Cat grin. He shook our hands. The skin was rougher than that of other Peruvian men (and that was saying something).

'You want to go to Mismi?' he asked hoarsely.

We nodded.

'I know Mismi,' came the gruff declaration. The grin never wavered. He planted his feet further apart, boot tips facing outwards, then folded his arms beneath the poncho. This was clearly meant to give him an imposing air.

'We need two donkeys to carry our gear for the climb up to the plateau,' I explained.

The grin vanished and he nodded slowly. I waited in vain for a further response.

'Do you have donkeys?' Colin prompted.

'Si.'

'How much for one day?'

Looking like something out of a spaghetti western, the

mysterious man rubbed his chin with thumb and forefinger.

'For me it is one day up and one day down. You must rent for two days.' This was fair enough, of course.

'Okay, sure. How much for two days then?'

As though he hadn't heard the question, the mysterious man swivelled his head and whispered to the deskman, who now stood behind him. Then he returned his gaze to us, grinning once more. 'We will leave at dawn tomorrow.'

'Great. So how much will it cost per day?' I pressed.

This time the question was shrugged off as unimportant. Deskman leant over to whisper quickly and quietly to Señor Mysterioso. I didn't like the conspiratorial atmosphere, and that grin was really beginning to bug me.

Scott voiced his thoughts: 'This guy is pissing me off. I bet he'll want a small fortune when we get there.'

It had all the makings of such a scenario. I pondered what else our enigmatic friend might be capable of doing. I tried once again to settle a price – the grin only broadened.

'Come here early tomorrow morning,' was all he said.

And with that, Señor Mysterioso walked back through the archway and out of sight. There was nothing more to be done. Slowly, everyone's attention returned to their activities. The doorman, smiling now, led us back into cold twilight. It was a smile that contained no hint of kindness.

Unsure even of where to spend the night, we aimlessly wandered Madrigal's windswept lanes, arguing over donkey options. As we walked beside a fence made from stones and hardened clay, a loud 'ee-ore' erupted from the other side. Several paces further along, there was a hole where the fence had crumbled. Leaning my head and shoulders through the hole, I came nose to nose with another victim of curiosity.

'*Hola.*'

'*Hola.*'

'Are they your donkeys?'

'Where are you from?'

He and I blurted out our questions at the same time.

We explained who we were and what we needed. Rufino, or Willy as he preferred to be known, was interested in doing business. His donkeys normally worked on the family maize plot, but there wasn't much lugging to be done at this time of year.

Scott lobbed in the inevitable question. 'How much?'

As if it were a grenade, I braced for impact. Cunningly, Willy threw it right back at us.

'How much do you think is fair?' he said.

Colin proposed 50 soles. Every Peruvian before now had claimed we'd be unlucky to pay more than 30 a day for a couple of donkeys. But Willy frowned.

'I will do it for 75 per day,' he stated firmly. He wouldn't budge from this. He viewed the journey as gruelling and perhaps dangerous if the weather turned foul. Any lesser payment was not worth his trouble.

I sighed. There seemed little hope of finding a better offer. Willy's price wasn't cheap, but it was a price nonetheless. Importantly, I sensed he was trustworthy. As a gesture of goodwill, he made us welcome to pitch our tent in the donkey enclosure for the night. Best of all, there was not a cheesy grin in sight.

I emerged from the tent and stepped in a pile of fresh manure. When I was growing up, my mother had always said that accidentally putting your foot in poo meant good luck – but then she'd also insisted that eating eggshells gave you warts. Certainly, this most recent promise of good fortune would only carry me so far in the coming days.

Like most Peruvians, Willy had risen with the birds. In daylight, I got a better look at our hired donkey-master. Beneath the well-worn peasant worker's hat was a young, soft-skinned face. His chin jutted out, looking all the more prominent for being freshly shaven. Overall, his head looked a fraction too big for his body. Unruffled by the cool morning air, he wore only a faded Brazilian football team T-shirt, canvas trousers and a pair of standard-issue rubber sandals.

The donkeys were busily munching on a stack of grass. Willy brought us a thermos of hot coffee to supplement our own breakfast of dry biscuits and fruit. Then he set to readying both animals for their unusual loads. Layers of thick woollen blankets cushioned their lumpy spines and bony haunches. A leather strap was looped around their bulging bellies.

Willy wrestled with the backpacks for more than half an hour, shuffling and rearranging them until he was satisfied. He complained that the bags were unevenly weighted. 'Sacks of corn are much easier to work with,' he grunted. From the entrance of their cottage, his wife and young son looked on in bemusement.

As an arc of molten sun trickled over the ranges bordering the upper Colca, Willy mumbled some coaxing words. The donkeys began to march.

Nosy faces appeared in the windows. Townsfolk ceased whatever they were doing to watch the odd procession. We skirted the plaza and passed the police station. Still in his pink beanie, Deputy Alvarez waved from the doorway. Thankfully, there was no sign of Señor Mysterioso.

Cobbles gave way to dried mud and gravel. Terraces lapped at the base of the mountain slope. The straight lanes between them suddenly became a zigzag of curving switchbacks. The thinner soil let nothing grow except for low shrubs and grass. Still hungry, each donkey tried sneaking a nibble here and there, but a gentle slap on the rump from Willy got them moving again.

Twenty minutes into the climb, the view of Madrigal already looked like an aerial photograph. Our initial ascent was fast. I studied my breathing – it still seemed normal enough. I asked Willy if he'd ever felt *soroche*. He shook his head but this didn't offer me much encouragement. I knew the people here had different physiologies.

'It is a problem for Peruvian people who normally live by the sea or in the jungle,' he added.

I already considered myself in the same precariously floating boat as both these groups, and the fact was, we were doing our best to rock that boat even more.

The problem had its roots in our small altitude gain between Huambo and Madrigal. Mismi's summit still soared almost 2500 metres above us. Mountaineering edict stated that when climbing above 3000 metres, the climber should not make an overall gain of more than 500 metres of elevation per day. We knew that by day's end we'd be camped on the Pampa plateau, some *1500 metres* higher than Madrigal.

No doubt many would maintain that we were fools for doing it, and perhaps, deep down, there *was* an element of 'It'll never happen to me.' But there was method to our madness: we knew that with every passing day, the Amazon's rapids grew in strength. By rocking the boat now, we hoped to reduce the chance of being dashed on the rocks in stormier waters later.

Even minus backpacks, hiking was difficult. Colin and Scott, as they had done from the outset, drifted ahead. I paced myself off the donkeys and made small talk with their master. My thoughts, though, never strayed far from *soroche*.

The possibility that symptoms might kick in with every upward step made it seem like wandering through a minefield. I remembered the words of a friend from Mackay who spent a lot of his time trekking in the Himalayas: 'At some point between 3500 and 5000 metres, I guarantee you will be vomiting.' He'd said it with a smirk, as if it was one of the joys of life.

One thing made me hopeful of *not* being sick as a dog. When I had last donated blood, the nurse testing for anaemia had raised an eyebrow at my high haemoglobin count. It made sense to think that blood brimming full of these oxygen-luring molecules would be able to rally against the thinner air. It was something to cling onto at least.

Willy handed over his prodding stick and motioned for me to keep the donkeys on track while he dashed off to the toilet. Both animals continued plodding up the trail just long enough for him to disappear behind a rocky outcrop. Then, in unison, they stopped. Their heads stayed low and facing forwards. They didn't move a muscle.

First I tried intimidation. I stood alongside them whipping the palm of my hand with the prodding stick. Neither donkey even twitched. Next I tried force, but my 'firm hand' translated into nothing more persuasive than tentative pats on the rump. I supplemented these with shouts of 'Yaa, mule!' One of the creatures turned its head towards me as if to say, 'Whaddya call that?' By the time Willy returned, I'd cemented my pushover status in the eyes of both donkeys. In Willy's eyes, I had probably labelled myself the quintessential city slicker.

By early afternoon, the sky had grown sombre. Cold rain turned into sleet. The trail flattened, first curving along a ridge-line, then traversing a slope that formed the Continental Divide.

The complexion of the land had changed. Here, it was exposed, regularly whipped and beaten by the harsh weather. As a result, it looked mean and bitter. At lower altitude the vegetation had looked something like the Mallee scrub of southern Australia. Now it had become a heathland of low-cowering shrubs. The landscape seemed prone to fits of rage, unwilling to cooperate with people. I began to suspect that we were approaching the limit of humankind's realm. Like trespassers, Peruvian folk made their dashes along this trail, between the hospitable lower lands on either side. And every time, they hoped to evade capture. During a past age, some had entered this place with no hope of being able to leave. In the wind, I imagined I heard their echoing screams, the cries of children who had been carried this way to be sacrificed. To quench the gods' intense thirst for blood, Inca priests had fought not only the frenzied struggling of their young victims but the often bitter mood of these mountains. On some of the Andes highest crags, where these days only Gore-tex jackets, designer fleeces and an expensive pair of Italian mountaineering boots are considered worthy apparel, archaeologists have found the remains of such Incan religious slaughter. I found it hard to imagine tackling summits even higher than Mismi sporting little more than a few llama skins and sandals, but that's exactly what the Inca did.

A flurry of snow whipped our faces as we slogged it up a last rise towards the Divide. I looked back at Willy and into the eyes of a man who regretted his decision to wear only sandals. My own toes were fighting hard to stay awake – Willy's must have been close to dropping off. He was a relieved fellow when I offered him Scott's sneakers.

We regrouped at the Continental Divide. While stamina slowly filtered back into leg muscles, there was time to savour a significant moment: our entry into the Amazon basin. Behind us, the snow and ice melt went only as far as the Pacific Ocean. From here on, every molecule of water we saw had the same intention as us – to keep a date with a far-flung Atlantic.

When my breath came back, something else arrived with it. An ache had planted itself in the central core of my brain and was making gentle probing jabs in all directions. It was a mild headache, but it was there.

'How are you guys feeling?' I asked.

Colin and Scott answered without hesitation.

'Great.'

'Fit as a fiddle.'

I would have preferred to hear less glowing self-appraisals. I felt doomed to be the burden on everyone else. If life imitated a movie script, then my name was about to be pencilled in beside one particular role, for no Hollywood portrayal of an adventure is ever complete without the poor sod whose body or sanity crumbles.

As we set off again, the trail sloped down sharply at first, then more gradually as we entered true Pampa plateau country. If the throb in my head was a sign of looming *soroche*, for now, any loss of elevation was more than welcome.

The snowfall got heavier and the temperature plunged with daylight's ebb. The thought of pitching a tent on the open Pampa did not appeal – there would be no fire and no hot meal. Willy had brought the Peruvian equivalent of a swag, but judging by his footwear choice, I doubted it would be sufficient. To avoid having our friendly donkey guide die from hypothermia, we would have to insist that he share the tent with us. Three was a tight squeeze already, four was getting ridiculous and guaranteed a terrible night's sleep.

Colin, Scott and I were ready to hunker down and make the best of it. Ideally, we wanted to have the tent erected before darkness fell but Willy insisted that we keep going further.

'There is a better place to camp,' he insisted.

He knew what he was talking about. Through the haze, a manmade structure appeared. It was a stone hut. I was both astonished and relieved. Alongside the hut, there were two animal enclosures, also made from stone. Only one creature could possibly be farmed in such an inhospitable climate – the alpaca.

The enclosures were empty. The hut was disused and had its own supply of firewood. Willy said it belonged to a herder who occasionally came to Madrigal to buy supplies. He lived in another hut close by. A chest-high wall, extending out from a corner of the hut, formed an alcove that was a perfect size for our tent. The alcove gave us complete protection from the wind. Inside, the hut was clean and tidy, the size of a modest bathroom. It was bare except for several alpaca skins bundled against one wall. Willy kindled a cooking fire in a purpose-built recess. If the air was already thin in these parts, the hut's interior quickly became more so. The sole outlet for the smoke was the low doorway, and this had a loose sheet of metal over it to shield out the draft.

'Why is there no chimney?' I asked the donkey-master, my eyes moist, my throat dry.

'Heat is precious,' he coughed.

Since the beginning of our trek from Camaná, almost a fortnight before, barely a couple of hours of waking, able-bodied time had passed without at least one of us pulling out the maps for a look. Accounting for another few centimetres on paper always felt good. But in trying to nut out the best possible path ahead we quite rightly became a little obsessive. The truth is that most planned journeys of this kind have the intended route drawn in with a permanent marker, on maps obtained several months beforehand. The only thing permanent on ours was the streaks left by dirty, probing fingertips, grubby monuments to our daily ritual of speculation, indecision and uncertainty.

That evening, we stared at the contour lines for much longer than usual. There was no labelling of Mismi's summit, only a ridge going by the same name. A bullseye of warped brown hoops indicated the location of the peak itself. From a dent in these hoops, the Amazon's first tributary – the Carhuasanta – headed off as a squiggly blue line. While we argued about the best way to approach Mismi, nameless nearby slivers of blue caught our attention. One in particular merged with the Carhuasanta, but appeared to be slightly longer up to this point than the Carhuasanta itself. The valley it flowed through was the same one we now camped in. It sprung from a different summit – Mount Quehishua – some five kilometres from Mismi.

'Hang on a moment!' I thought aloud. Was *Mount Quehishua* the true source of the Amazon? Or was this just another boo-boo made by the not-so-trustworthy cartographers in Lima?

Willy shrugged. I could tell he was still trying to figure out why three westerners believed that the start of the Amazon lay right on his doorstep. It certainly wasn't common knowledge. For decades, a tributary 500 kilometres north of our present location – the Marañón – was believed to be the farthest origin. Only recently, improved aerial photograhy and satellite imaging had shown otherwise.

I was no slouch when it came to geography, but I didn't know the name of the Nile's ultimate source. And, admittedly, before receiving Colin's letter, I'd never given any thought to where the Amazon began either.

As it turned out, Colin had only heard Mount Mismi quoted in relation to Mike Horn's Amazon foray. Three years before us, the South African Special Forces ex-serviceman had come this way, alone, and kicked off his voyage by paragliding from the mountain's summit. The 1986 Chmielinski–Kane expedition had considered the Divide pass (where we'd crossed earlier in the day) as their starting point. Horn's approach at this stage couldn't fail to inspire the likes of Colin. Despite leaving the paragliders at home, we wanted a mountaintop to be our beginning as well.

But had Horn really done his homework, or was Mismi selected because it offered a good launching pad? There seemed nothing else for it. In order to feel sure that we would clap eyes on the baby Amazon's very first dribbles, we must climb both peaks. Mismi would be first.

I turned in for the night and for the first time needed to zip up my sleeping bag as far as it would go. For added insulation, we had stuffed backpacks along the inside edges of the tent. Willy was happy to sleep in the hut beside the fire. I worried we might find him dead from smoke inhalation in the morning.

My headache was no worse. However, Colin and Scott had started complaining of something similar. The three of us lay there like sardines, discussing whether or not the coming day would be kind to us. A strong wind made the tent fabric crack like a whip. On my mind, more than anything else, was the persistent belief that I remained an intruder in these highlands. Perhaps chronic *soroche* would hit me as I slept and I'd never wake up. I might have tossed and turned all night contemplating this had I not (a) been wedged in so tightly, and (b) been claimed so quickly by the slumber of exhaustion.

Morning arrived without pain or nausea but with lingering images of some of the strangest dreams of my life, that I thought were symptoms of the thin air. Lying flat, everything seemed in good working order. Ten minutes passed before I dared raise my head. Even then, there was still only the same faint throbbing, like a muffled emergency beacon, echoing from the middle of my brain. Hopefully it was simply a gentle reminder that caution must go hand in hand with having your head in the clouds.

Colin and Scott wished their heads were numb, and the two men barely found the energy to put their clothes on. They tumbled from the tent looking as pale as the fresh snow that coated everything. Both stuffed their mouths full of coca leaves and chewed. It brought them some welcome relief. But while I later gulped down two bowls of porridge for breakfast, the pair could do nothing apart from empty their bellies of last night's meal. Like a prowling demon, it seemed *soroche* had stolen into camp and filtered into the bodies of my two companions.

Slightly less sinister was a visit by the hut's owner and his enormous woolly dog. He knew nothing except herding alpacas across the Pampa. The story of his life was etched in facial skin the texture of cooked meat; then again, if his home boasted the same standard of fireplace ventilation as this hut's, it was fair to say that his flesh had been well smoked over the decades. I was sure that not even driving animals through blizzards day after day could beat what that smoke must do to the complexion.

The old herder's name was Rilca. Willy knew him. You'd think that either this fact alone or the hut's disused status, or a combination of both, would have guaranteed us a free stay. Not so. Plateau hospitality came not only with a warm handshake and a broad smile, but with a price tag.

Debts settled, Colin staggered off in search of a good spot to loosen his bowels. Rilca's dog followed. The Canadian returned more nauseated than ever. 'He sat and watched me while I crapped. He was even drooling,' Colin reported. Minutes later, the dog came trotting back into view, licking his jowls and looking satisfied. As both man and beast had just demonstrated in their different ways, living high in the Andes was about being able to make the most of your opportunities when they came.

By 8 a.m., we were ready to go.

'It should take you no more than six or seven hours.' This was one of two pieces of advice with which Willy sent us on our way to scale Mount Mismi. The other was his insistence that leaving backpacks unguarded at the alpaca farm base camp was too risky. No problem, though. For an extra 50 soles he would gladly wait with them, and even have food prepared when we got back. Had we not had such a good feeling about Willy's honesty, I might have mistaken all this for extortion.

Colin and Scott's condition had improved since breakfast but things fell apart quickly for them once the hiking began. Not even the warm sunshine could throw off *soroche*'s fast-descending cloud. The snow crunched under my feet. Colin and Scott bulldozed through it. Fifteen minutes in, Scott turned around. Five minutes after that, Colin was doubled over and dry retching. He, too, could go no further. I knew Colin as someone who revelled in the challenge of forcing his body onwards through constant pain. For him to concede showed just how paralysing *soroche* was.

At no stage over the past three weeks had any of us considered going solo. Either we all hiked together or we didn't go anywhere. Safety and security were in us keeping close together. More critically, we didn't carry enough spare equipment for each of us to be self-sufficient. There was only one set of maps, one tent and one Spanish phrase-book.

Right now, the equipment factor was no longer an issue. That was the beauty of having a base camp. Going solo was an option here. A streak of independence awoke in me. Strangely, given my last thoughts the previous night, I wasn't gripped by dread at seeing the state Colin and Scott were in. If anything, my confidence grew, as it became more apparent that my body was able to ward off the lurking demons.

Looking at it from a level-headed perspective, the odds were stacked in my favour: the weather was superb and the climb to Mismi's summit was not supposed to be a particularly difficult one. That said, there was still no visible mountaintop to head for. I spent half my time during the first couple of hours matching contour lines to landscape features. Sometimes my gaze would flick between paper and the same rocky spur for several minutes, until I was convinced that they were one and the same. I knew that if I lost my position on the map, I would feel paranoid about losing Mismi's identity among half-a-dozen other peaks.

I skirted a grass-choked marsh then attacked the ridge slope that I hoped would give me a first glimpse of my goal. Over the final hundred metres up to the ridge-top, I climbed a staircase of boulders that had spilt into and filled a deep gully. Like the entrance corridor of a temple, it ushered me into the presence of Mount Mismi. Again, my thoughts returned to a Tolkien adventure. Mount Mismi didn't have a craggy castle stuck on top of it, yet I half expected to see a battle raging between the goblin and troll hosts.

The caramel-coloured terraces of the Colca Valley were visible more than two kilometres below. I looked at them as though through a portal to another dimension. It was a different planet down there.

With the summit in view, I picked up the pace. The ridge-line stretched away towards Mismi, looking like a sharp-angled rooftop. The right-hand side, dipping into the Colca, was buried under a snowdrift. At the ridge's apex, this hardened snow ended as a three-metre-high wall. Falling away towards the Carhuasanta River, the left-hand side of the ridge was a mess of boulders and plate-like scree.

Crossing the ridge drained the stamina from my legs, and my calves, shins and feet were soon aching. The ground moved with each step. Every scree fragment had sharp edges, slicing into boot leather or ankle flesh if my foot sank too deep. Twice I landed on my hip and shoulder when a plate slipped and slid downhill. Only my gloves prevented the Nevado Mismi from drawing blood.

Eventually, I reached the base of a ledge leading up to the peak itself. I was happy to swap the spiteful scree for a field of abstract ice sculptures. Scoured and shaped by the wind from a sheet of frozen snow, some of these rose up to my waist. Beyond the ice sculptures, I can only describe the rest of the climb as pure hell. Although the terrain became more solid, it also got steeper. My leg muscles, whether from overwork or lack of oxygen, felt like they were on fire. Soon I needed to stop and rest every 30 seconds, the burning sensation came and went so quickly.

Thick clouds had blanked out the sun completely now, but conditions on the ground were still good. I hadn't worn a watch in years (to Colin's occasional annoyance) and I'd paid little attention to the sun's position before it disappeared. I had no idea what the time was, and it was hardly as if there was anyone around to ask. I felt very lightheaded and my body clock could do no better than be certain it was sometime between 11 a.m. and 3 p.m.

By the time I made it to the false peak, my legs were

struggling to power on. The false peak itself hadn't caught me out – I'd expected it. Most mountains have one and I'd learnt never to start celebrating ahead of time.

The highest point lay a few hundred more metres away. An axe-blade ridge, known by mountaineers as an arête, was between me and it. As a slender wedge of rock, it linked the false peak to the true summit of Mount Mismi. And, as with the much larger ridge behind me, blown snow had heaped on the arête's right-hand side. This snow's face fell away sheer for at least a kilometre. The other face of the arête was home to more ice sculptures. These ones licked upwards out of the scree, like the frozen flames of a hillside inferno.

I crawled, ape-like, along the tightrope sliver of rock that divided the two sides. The wind gusted up from the void to my right. My heart raced more out of terror than from the effort. My thighs cramped. I began to doubt whether I'd have enough physical reserves to make it back down again. I couldn't bear to look any further than where each foot was going.

Then, sooner than expected, the cairn was up beside me. The pile of stones was not only the end of my climb, but a reminder that there were other people in the world. Instead of puffing my chest out (or crying with relief) I pondered on who had stacked these stones. Six rocks meant six people. Conquistadores perhaps? Maybe Incan mountaineers had started the cairn. I knew for certain that Mike Horn had supplied one. Another one represented an American named Loren McIntyre, who came to this region in 1971 seeking the source of the Amazon. He had ascended Mismi, but proclaimed a small lake 300 metres below the summit as the source.

I could see this lake now – Lake McIntyre. It was tiny, no more than 50 metres across, cradled in a rocky lip overlooking the head of the Carhuasanta Valley. Almost perfectly parabolic in cross-section, the valley curved left before I could see where the Quehishua-born stream intersected it.

Suddenly, my view of the valley began to fade, and was then steadily absorbed into whiteness. Menacing clouds were rushing upwards from below, as though by reaching the summit I had triggered some kind of booby-trap. The weather, after being good to me for so long, was about to get nasty. I didn't care. I sat feeling a sense of triumph that even eclipsed what I'd known on getting a hat-trick in school cricket. (Those who play the game and have snared three wickets in a row know that this is saying something.)

The clouds arrived. Falling snow stirred me to action. I set up the tripod and took photographs. I put my rock on the cairn. Perhaps breaking some code of mountaineering, I added a second trophy – a jade necklace, engraved with a Celtic rune. Sacrificing children to the gods might not be my style, but some kind of offering seemed right for Mismi, nonetheless.

I could see just a few dozen metres ahead through the mist. The loss of visibility made me acutely aware there couldn't be too many hours of daylight remaining. I retied my bootlaces then set off on a beelining scramble for the Carhuasanta and base camp. Bearings weren't a problem. I simply had to go straight down, parallel with the direction of the slope.

The ice sculptures demanded patient negotiating, but on the bare scree I bounded freely. Even over the sharp-edged plates, I made good time. I took each stride with an exaggerated heel-first motion, allowing for the rubble sliding under my weight. In this way, I half leapt, half surfed down the north face of Mount Mismi.

The slope flattened into the shelf on which Lake McIntyre sat. Scree became boulders the size of cars and buses. With no gradient to confirm a direction, I concentrated hard on keeping to a straight line and taking the shortest route. Engulfed by mist, the terrain seemed otherworldly.

The shelf ended at a cirque. My heart somehow managed to thump still harder. From the lip of the cirque dropped the sheer wall of the valley head. Over millennia, a sloping pile of boulders had built up against the wall. Twenty metres to my left, there was a place where they almost reached the lip.

I hurried over and quickly assessed my chances. It was three metres to the nearest boulder. There were no foot- or hand-holds, but a one-metre-wide cleavage in the wall meant I could probably lower myself halfway by bracing my feet and back against sheer rock.

My instincts were to scour the area for alternatives, agonise over the best technique to apply, then spend time steeling my resolve – but there was no time for any of that. I didn't hesitate for an instant. As far as I was concerned, the worst thing that could happen to me was to be caught short of base camp when darkness fell.

The wall face had a texture like fine-grained sandpaper. Although wet, it proved excellent for gripping. Thank goodness for small mercies, but that was where they stopped. The surface of the boulder I planned to drop onto glistened like wet concrete – treacherously smooth. Because the cleavage doubled in width halfway down, I was forced to try landing on it from a height of nearly two metres. If I didn't slip and snap a leg on impact, the likely event of me tumbling into one of the gaps between the boulders would surely end in a broken neck, I thought.

With feet and shoulders pressed hard against either side of the cleavage, my body was in anything but the ideal starting position. Mustering every feline instinct I could, I let go and twisted my torso in mid flight.

Both boots planted flat and stuck. Scree-jumping and plate-surfing had been kind to neither leather nor stitching, yet the soles were showing toughness. I gave silent thanks to the god Vibram. Snow dusted every boulder, like the icing on bread buns. Not keen to push my luck further, I crawled down over them very gingerly.

At the valley floor, I heaved a sigh of relief. No more risk of strains or fracture and the chance to run on level ground. Wrong! First step, I slipped and fell flat on my back. Beneath a layer of snow, marshy earth had frozen into a patchwork of little ice-skating rinks. Pools of anoxic mud festered between clumps of grass. A crust of ice sealed off the putrid contents, until my foot came along, and broke through the ice and stirred things up. I passed on my first opportunity to drink Amazon water.

The upper Carhuasanta defined itself as a tiered chain of boggy puddles – 'humble' certainly described the beginnings of the Amazon. And if the standard was being set for ease of travel down the remainder of its length, Colin, Scott and I were in for a nightmare of a time.

I zigzagged across the floor of the valley, chewing up valuable time in search of solid ground. When I found some, it rarely lasted more than a few hundred metres before I was back up to my shins in slop. The sharply rising sides of the valley put paid to any hope of moving laterally across the slope. Accepting my lot, I settled into a style of motion that was something between a walk, a run and a shuffle. It seemed to maximise speed while at the same time minimising the chances of injury.

Day's end, however, was always going to beat me. I invested the last few minutes of half-light into pulling out the map for a last review of my position. The uniform slopes and poor vision made this almost impossible. At a guess I figured it was about a kilometre to the valley containing the nameless Mount Quehishua stream.

I knew that somewhere up the valley was the herder's hut and my mates. I also knew that with no moon out tonight and a leaden sky, the coming night would be especially black. Hiking in darkness didn't frighten me as much as the possibility that I might simply not find the hut. The Quehishua valley was much broader than the Carhuasanta and its sides gently sloping. Getting orientated would be extremely hard. I could easily walk within 50 metres of the hut and not notice it.

The desperate hiking made me warm, even sweaty. At some point, though, physical exhaustion would replace nervous energy and make me stop. Hitting that brick wall was sure to happen well before morning came. And in the conditions, cooling down might prove fatal. Without rock overhangs and ledges, the only place to take shelter from the snow and wind was at the hut.

When the last flickers of daylight were gone and the mountains slept as faceless giants, I turned left into the valley carved by the Quehishua tributary. Above the wind, I heard a fledgling Amazon gurgle her first sounds. My head-torch illuminated the first of 15,000 confluences. Here, for the first time, the Amazon expressed a personality. Before now, it had seemed embryonic, not quite alive.

The head-lamp was crucial. I aimed it forwards, straight up the valley, not at the ground where I trod. Forgetting to pack my little alarm clock had been careless but at least I'd been cluey enough to bring light. It was a beacon for Scott and Colin, as the conditions would muffle our shouts.

I didn't want to think too much about the possibility that their *soroche* had worsened to the point where Willy had put them on the donkeys and taken them back down to the Colca. That meant things were bad for all of us.

Half an hour passed. Then I saw what I wanted: a pin-head of torchlight in the veil of gloom.

Another half-hour later I'd finished gobbling down a hot bean casserole in front of the fire. My toes thawed. I coughed contentedly on the smoke while telling my story. It was past eight o'clock. So much for a six-hour round trip.

'Sorry to get you guys worried,' I said, rubbing smoke out of my eyes.

Colin's eyes were watering too. 'I'm just glad I didn't have to ring your mother to tell her you croaked,' he replied.

'Well, I'm happy you two got off your arses to come look for me!'

Most of their day had been spent lying flat on their backs, chewing coca, and taking turns to throw up. By late afternoon, the acclimatisation process had kicked in and they felt much better. Their strength had returned, and with it the desire to get among the action themselves come the morning.

The next day, while I nursed two very stiff legs and some brittle nerves, Colin and Scott made a successful attempt on the summit of Mount Quehishua. As a team, both mountains were now under our belt. We were confident that, somewhere along the line, one of us had stood at the ultimate source of the Amazon.

Last word on the matter comes from a *National Geographic*–funded research expedition that came to the

Madrigal region in mid 2000. An exhaustive survey of all the watercourses in the area concluded that because the stream issuing from Mount Quehishua does not flow all year round, it cannot lay claim to the title of furthest tributary.

It sounds technical, and it is, but after all the injured joints, frantic heartbeats and grey hairs of those three weeks of trekking, I won't argue with anyone who says the Amazon 'officially' begins at the top of Mount Mismi.

SIX
THE APURIMAC

6 October 1999 (day 24):
Pilpinto, 6790 kilometres to the Atlantic Ocean

The old man puffed on his pipe, then used the end to point at our bundled-up raft.

'What did you say that was?'

'It's a boat.'

I didn't know the word for 'inflatable' so I made pumping motions (like detonating an explosive) and blew air out of my mouth. Scott handed down another of the heavy 'dry bags' from the roof of the bus.

The old man's laugh turned to a smoker's hack. He spat onto the pavement, then levelled a cynical smile at me.

'The river is nice here. But down there . . .' He shook his head and slapped the air in dismissive fashion.

Scott tossed down one of our five paddles. I gave a few sweeping motions and added '*Todo rio*' – the whole river.

A couple of younger men wandered over for a closer look at the paddles.

'They're going down the *whole* river,' declared the old man in a mock-serious tone.

Clearly he wrote us off as simply naive, joyriding gringos. I was yet to quash that notion in my own mind.

'Are there big rapids near here?' I asked one of the young men.

He nodded. 'I have not seen them, but –'

'Amigos,' the old man interrupted, 'the church is not far from here either. I think you must go there first.'

Pilpinto didn't offer much besides a place to access the Apurimac with our boat. It certainly didn't offer encouragement. People were perplexed by our plans, some seemed almost disappointed they would not be there to see us pulverised by the first monster rapid.

The plaza sported a sculpture of three huge clay butterflies. They were symbolic of the ones fluttering about in my stomach. It was a sensation that had plagued me in every cricket match as I waited to go in to bat. My coach would always say that butterflies were good to have, as long as they went away by the time you were about to face your first ball. I imagined those inside me now with sharp teeth and claws, poised to tear their way out of my belly.

Familiar thoughts laid seige to my brain as well. Would I be out first ball? Would I take some blows on my body, smash a few boundaries, then get clean bowled just when I looked to be getting my eye in? Or would I manage to get through the entire innings unbeaten? Problem was, I'd never scored a century in my life.

While I wrestled with all those long-held doubts, Colin gave out plenty of positive energy and enthusiasm. This was the day he'd really set himself up for. Trekking to the source had satisfied an urge for some completion, nothing more. The Apurimac was his inspiration.

It seemed Scott, too, could barely wait to pit himself against the rapids. The exhilaration of a rafting trip down Africa's famous Zambezi River when he was younger had stayed with him. He loved the idea of revisiting that feeling, and he was no stranger to getting splashed. Scott had done a lot of waterskiing in his time and could handle a jet ski quite nicely too. Fast and furious watersports, they were his thing.

The river eased its way gently past Pilpinto, as though trying to rebut all the bad press levelled against it. It was about 30 metres wide, and shallow. We launched from a pebble beach in front of the town. Five seconds later, the boat scraped to a halt and had to be walked into deeper water. The canyon's right-hand side rose almost vertically from the water's edge. The left bank ascended sharply at first, then flattened off for ten metres or more before again striving for the sky.

It was mid-afternoon and a dozen schoolchildren hit the edge of town at the same time we did. They scampered home along the precarious road linking Pilpinto to an even smaller settlement further along the canyon. From high above us came yells, whistles and waves.

There was barely a ripple on the river surface apart from those made by the paddles breaking through it. If you closed your eyes, nothing betrayed the fact that you were moving. Only the shore sliding smoothly by gave it away. My knees, feet and shoulders quietly celebrated. This was a well-greased slide, a world of negative gravity. Even when we stopped paddling, the current pulled us along faster than we had been going at any stage of the hike. Above, the schoolkids had to mix running with walking to keep pace.

I relaxed. The mid-afternoon sun had already slipped from the strip of sky overhead but it left an ambient warmth lingering in the still air. The raft looked strong, the rest of our equipment well ordered and secure. Just getting it all to this point, intact and on time, deserved a pat on the back. We joked and chatted like old school chums. The camaraderie between the three of us was the best it had been.

We felt comfortable around each other. There were no fundamental differences in our outlooks on the universe and we each prided ourselves on maintaining a sense of fair play. And politically speaking, we marched to a similar beat. Most important of all, none of us had a girlfriend whose name cropped up every five seconds. No topic was taboo. However, while we openly speculated on what gruesome fate might befall us during the next 400 kilometres of whitewater, never once had any of us gone beyond cosy banter to reveal our raw state of mind.

For me at least, the immediate future had never promised so much risk. No matter what our level of skill or degree of confidence, incidents would happen. That much was a certainty. The Apurimac has a reputation as one of the most treacherous rivers on the planet. A French kayaker drowned in 1953. In 1976, a German expedition was abandoned after the team leader died in a boulder sieve. And two Swiss rafters went to a watery grave in 1997. There are a dozen scenes in Kane's book that could give even the most seasoned armchair adventurer nightmares about the Apurimac. Before 1986, no one had successfully navigated its length. All up, a disturbingly high proportion of attempts to run the Apurimac have ended disastrously.

We admitted to finding the challenge awe-inspiring but none of us had really expressed the emotions evoked by such a tragic history. Maybe there was no need. A kind of motto had been coined, from which we drew peace of mind: 'We'll portage the bad stuff.' In other words, at the rapids that looked most dangerous, we would haul everything out of the river and go around them. It was a statement each of us had made a number of times already. Every time someone said it, the other two would agree enthusiastically, as though it was a key factor being noted for the very first time. That word 'portage' seemed like a 'Get out of jail free' card. Strangely, but perhaps helpfully, we spoke as if those killed by the Apurimac had never recognised it as an option.

A hamlet came into view an hour (and no rapids) after leaving Pilpinto.

'Should be a shop here,' I observed. 'Anything else we need?'

One of the big dry bags contained about 50 kilograms of food. The fact that it had almost given the poor old bus driver a hernia back in Cuzco (where we'd retrieved our gear from the South American Explorers Club) seemed a good indicator of how thorough we'd been. It was sure to hold out for the better part of two weeks, and meant that for the first time we could prepare substantial meals.

'More Sublimes?' Our favourite comfort food, a must-buy.

'Good idea.'

'Fish bait.'

'Ah, yes!'

Trucha, an Andean variety of trout, ranked highly as a topic for small talk between us and the locals. Maybe the Apurimac promised as much fish as it did rapids.

As we nudged shore, the children returning from school in Pilpinto ran down and skidded to a halt at the river-bank. While Colin and I told our story so far, Scott went in search of the chocolate and a hunk of meat. More than any others we'd met, these kids were full of questions. A boy of about ten stepped forward and indicated three teenage girls at the back of the throng.

'They like you,' he winked.

Several other youngsters nodded and said it was true. Yet instead of going into fits of giggling as girls of a similar age in the west would be likely to do, the three tossed their heads back and pouted provocatively like catwalk models. Thoughts of gringos for husbands, perhaps.

I studied the other faces and wondered how many of them would ever have the opportunity, or the desire, to leave this valley. How would they cope with moving from a place where the sense of community was everything? Even modest Pilpinto dwarfed the hamlet. Cuzco must have seemed impossibly big and so far away. And us, we were envoys from another planet.

For the community members old enough to have tasted the bitter fruits offered by the Peruvian class system, we were probably regarded as *Viracochas* (the Quechuan word for the Conquistadores). In the minds of those people, we were not so different from the brutal Conquistadores. We were white-skinned and ready to shoot anything, even if only through a video-camera lens.

For centuries, the Quechuan people have received only scraps. The distribution of wealth and respect is heavily lopsided, favouring the *Criollos*, or people of pure Spanish descent. The Quechuas and the *Mestizos* (people of mixed blood) are left with almost nothing. I could feel a resentment, both in Pilpinto and in the people of this hamlet who stood watching us from afar. Their cold, sceptical attitudes contrasted with the excitement and wonder on the faces of these children. Perhaps we captured imaginations and spirits that were yet to be shot down and trampled into the dirt at the base of the social ladder.

We waved goodbye and continued. A half-hour later, Scott bolted upright from his slouch over the paddle.

'Oh, shit! You know what we've forgotten, don't you?'

'No, what?' I cringed, waiting for him to say 'a can opener' or, worse still, 'matches'.

'To give this boat a name.'

'Oh,' I said, a little peeved that I'd almost skipped a heartbeat over that.

'It's bad luck to sail a boat without naming it first,' Scott insisted.

'Is it?'

'Probably.'

'Funniest-looking sailboat I ever saw,' Colin chuckled. 'The christening bottle of champagne would end up bouncing off and smashing your skull. But I see your point. We're going to get to know this baby quite intimately.'

This was very true. For the sake of solidarity at least, our little red raft needed a name. And I'd always given names to my cars and bicycles. (My first car, an orange Datsun, was named Ernie, after the *Sesame Street* puppet.)

Since getting our hands on the raft, we'd been tossing a few ideas around, but suggestions like Red Bull (because she'd get the heart racing) and Atlantic Bound (as a show of confidence) didn't really seem to suit. Ultimately, it took being surrounded by craggy rock walls to promote the right amount of lateral thinking on the issue. I pondered this: to a Peruvian, staring down into this crack in the earth from the brink above, what would we look like? Answer: a pair of giant red floating lips. The fat round tubes, tapering to a point at each end made a gaping mouth in which the three of us sat.

'The Lips,' I offered.

'The what?'

I explained my rationale.

'How do you say it in Spanish?' Colin asked.

I looked it up. '*Los Labios.*'

'Perfect,' nodded Scott.

Los Labios boasted the latest material and design technology. At just over four metres from tip to tip, she rivalled commercial tour boats in length. Width-wise, she was slimmer and tapered in the fashion of a viking longboat. Although it made her significantly lighter when bundled up, she was less of a stable platform in violent slosh, more vulnerable to tipping right over. At the same time, her advantage over bigger boats was manoeuvrability. *Los Labios* could turn and accelerate quickly, weaving around mayhem that commercial-size rafts had no choice but to barrel through. Colin could vouch for it.

'She's a sportscar. Turns on a ten-cent piece,' he marvelled. 'Not like those pigs of boats I spent all summer guiding.'

Our selection had been no fluke. By all reports, the Apurimac rewarded technique over power, finesse over simply charging through. The river's medium volume did not pose as great a threat as her extreme rockiness. Apparently, rafting the Apurimac wasn't so much an exercise in hanging on to the back of a bucking bronco, it was more about finding a way through a tricky obstacle course without losing your head or getting stuck forever.

There was more to *Los Labios* than just sleekness. Beneath the tough outer skin, inner air-bladders were made from a soft transluscent plastic. In the event of a puncture, they could be accessed by unzipping the outer shell, and patched easily. The pontoon itself contained three separate bladders, meaning that if one suddenly ruptured, the other two would still keep us afloat.

Secured between the port and starboard sides (left and right, respectively) of the pontoon were two inflated cylinders called 'thwarts'. Grey-coloured and roughly a metre apart, they divided the raft into three compartments. The lens-shaped floor was inflated to about ten centimetres at its thickest point and attached to the pontoon via a long length of cord woven between the two. A purpose-designed gap between pontoon and floor allowed any water coming into the boat to escape immediately. The manufacturers boasted that, in the event of the raft completely filling with water, this 'self-bailing' system would drain it all away in less than four seconds.

The first evidence of whitewater was a series of riffles – small, shallow waves tumbling down a modest gradient. They brought shame to the fraternity of rapids. Not only was each set a model of uniformity and refined order, they were more or less spaced evenly down the river. Utterly benign, each lowered us gently to the next level like an escalator, but the machinery running them was in need of a good lube job. Eerie sequences of short whines filtered up through the floor as smooth river rocks buffed against slick rubber. Twice we ground to a standstill altogether, and were forced to get our feet wet. Our combined body weights plus food and all the equipment measured close to 400 kilograms but such was the raft's buoyancy that her draught (or depth taken in the water) didn't amount to more than a dozen centimetres. It was still enough to run aground, though.

Careful thought went into the distribution of weight. One man sat on the forward left and one on the forward right of the pontoon, just in front of the bow thwart. The third assumed the all-important 'guiding position' at the raft's stern. Our gear fit snugly into the middle compartment. Four 115-litre dry bags, stacked two high, were held firmly in place by cam straps that threaded through the pontoon-floor gap and around the bottom of the boat. A host of bits and pieces was either hooked onto these cam straps or stuffed tightly into nooks – because they wouldn't fit into the large dry bags or needed to be accessed quickly. Such items included the pump, two spare paddles, shoes, collapsible water container and a couple of foam sleeping mats. Smaller waterproof bags contained cameras, journals and the first-aid kit. The dry bags, big and small, were crafted from a similar material to the raft. In theory, nothing inside them got wet, even if the boat flipped.

There was little risk of that happening on the first afternoon. We arrived at an ideal place to camp, singing 'New York, New York' at the top of our lungs and enjoying the sound of it reverberating through the canyon. To the right, a concave length of cliff, with a high overhang, gave our chorus an almost concert-hall effect. To the left, a sand beach cried out to us as the first offering of flat ground in over two hours. The beach was stepped – denoting two distinct water lines – and fringed by a tangle of shrubs and crooked-limbed trees.

Without debate or fluster, we went to work. Colin put up the tents. (The one that had been stored at the South American Explorers Club was now in service too. Identical to the first, our second tent guaranteed more spacious sleeping arrangements and the luxury of a tent to oneself every third night. It was promptly dubbed the 'masturbation tent'.) I scavenged for driftwood and got a fire going. Scott paddled across to the pool at the base of the concave cliff and fished, using the raw beef recommended to us as bait.

It seemed an almost Utopian setting, like something out of *Swiss Family Robinson*. There was no friction in anything we did, as if we'd known this place and each other our whole lives. As late afternoon became night, the temperature hardly dropped. The insects weren't biting, nor were the fish, for that matter. Boiled rice, fried vegetables and a can of pilchards constituted a meal that could have been prepared in the Royal Kitchen itself. The river was silent. I ran my hands through the cool, dry sand and felt myself being caressed in turn by a splendid drowsiness.

Try as I might, though, I could not for an instant be lulled into a feeling of security, by this tranquillity and harmony. The future wouldn't leave me alone. Deep down in this crack in the earth, what had we as yet really done to make ourselves feel in contol?

More riffles teased us during the morning of our second day on the river. They became irregular in shape and variable in depth, but again posed no threat. The only danger was in slipping on the slime-coated rocks we had to stand on when hauling the raft off a snag. The routine intensified – drift, slide, snag, slide, drift, slide, snag, slide – and became quite wearisome. I caught myself looking forward to running something a little more thought-provoking.

On a positive note, we covered a good distance and there was no shortage of opportunity to lounge and soak in the essence of the Apurimac Canyon. Many regard it as second in depth only to its neighbour, the Colca. It was once the barrier that sheltered a fledgling Inca state from more powerful Indian nations, allowing the Incas to amass strength before they initiated the formation of the greatest empire ever seen in the western hemisphere. Decades later, when the Spanish invaders pushed west into the Andes, seeking to take Cuzco – the heart of the Incan Empire – the Apurimac was one of the main reasons they succeeded. The river that year was uncharacteristically low and enabled Pizarro's army to cross as they pleased.

The Apurimac is a dry valley. The dusty haze that hangs low in the sky over lands on the Pacific side of the Andes can be seen here too. The walls of the valley are a mosaic of browns, oranges, greys and yellows, and, where they are willing to allow moisture and the formation of a little soil, pale green vegetation clings. These plants are squat and mean. Narrow ledges support gnarled trees that would look more at home on Africa's Serengeti Plain than on the banks of the Amazon. The Apurimac contrasts starkly with the Urubamba, a lush river valley running parallel to it, less than 50 kilometres away. Machu Picchu, one-time Inca fortress and present-day archaeologist's treasure, hid for centuries in thick rainforest verging on the Urubamba River.

After lunch, the valley widened and lent itself to agriculture. Tiny settlements of mudbrick and thatch occupied flat expanses at the base of the still rugged range of peaks that flanked the Apurimac like an honour guard. Here the mountains seemed to take a step back out of deference. It was an unexpected interlude and, in hindsight, perhaps the last chance for us to shelve our plans to raft the Apurimac and become subsistence farmers instead.

The canyon closed in again and the first boulders began appearing in the river flow. Their presence coincided with the first real chutes and cataracts we'd seen. Water slid between them, shaped into licking tongues, curled at the edges; or it crashed abruptly onto the next level, up to a half-metre lower, as a white foaming mess. *Los Labios* took it all in her stride, and we whooped through each rapid as water slooshed over the sides and sprayed our faces. I welcomed both the change in the nature of the river and the nervous exhilaration that it triggered inside me. Not only did boulders rise out from the water, but they lined the banks too. It seemed as though the mountaintops had been detonated, the debris having rained down to litter the base of the canyon.

One dictionary defines rapids as 'a part of a river's course where the water rushes quickly, often over rocks near the surface'. To be more precise, rapids are produced by sudden drops in the level of the riverbed. Without a doubt, the submerged relief of the channel was now warped and uneven, rising sharply, falling away just as severely, predictable only in its desire to lose altitude fast. It is this tendency to be in a rush to descend that marks the Apurimac as a brute. No river could possibly drop more than 2500 metres over a distance of 500 kilometres without losing its temper.

About the scattered boulders, the flow was contorted, split, funnelled, harshly diverted. In quick time, the kindly Apurimac began to show sure signs of grumpiness. I had the sense that its mood would only get worse.

Now that we were limbered up, the river got serious. The haphazard scattering of boulders turned to pure congestion, tormenting the water still further and obstructing our view of what lay downriver. The loudest roar I'd heard so far drifted up to meet us on the back of a light headwind. We could see nothing except the odd plume of misted spray. It was time to get out and scout.

Colin angled the raft to face upstream and we ferried into an 'eddy' by the near bank. The eddy is a sanctuary offered by even the most ferocious and hateful whitewater river. Physics aside, it is basically a current moving in a direction opposite to the main flow. Eddies form behind outcroppings of the shore or behind any object (namely a rock) that obstructs the main flow downriver. 'Catching the eddy' was a technique we'd practised often in Canada, and one of the most important manoeuvres employed by whitewater rafters and kayakers. Recognising eddies and being able to slip into them can mean the difference between pausing safely to inspect the river ahead or careening blindly over a waterfall. They are a time-out option above wild rapids, but also invaluable for executing quick changes of direction and traverses across a river.

We secured the raft and ambled over the rocks to a point from which to survey this particular rapid.

'Okay, lads, the good stuff starts here!' Scott cried, rubbing his hands together.

Colin, also, was champing at the bit for action. He chattered excitedly as his finger traced the route he'd guide us down. But he stopped midway, peered across at a point downstream for several seconds, then shook his head. 'Shit! I think we'll have to portage this one.'

Scott shrugged. 'Doesn't look too bad to me.' I had to agree with him. It looked like a good clean run.

Colin's expression turned grim. 'You don't want to fall out in there,' he said.

'Why not?'

'See that rock?' he asked, pointing at a caravan-sized boulder on the left against which the roiling flow seemed to collide but not explode. 'Most of the water gets sucked underneath it.'

I didn't need to hear any more. This was something I'd read about. 'Boulder sieves' are a rafter's nightmare. Although harmless for boat occupants, they can kill a person who falls overboard and drifts into them. Water spits out of the other side of the boulder but only after it has squeezed through a barricade – 'the sieve' – of smaller rocks. A swimmer, swept down beneath the boulder, gets pinned against these rocks by the force of the water and can only drown.

There is so much more to a river than meets the eye. Being able to read possible danger is the first prerequisite for safe whitewater rafting. At this stage, Scott and I were more or less illiterate so it was a good thing that one of us understood the language.

Portaging around the boulder sieve proved an incredibly energy-draining exercise. Although only about 40 metres as straight-line distance, the unkind arrangement of shore debris forced us to take a detour that was closer to 100. The bulky dry bags restricted our movement over the rocks to a crawl, scramble and bent-double stagger. The already infamous food bag threatened to rip its carrier's arms off at the shoulder. Transporting the raft took half an hour alone and earnt me a hard knock on the knee when I lost my footing. By the time everything was repacked and fastened securely, the better part of two hours had slipped by.

For the next hour we fumbled through a boulder garden maze. The raft's width meant she could squeeze through gaps between rocks that would have stalemated a larger raft. Even so, we scraped and clawed our way downstream, more at the mercy of an intricately woven flow than by deciding a path for ourselves with slick, precise turns and even paddle strokes. It wasn't pretty. We bounced off rocks like a pinball, or wedged sideways between them. Misjudged cross-currents spun the raft around and shunted us through less desirable avenues. We slid backwards down chutes when the intention had been to go forwards. Essentially, we lacked the control that would be needed to survive the bigger rapids I knew lurked further downstream. Knowing how to manoeuvre the boat is the second prerequisite of safe whitewater rafting.

Another roar indicated that it was time again to stop and scout. My knee was stiff and tender so I waited in the boat for Colin and Scott to return with a verdict.

'How does it look?' I asked.

'Piece of piss, mate,' Colin replied.

'No boulder sieve?'

'Nup. But there's a one-metre-high drop-off that we want to be on the left side of when we go over.'

'No danger?'

'As long as we keep left, it's not a problem.'

I was satisfied with that.

As the only one of us in possession of something resembling experience, Colin initially monopolised the task of guiding. He steered from the back of the raft. Upfront, Scott's and my role was to supply the power and the braking. At Colin's shouted commands of 'Forward paddle!' or 'Back paddle!', we would immediately do so. If more speed was needed, he would yell 'Hard forward!' or 'Hard back!' And we mustn't stop paddling of our own accord; when he wanted us to stop, he would cry 'Stop!' Whoever held the guiding paddle was captain. The other two did what they were told.

We pushed off and jostled our way through the crowd of stone faces some more. A wide gap opened up to the left.

'Ben, we're going left here first,' Colin announced.

He aimed the bow squarely at the gap.

'Forward paddle.'

We dug in, but the current had other ideas. It was pulling us quickly to the right.

'Hard forward!' cried Colin, swinging the bow to point 45 degrees upstream. Scott and I quickened our strokes. It wasn't enough. We missed the gap. Nothing new. 'Stop.'

The stern hit rock and we pivoted hard to port so that the bow now faced the right bank. On our immediate left, a chain of four boulders bullied the water towards the right bank also. We curled around the edge of the fourth boulder and pointed downriver again. Fifteen metres ahead, the river seemed to disappear at a line between two more hunks of granite. Like overweight nightclub bouncers, they stood guard at either side of the drop-off.

Much of the flow headed to the right, and was forced through another gap, too narrow for *Los Labios.* We were being pushed in that direction. Colin angled the raft to port.

'Hard forward!'

We countered the current. Five metres from the lip, we were set to split the middle. Then Scott stopped paddling.

'Scott, keep going!'

The South African's paddle stayed out of the water.

'FORWARD PADDLE!!' Colin screamed.

Still he didn't move.

Powered from only one side, the raft lost forward momentum and skewed left. Despite Colin's last-ditch attempt to straighten up, we tipped over the edge of the falls at a 30-degree angle. Instead of the bow charging over the left side of the falls as originally intended, we tipped over sideways and too far right. The starboard side of the raft stuck firmly in the bubbling water at the base of the falls, flipping us in a moment. I was catapulted clear of the turbulence and into water still coming to its senses.

Then the current recovered and I was whisked away. Upside down, *Los Labios* kicked clear of the falls and followed close behind. I grabbed at her perimeter rope and scanned downstream with wide eyes for anything resembling a boulder sieve. After 20 metres or so, my fingers caught hold of a doorknob-shaped outcrop of granite. Still clutching the boat rope, I managed to scramble onto a submerged ledge that sloped gently out of the water.

I played tug of war for the raft with a strong current, the tacky rubber soles of my neoprene boots being all that kept me from being yanked off the ledge. Scott and Colin arrived a few seconds later to lend a hand.

'Fucking hell, Scott! Why didn't you paddle?'

Colin was shaking. At the falls, he had tumbled from the raft and smacked hard against a rock platform just below the surface (the reason for his insistence on our keeping to the left in the first place). Scott looked embarrassed. 'I thought I remembered the rock being on the left.'

That wasn't good enough for Colin.

'But we saw it together! We agreed that the rock on the right was bad news.' He rubbed a bruised forearm and scowled. 'Shit!'

'Hey – I'm sorry, okay? I fucked up. What more can I say?'

Still jittery from the shock, I needed to vent some of the strain myself.

'I thought you guys said it'd be easy. I wish I'd gone to check it out as well. That was a fucking comedy!'

'It should have been easy,' Colin growled.

Cooperating effectively as a tight team unit is the third and most crucial prerequisite for safe whitewater rafting. We weren't doing so well in this department either.

I felt ashamed for another reason too. Amid all the confusion, I'd lost my paddle. Back in Canada, when the boat flipped or I'd fallen overboard, my reaction had often been to let go of the paddle. More than anything else, that had convinced me I wasn't a born rafter. Although it had been relatively easy to locate and retrieve my paddle from open rivers like the Bow and Kicking Horse, I knew that in this maze, the bloody thing was gone for good.

As well as my feelings of failure, the loss left us with only one spare. That evening, I wallowed in regret that I had partly condemned us to a likely scenario of being halfway down the Apurimac with no paddles. By the time one of us struggled out of the canyon and found something even remotely useful as a substitute, it would be too late.

Our campsite was a cramped alcove between the rocks, and the ground was sloped and lumpy. The day's last rapid filled the air with thick hissing. A sombre mood prevailed. The only thing that hadn't changed in 24 hours was our luck with catching fish.

Our third day on the water began with us implementing an idea that Scott had come up with to solve paddle concerns. It involved reappropriating the 'flip line' – the length of rock-climbing strap with carabiner that each of us carried for righting the boat if it flipped. Instead of coiling the strap around our waist, we now clipped the carabiner end onto the raft perimeter rope and tied the other end around the neck of each paddle, just above the blade. In this way, whether we let go of the paddle or had it torn from our grasp by the most frenzied water, it would remain connected to the boat. This arrangement would also make pulling the boat right side up a quicker process because the strap was already clipped onto the side.

It was an unorthodox move and not without drawbacks. Pro rafters would have frowned on it for safety reasons. The risk was that the two metres of loose strap needed for freedom of movement could easily ensnare a team member caught under the raft in a flip situation. We agreed to take our chances. Scott's idea lessened the probability of losing all of our paddles and removed a niggling disquiet from the back of my mind.

The river behaved as it had the previous afternoon, but a new day wiped the slate clean. We tried harder. We acknowledged the gaping holes in both our individual techniques and overall cohesiveness. Each of us made a special effort to tighten up, to at the very least *look* like we knew our stuff.

The proper technique for paddling a raft is to sit as far over the pontoon as possible, lean right out over the water then thrust your blade in deep. It flies squarely in the face of one's instinct to go the other way and crouch in the bottom of the raft. It takes time to be convinced that exposing your body to the river like this is ultimately the only way to preserve yourself. Your legs assume a sprinter's stance, frozen in mid stride; the back foot wedges into the tight space where floor meets pontoon, while the front foot slots into a 'foot cup', a slipper-like pouch of meshed plastic that is glued to the floor.

We bumped with assuredness, scraped with unflinching purpose, and spun around far more elegantly. We even swore with a passion that had been lacking the day before. And we didn't flip. Instead of contemplating what lay downriver, I tried hard to focus on what was immediately before us. I put aside my concerns that on current levels of progress, we'd be running rapids well into the New Year, and settled into a routine of mentally ticking each one off a finite list.

At about midday, the geology changed. The boulder-studded waterway fell behind us and we returned to alternating between gently tumbling cascades and flat glassy expanses. In the space of 30 minutes, we covered more ground than in the previous seven hours.

We passed a lone fisherman. Cane rod in hand, he squatted silently on a gravel bar. Like a wildlife specimen, he was camouflaged, not moving a muscle for fear of drawing attention to himself.

'Any fish?' we asked.

A shake of the head. In the shadow of a floppy-brimmed hat, his face split into a broad smile of bashfulness.

'Is there a village nearby?'

An arm pointed downstream.

'*Gracias, señor.*'

He raised his hat.

Minutes later we came across two girls sunbaking on a sandy beach. They appeared to be topless. Catching sight of us, they both squealed with surprise and hurriedly pulled up their bikini tops. We waved. Giggling, the girls waved back, then motioned for us to come to shore.

'Where did you come from?'

'That way,' Colin said cheekily, gesturing upriver.

This seemed to be enough information for them.

'We're not used to seeing people come in boats.'

'So it seems,' I noted in English.

They were university students from Cuzco, on a break from their studies. A real seaside beach was too far away for a visit. The Apurimac supplied the next best thing – and a good view too. Still smirking, Colin agreed with that.

We invited them aboard *Los Labios* then paddled about in circles while they giggled some more, snapped photographs and passed around a large bottle of soda. In turn, they invited us to share their picnic lunch of crackers, tomatoes and roasted corn. We declined. The prospect of heartier fare close by overwhelmed the urge to sit and spend time with a couple of nice-looking girls. Just as a trip to the seaside does, the river gave us constant huge appetites.

Around the next bend, a steel bridge came into view. And sure enough, an el cheapo diner serviced the road going over it. We parked the raft, scaled a high and unstable bank, raced inside and ordered three 'menus'. The dim interior was a welcome change from bright sunshine. We seated ourselves at a table and smiled at two bewildered truck drivers. The woman who'd taken our order went to the doorless entrance, looked about in vain for the car we must have arrived in, then returned to the counter scratching her head.

Scott walked to the counter and returned with three Sublime chocolate bars.

'No point going hungry while we wait, eh lads?'

Our meals of steak and rice arrived. We gorged ourselves while chickens pecked scraps off the dirt floor. When the plates were empty, I wiped my mouth on my arm and grinned.

'Fancy some dessert?'

Colin and Scott raised their eyebrows as if to say, 'Stupid question.' I bought six more Sublimes. If it's true that chocolate cravings indicate a form of nutritional deficiency, then we must have been in a bad way.

After lunch, we drifted on again, our full bellies settled. The easy conditions allowed us to lie back and tan the skin under our chins. Our heads tilted back, we marvelled at the most spectacular crags to date.

Late in the afternoon, a second great garden of boulders welcomed us. This one seemed kinder than before, however. Several inflowing tributaries that day had boosted the Apurimac's volume. The rapids were bigger, but now less difficult to ride. Although a more powerful river would not be so forgiving of mistakes, our chances of making them would also lessen.

A final session of blood-pumping action saw us dance over standing waves that reached a metre in height, and barrel through 'holes' at the base of cataracts. It culminated in Scott and me being flung overboard when the raft slammed into a rock and spun sharply. Colin hauled both of us back on just in time for me to steer the boat through a last cascade.

At breakfast, two fishermen and their squawking children destroyed our claims of having found the ultimate in seclusion. To the untrained eye, the canyon seemed impenetratable to anyone on foot, but when asked where they had come from, our visitors pointed over the mountains. Did they have any fish? No.

We set ourselves to getting video footage of us tackling the rapids. I couldn't see our efforts being appreciated by anyone other than family and friends. Colin, on the other hand, envisaged a possible documentary.

First up, we took turns filming from shore while the others came down a section of river as a duo. Minus a man, the loss of power, control and overall balance was obvious. Then the rapids grew in size, becoming too big for just two men. We adjusted our filming technique. One of us would scramble along the bank, set up the camera, press record, race back and jump in the boat. Then we'd sloosh past the lens as a threesome. For a while, the locals followed and watched us as we leapfrogged downriver.

The fishermen had seen gringos here only twice before. Two years earlier there had been a soloist (who sounded like the South African, Mike Horn), and five years before that, a raft with four people. We hadn't heard of anyone going down the Apurimac in 1992. Of course, that didn't mean anything – they might have travelled only a short distance or simply not bothered to make their journey known.

'Or maybe they never got out to tell anyone,' Scott suggested.

It was a comment that emphasised the air of remoteness about this canyon, and it highlighted a sobering truth. Even our parents had only a vague idea of where we were. All anyone knew was that we'd probably be out of contact for months.

That raised some interesting questions. If something happened to us, when would the whistle get blown? Who would come looking for us? And where would the search begin? We joked that perhaps one day, far into the future, someone would stumble on a tripoded video camera. They would find it perched on a riverside boulder overlooking a watery hell. Played back, the tape would show a red raft and three men being smashed to smithereens.

At the very next set of rapids, such a scenario almost came to pass.

Even before leaving Canada, we'd got into the habit of rating the strength and difficulty of a rapid according to the following standard classification system:

- **Class 1 – easy:** Fast-moving with riffles and small waves. Few obstructions, easily avoided. Low risk. Easy self-rescue.
- **Class 2 – novice:** Straightforward rapids; wide, clear channels evident without scouting. Occasional manoeuvring. Rocks and medium waves easily avoided by trained paddlers. Swimmers seldom injured.
- **Class 3 – intermediate:** Rapids with moderate, irregular waves that can swamp open canoes. Strong eddies and currents. Complex manoeuvres and good control required in tight passages and around ledges. Large waves or strainers easily avoided. Scouting advisable for inexperienced parties. Self-rescue usually easy; group assistance may be required. Injuries while swimming are rare.
- **Class 4 – advanced:** Powerful, turbulent and predictable rapids; large, unavoidable waves and holes or constricted

passages. Fast, reliable eddy turns and precise boat handling needed to initiate manoeuvres, scout rapids or rest. Rapids may require 'must' moves above dangerous hazards. Scouting necessary first time. Self-rescue difficult; skilled group assistance often needed. Moderate to high risk of injury to swimmers.

- **Class 5 – expert:** Extremely long, obstructed or violent rapids with exposure to added risk. Possible large, unavoidable waves and holes or steep, congested chutes. Eddies may be small, turbulent, difficult to reach or nonexistent. Proper equipment, extensive experience, high level of fitness and practised rescue skills essential for survival. Scouting recommended but may be difficult. Swims are dangerous. Difficult rescue for experts.

- **Class 6 – extreme and exploratory:** These runs have almost never been attempted and often exemplify the extremes of difficulty, unpredictability and danger. The consequences of errors are very severe and rescue may be impossible. For teams of experts only, at favourable water levels, after close personal inspection and taking all precautions.

Our next taste of rapids occurred where the river dropped by about six metres over a distance of no more than 50 metres. That was huge. The rapids were three-tiered – composed of two chutes and a large hole – and bordered on the left by a vertical cliff face. A thunderous roar drowned out even the sound of the blood pumping in my ears.

'What is she?' I yelled.

Colin rubbed his chin. 'Four plus.' He grinned and added, 'Looks exciting.'

'Yeah,' agreed Scott. 'I'll go set up the camera.'

I pointed to where the water 'boiled' and spat at the end of its tortuous descent.

'What about that hole at the bottom?'

'I don't think it's a keeper.'

Colin continued his sales pitch. He was keen to run this one: 'It's not that long, and there's a long stretch of calm afterward. We'll be fine.'

I wasn't convinced. It was the biggest and wildest rapid the Apurimac had shown us so far. I'd tackled class 4+ in the past, though never as the boat guide.

'You okay to keep guiding, Ben?'

That was the challenge I needed. Being seen as a piker was the greater risk. 'Sure,' I replied.

To exit the eddy, I braced my paddle against a rock and pushed. As we crossed the eddy-line – the interface between gentle swirl and raging torrent – the front of the raft was sucked towards the first chute.

'Easy forward!' I barked. Jamming my foot even tighter under the thwart, I leant back and over the side, using the paddle as a rudder to keep the bow pointed directly forward.

We careened down the first chute perfectly. The second was much wider, spanning the left half of the river. Water gushing down the first chute deflected left from a knobbly outcropping of the shore. We were being carried towards it, fast. Using my hip as a fulcrum, I pushed the blade away from me, swinging the boat left.

'Hard forward!'

Too late. We were upon the outcrop quicker than expected. The back end of *Los Labios* slammed, recoiled and bucked me overboard.

I surfaced a metre behind the boat and watched helplessly as we sped on a collision course with the cliff face. An undertow grabbed my legs. It swept me alongside the raft, teasingly just out of reach of the perimeter rope. Not that it would have mattered. I couldn't even free an arm from the churning water. All four of my limbs were at its mercy.

We were much too far left. I was facing backwards as we dropped laterally across the second chute. Then, seemingly with an almost gloating intent, the river spun me around and presented the jagged base of the cliff, on which it meant to dash me. At that moment, for the first time in my life, I thought I was truly going to die.

I hit hard, the air exploding from my lungs. My eyes blinked clear in time to see the red pontoon bearing down, about to sandwich me against the cliff. I was pulled under. The mayhem at the foot of the chute was more air bubbles than liquid – that meant no buoyancy. I saw nothing, but my eardrums screamed. I had no idea how deep I was, nor which way was up. In whitewater-rafting terminology, I was being 'Maytag-ed' – a term coined from the similar fate of clothes in a washing machine.

While I floundered, the out-of-control raft carried on, with Colin and Scott still aboard. It plunged down the last tier and burst through the worst of the massive hole. But like tentacles of the Kraken, the recirculation seized hold and began pulling her back in. Somehow, Colin and Scott regained enough balance to paddle like madmen and break free.

Then came a tug on my arm, and the joyous reminder of my lifeline. One hand still had hold of the paddle, a subconscious and white-knuckled grip. The raft's momentum yanked me down into the hole for a brief tour of the Kraken's lair, then hauled me onwards and into tranquil waters. I broke the surface, gasping. I had been underwater for 20 seconds, the better part of an eternity.

I crawled out of the water and lay prostrate on a warm slab of rock. My hip was in agony from where it had struck the cliff. Colin slapped the top of my helmet.

'I take it back,' he beamed. 'That was a class 5 for sure.'

SEVEN
INSTINCT

10 October 1999 (day 28): middle Apurimac, 6730 kilometres to the Atlantic

Oddly enough, my hip showed few signs of soreness or bruising. More surprising still, my nerves were intact. I put it down to a kind of euphoria at having survived a situation that had convinced me I was a dead man.

I didn't see my ordeal in that class 5 rapid as a warning of impending doom. It was just another example of the Apurimac probing latent regions of my brain. If anything, it boosted my confidence. I felt that my survival was less about luck and more about the gritty, subconscious will to hang on.

Delusional? Maybe. Nevertheless, I tried to nurture those beliefs. The Apurimac puts on trial your mental strength as much as your reflexes and skill. A positive outlook is precious but, on this river, a slippery thing to keep hold of. From day 1 of this whitewater stage of the journey, my moods had seemed as transient as the clouds of mist thrown up by the cataracts.

We arrived at the top of a set of rapids that looked similar in potency to the brute from the previous day. I said I was prepared to have a crack at it. Colin was more than keen. Scott, however, was adamant that we were tempting disaster and refused to raft it. His doubts were a sobering slap across the face for me, and I was more than happy to agree. Colin conceded, but only grudgingly. After yesterday's close shave, he had expected me, not Scott, to stonewall. 'We're being too cautious,' he complained.

A gruelling portage wasn't necessary. For the first time, we employed a technique called 'lining'. We tied one end of a long climbing rope to the raft's stern. With the other end, Colin and I worked our way down the right-hand bank as far as we could. Both of us found a good bracing position among the rocks and took firm hold of the rope. At the thumbs-up signal, Scott kicked *Los Labios* out of the eddy. The unmanned raft gathered speed and hurtled through the rapid. Colin and I reeled in the slack as she came towards us. As the raft shot past, we tensed muscles, leant back and took the strain. Simultaneously, we began to ease the rope out again, making sure that she maintained enough momentum to blast her way through consecutive holes at the end of the run.

The entire procedure was executed to perfection.

For the rest of that day and well into the next, the Apurimac gave us few troubles. We covered a lot of kilometres. Despite there being no shortage of rapids, some of them quite substantial, we were rarely forced to stop and scout. We discerned the most prudent routes simply by standing up in the raft as we drifted towards or hovered above the brink.

We reached the Military Bridge in good time. We were in high spirits too because this was the first major milestone we had set for ourselves. Deep down, though, I felt we were being buttered up, and that the faster we travelled, the sooner we'd be knocking on the door of the dreaded Acobamba Abyss. With our current progress, it was only a few more days away. If we were destined to be destroyed by the Apurimac, chances were greatest that it would happen there.

Scott drew the short straw, earning him guard duty while Colin and I headed inland to buy supplies at a small settlement indicated on the map. When we got back, there were two Nissan vans parked by the bridge, and the riverbank below was bustling with activity. Four whitewater rafts were being pumped up. An assortment of backpacks, wetsuits, life jackets and plastic containers lay scattered over the rocks. A total of eighteen people were getting ready. Four were Peruvian river guides, the rest were Israeli tourists, all in their early twenties.

The name 'Instinct' zapped like a lightning strike across the side of each raft and on various pieces of clothing worn by the guides. The company was based in Cuzco and regularly offered whitewater tours on the Apurimac, between the Military and Cunyac bridges. The lead guide, an affable man called José, was intrigued by our story. He seemed fed up with the Israelis already and welcomed the idea of us tagging along for the two-day journey to Cunyac.

Three of the Instinct rafts carried paying customers. Each craft was captained by a clean-cut, well-groomed Peruvian. The fourth raft lugged most of the food, tents and dry bags containing personal gear. It was black, scarred with patches, and resembled the inner tube of a tractor wheel. The stubbled oarsman for this supply boat went bare-chested, and sported long curly black hair and a bandana. His name was Dante.

Only one of the boats was steered like ours: by a paddle-wielding guide at the stern. José and the other guide sat in the centre of their respective rafts and manned the long oars attached to a rowing frame. The supreme power and control bestowed by a set of oars meant the Israelis on board were relegated to the role of mere token paddlers. Many commercial raft guides use oars to overcome the problem of punters not listening to commands or freezing up in the middle of a big rapid because of fear.

Below the Military Bridge, the geology changed dramatically. From Pilpinto, the rock strata had been dark in colour, heavily cracked and fissured, and erosion had produced canyon walls that were chipped and splintered along their layers. Every formation was composed of sharp angles and small cubical blocks. Now, the walls of the canyon were smooth and curved. Shades of cream and grey blended into smudges of black. Boulders glistened in the surf, like marble sculptures. The river appeared more epic in scale, almost theatrical, as we bobbed down boulevards of tall-standing waves.

Above each rapid, the Instinct boats gathered in an eddy, then descended one by one. We trailed the last boat in the convoy, at a distance far enough behind so as to not get in the way and near enough that we could copy their exact route and manoeuvres. We would otherwise have invested a lot of time scouting each run first.

Just before dusk, the four tour boats reined in above the meanest, most savage rapids I had ever seen.

'We portage this one,' José announced to us.

In the failing light, our wide eyes followed the river over two successive drops, each about two metres in height.

'No shit,' Scott murmured, still transfixed.

Around dinner, word of our intentions spread. The Israelis asked very few questions and spoke to us in flat tones, as though writing us off as a trio of sad dreamers. Only the guides seemed to take us seriously. They were clearly impressed by what we aimed to achieve. Between them, they had rafted the Apurimac, from the Military Bridge to Cunyac Bridge, a total of 150 times.

While the Israelis chatted in their impermeable groups, we grilled the Peruvians about what they knew of the Apurimac below Cunyac Bridge.

'The Acobamba Abyss is very bad. Very bad.'

'An absolute nightmare,' added another guide, who'd gone through once as part of a kayaking group.

'Will you go through it?' asked José.

There was a short silence, during which Colin, Scott and I shot each other looks.

'We had been planning to, up until now,' I replied.

The less-than-rosy appraisal, from veteran river guides, corroborated both what we'd read and the general word on the street. And once you entered the Abyss, for 40 kilometres there was no option to quit. The sides are that steep.

It was clear that, on paper, our skills very likely wouldn't measure up. We might fluke it but we could very easily die. And for what? A careless show of bravery? Or for being too lazy to do a 40-kilometre portage?

A lone kayaker arrived early next morning to join the Instinct tour party. He was Benjamin (in Spanish pronounced *Ben-hamin*), the company director. Benjamin was in his mid-thirties, well educated and had travelled throughout Europe and North America. He was the first Peruvian I could remember meeting who'd gone beyond the country's borders.

Apart from relishing the opportunity to play in rapids and simply enjoy the Apurimac's beauty, he liked to be there for the added safety of his clients. In his kayak, he could nimbly scoot in and rescue anyone who fell out, before they got into trouble. Naturally, this applied to the occupants of little red rafts as well. For the first time since Camaná, I felt as though someone was looking out for us.

As the company rafts lined up to run the day's first rapid, (known as 'Space Odyssey'), Benjamin paddled alongside us.

'Be careful here. On the left, there is an undercut rock,' he said, motioning downriver. 'Two years ago, an Australian girl was caught by it. She is still there.'

I shuddered, imagining the pulpy, waterlogged flesh and her body still pressed against the sieve. As we passed within metres of the killer rock, my heart drummed a primeval rhythm against the wall of my chest. Within the rumble and bubble of the water gushing around that rock, I could all but hear the poor girl's muffled screams.

Fleur Fraser was a beautiful, outgoing young woman from Melbourne. An adventurous spirit had led her first to South America and then on Instinct's rafting tour of the Apurimac. Just above the rapid known as 'Space Odyssey', she'd moved to the back of the raft to give someone else a go up the front. When the raft collided with the undercut rock, Fleur fell overboard. A memorial to her exists near the site of the tragedy.

The rapid looked like many we'd run in the previous few days. Knowing this one's lethal capabilities highlighted just how narrow our tightrope had been.

The men from Instinct gave the impression of having tamed this stretch of river. In their presence, the Apurimac seemed to lose a good deal of its threat; not even the ineptitude of the Israelis could unsettle their expert boat-handling skills. Colin, Scott and I relaxed. They wouldn't let anything bad happen to us.

At the bottom of a routine class 4, we slid sideways into a hole. A few power strokes would have been enough to allow escape but we were angled too horribly for them to be effective. Boiling swirls pulled the port side of the raft back into the cascade that had created the hole. 'High side!' yelled Colin, as the torrent battered the starboard pontoon, forcing it beneath the surface. Scott and I flung our weight on the rising port pontoon, desperate to force it back down. It worked, but as the tube slumped, Colin lost his balance and tumbled overboard. He disappeared from view. This left Scott and me at opposite ends of the boat, and no real way of coordinating an effort to paddle free.

Abruptly, the raft swivelled 180 degrees and this time the port pontoon was swallowed downwards. *Los Labios* tottered for several seconds with the South African and me leaning over starboard as far as we could. Again she slumped. Again the flip was aborted.

And so the loop continued. Meanwhile, Colin remained in the chaos below, tangled up in his paddle strap. He was running out of air and couldn't fight his way to the surface.

Then, out of the corner of my eye, I sighted the black supply boat bearing down on us. Dante had lined us up for the rescue hit. Slap. It was like the collision of two snooker balls. The transfer of momentum fired us out of the hole and left Dante rooted to the spot. Now the hole tried flipping him. As the bow lifted out of the water briefly, the Peruvian looked like an outlaw astride a rearing black stallion. Laughing, he loosened two quick oar strokes and broke free. Gasping for air, Colin was hoisted back in.

It was clear that the Peruvian guides, in their big Avon boats, were enjoying the role of big brother to our little red raft. Benjamin spent a lot of time paddling alongside us, sharing advice and his knowledge of potential hotspots beyond the Acobamba Abyss.

'What is the Apurimac like at the end of the wet season?' Colin asked.

Benjamin made a low whistle and shook his head.

'It is crazy. No one can survive.'

'See that?' He pointed up to a deep, rounded hollowing-out of the rock wall. It was five metres above our heads. 'That is made by a whirlpool.'

Our third day with Instinct brought the biggest whitewater to date. The Apurimac was growing – not yet as a result of the rains and melting snow, but from the persistent inflow of streams. They poured over the lip of the canyon as breathtaking waterfalls. Some fell from such a height that they turned into clouds of spray.

The whitewater behaved in the same way. Everything just got larger. Water flowing down a roadside gutter after rain obeys the same rules of fluid dynamics. Outside every suburban house you can see miniature chutes, waves and holes.

The bow of *Los Labios* lunged at the sky as we ramped off huge standing waves. We charged them like surf lifesavers do the incoming breakers aboard their Zodiacs. Even the once benign waves now had the power to toss an unwary raft upside down. The sucking power of the holes increased. We dug in and smashed through them, our heads bowed and hearts fluttering.

In the mid afternoon, the river doglegged to the left. Just before the bend, the Instinct rafts pulled into shore and we followed. Benjamin paddled over to us.

'Afternoon tea stop?' queried Scott.

'No. We must scout this one.'

'Scout?'

'Yes.'

It was the first time the Peruvians had done that around us. And it spoke volumes about what lay around that corner.

Over a distance of 100 metres, the river looked like an avalanche of snow. For an hour, the three guides and Benjamin surveyed the rapids, skipping backwards and forwards along its length, chattering in fast Spanish.

Colin, Scott and I initially murmured the 'p' word to each other but then we began psyching ourselves for battle. Not one of us said as much, but we each baulked at the idea of being seen to cower. There was a long way to go. Here was an opportunity to demonstrate our resolve and the skills we'd need to rely on to get us through the rest of the Apurimac.

We made our own survey then bounced a plan of attack off José. It was more or less the same as the Peruvians' strategy, but he recommended a couple of changes that would suit our smaller craft.

Rafting is all about judging angles and speeds. Just as astrophysicists need to calculate the effect of the planetary orbits they use to catapult space probes, the rafter must reckon on the pulling and pushing power of angry water in order to decide where to point the raft and how to paddle. Holes and eddies, crosscurrents and whirlpools, all exert forces on the raft. Predicting what each will do is crucial for staying on course in a rapid.

The first 95 metres could best be described as a complex arrangement of chutes – the worst was saved for the final five metres. A demonic cataract blocked the right-side exit. An awkwardly shaped hole guarded the left. Precision entry was needed so as not to fall foul of the recirculation and then of two jagged-edged boulders immediately beyond it, waiting like assassins.

The long delay puzzled and disturbed me.

'If you've rafted this rapid 60 times, why do you need to scout it for such a long time?' I asked José.

'Because every time it is different,' he said in a tone of calm acceptance. 'The water level is never the same twice. It means that perhaps a route which last time was safe, is now dangerous. And a hole which could make big problems last time is now okay.' His normally poker face cracked into an odd grin. 'I am always a little nervous about this one.'

'Have any customers ever died here?'

'Not yet.'

Half the Israelis refused to go down by raft. The first company boat lost two people overboard when it twisted in the final hole. The second flipped, stern over bow, in exactly the same place. Fortunately, no one landed in the embrace of either hole or assassin.

Los Labios went next, Scott and I up forward, Colin at the helm. We took the first chute, no problem. Then the water defied prediction, dragging us past the next chute on our itinerary. Our plan dissolved into the foaming, hissing river and the rest of the rapid would need to be taken as it came.

We tried correcting things through a couple of gentle drops, but still found ourselves too far right as the second major chute loomed. The lip of this chute was shaped like an 'L'. We plunged down it through the apex. At the base of the apex, the water got compressed and the resultant swell delivered an uppercut punch to the raft's floor that jarred my knees.

Colin's yells from behind me stopped but I barely took any notice. Scott and I were already at it. We paddled like crazy to get the raft over to the left and away from the clutches of the cataract. We got left, but the raft didn't turn to face downriver. Over an even, tilted stretch of riverbed, water rushed towards the final hole. We were in a terrible position and the gap was closing fast. While Scott continued to paddle forwards, I locked the paddle against my hip and stroked backwards. As hoped, the bow spun around to point downstream.

Scott and I were mesmerised by the scene ahead. We dared not take our eyes off it to turn and ask Colin what the hell he was playing at. Just metres above the hole, the raft skewed left.

'Bloody hell! What's he doing?!' cried Scott.

I leant out as far as I could, stabbed the paddle blade parallel to the flow and ripped it towards me. The bow entered at an angle of about 20 degrees. *Los Labios* punched through but the recirculation grabbed hold long enough to again jerk us left. In fact, we were pulled around to face the upstream left bank.

Fortuitously, it proved the ideal position to be in for our last obstacle – the two assassins. The starboard stern lifted up on water pillowing in front of the right-hand assassin. Simultaneously, whitewater being spat out of the hole slammed against the port bow, knocking it around to point downriver. My heart leapt as I saw that we were aimed to safely pass between the assassins. The stern slumped off the pillow and we coasted between the two boulders.

I was ecstatic, and amazed by our good fortune. Had we hit the hole dead on as originally intended, we probably would have been smashed on one of the assassins.

I turned to Colin. 'You had the right idea, angling left at the end there. But what were you do –'

'Mate,' he interjected, 'I wasn't even *in* the raft at that point!'

'Eh?'

'Didn't you notice me missing?'

Scott and I looked at each other.

'You did go quiet – and you lost control,' I recalled.

'But then you're a bit wonky at the best of times,' Scott added with a smart grin.

'I got bucked off halfway down!' chuckled the Canadian.

First, he explained how he had fallen backwards as the raft went down the second chute. What he described next made my jaw drop.

From trailing two metres behind the boat, he had pulled himself, hand over hand, up the paddle strap. He had then grabbed hold of the perimeter rope, hauled himself back on board and resumed his position just as we struck the hole. Colin's stunt reinforced what I had long suspected: he was an athletic *freak*.

An hour later, the Nissan vans came into view. Our 'big brother' escort on the Apurimac had ended. It was time to go back to fending for ourselves. We bid fond farewells to the Instinct crew, then wrapped up the last few kilometres to the Cunyac Bridge. And with that, the curtain fell on the second act of our whitewater drama.

EIGHT
THE PORTAGE

13 October (day 31):
the Cunyac Bridge, 6680 kilometres
to the Atlantic

The show was far from over, but we had an urge to celebrate what we had achieved up to now. Our bodies and minds could abandon the pressures of whitewater for several days, as we portaged the Acobamba Abyss. That fact alone warranted a few cold beers. A cold brew was pure fantasy, and the only substantial food available at the tiny settlement of Puente Cunyac were deep-fried balls of mashed potato.

But we did find people to help us party. Sergeant Oliveira and a stall owner named Felix joined us at the roadside table where we sipped warm bottles of Cusqueña beer and indulged our egos. Oliveira had just come off duty and was ready to drink. His good mate Felix was already incoherent.

Another bottle of beer materialised. So did a plastic cup. The patriotic sergeant said we would drink beer the Peruvian way. He filled the cup and handed it to Scott, who sipped at it.

'No, No!' cried Oliveira. 'Like *this*.'

He took the cup, put it to his lips and threw his head back. The beer disappeared in two gulps. He poured again. This time, Scott sculled too. As the South African moved to hand Colin the empty cup, the sergeant again protested: the sculler had to refill before doing the baton change.

Oliveira was one of six policemen stationed in Puente Cunyac. Their job was to monitor the flow of goods and people traffic between the provinces of Cuzco and Apurimac. Though quiet now, the position had promised danger only half-a-dozen years earlier. Along with neighbouring Ayacucho province, Apurimac province had been a spawning ground of the *Sendero Luminoso*, the guerrilla movement that terrorised all of Peru for more than a decade.

The Cunyac settlement had grown up to take advantage of hungry and thirsty motorists who stopped to have their papers checked.

'Is there much to do here?' I asked the sergeant.

'Only work and drink,' he replied, gesturing that I was holding things up. I sculled, repoured, and handed the cup to him. My posting here is almost finished.'

Then he indicated his bleary-eyed friend. 'He has lived here all his life.'

Felix slurred something about this being true.

A plump woman lumbered across the road. She saw Felix, put her hands on her hips and screamed abuse. Felix stood, swayed, shook his fist at her and yelled back, his words accompanied by a hail of saliva. 'That is his wife,' explained Oliveira.

The cup did many rounds of the table. We ate countless potatoes. Oliveira recalled stories from livelier postings he'd known during his career. Felix asked what our names were perhaps 20 times, and stated his own just as many.

A truck arrived. Oliveira went off for a drunken chat with the driver, whom he knew well. Felix staggered away to man his stall in case there were any passengers who wanted to buy a drink. We stumbled back to the tents like blind men. The moon had not yet risen above the canyon wall. In the pitch-blackness, we almost broke our necks getting down the rocks to our sand beach at the foot of the bridge.

I slept as one who knows he doesn't have to wake up and go to work the next morning.

Our time off began deliciously. The police commander invited us to breakfast at the station house with him and his men. We ate fruit salad and yoghurt, prepared by Sergeant Oliveira, followed by freshly caught catfish, gutted and fried whole.

For the rest of the morning, we drifted lazily downstream. Our aim was to get as close as possible to the start of the Acobamba Abyss. As foretold, a cluster of buildings emerged on the left bank, just before the canyon closed in to throttle the river. They marked an opportunity to revitalise our tender bodies – hot springs.

I had imagined soaking away my aches in a steamy rock pool. The reality didn't even come close. Tepid water had been channelled into concrete basins; a thin layer of slime coated the sides. The basins were filled with dozens of shrieking, splashing children, there on a two-day school excursion.

Their interest in *Los Labios* did create some room in the basins. To keep the children honest, we strung her out in the current at the end of a long rope tied to a tree. After half an hour in a basin, we got out, shivering. I doubted that water from the spring could cure any of the afflictions that the peeling sign claimed it could. The bulk of the minerals probably came courtesy of kids' bladders.

Four schoolteachers invited us to join them in a session of drinking beer – Peruvian style, of course. As the children ran amok, we discussed the lives of teachers in Peru. Although they liked their jobs, they lamented the fact that teachers are among the poorest paid workers in the country.

We explained our plans to trek to Cachora, the village closest to where the Acobamba Abyss finishes. Such a lengthy portage would not disqualify our attempt to travel the Amazon from source to sea since skirting a length of river by land is considered the same as rafting or kayaking it, so long as you continue to travel under your own power. In terms of officially running a river, a 40-kilometre portage is no different from one of 40 metres.

Logistically, it invited headaches. Carrying everything that far would cripple us. We had decided that before starting the portage proper, we would transport all our gear to Abancay, the capital of Apurimac province, and get it stored safely for a few days.

Ronald, a swarthy teacher wearing dark sunglasses, said they could help with the transport. In the morning they'd be returning to school and we were welcome to hitch a ride as far as Abancay. He poured the dregs of the last bottle of beer into the cup, then called over a young girl who was sprinting past. He handed over money and instructed her to go fetch another bottle of Cusqueña from the 'hole in the wall' store.

For the second night in a row, we made our way to camp drunk and in darkness. This time, we paddled in circles across to a secluded sand bank on the other side of the river. The children's squeals and the inebriated shouts of their guardians wafted across the river well into the small hours.

Early the following morning, the raft was deflated and dry bags neatly piled awaiting the school bus. During the process of deflation, I noted the condition of the rubber, especially around the exposed sides of the pontoon. For all the pokes, scrapes and crashes she had endured over the past nine days, *Los Labios* still looked in pristine condition. I recalled several occasions where I had shut my eyes and waited for a fast-approaching, dagger-like rock edge to hit and slice through her red skin. At the worst came harsh, squeaking noises, like fingers across a party balloon. And barely a mark betrayed the point of collision. The biggest danger had come from the hot ashes falling from the end of Scott's cigarettes.

The school 'bus' arrived. It was a flatbed truck. The raft and bags were loaded in first, followed by the 45 students. Scott, Colin and I squeezed aboard, and like cattle, we were transported to Abancay.

Although regarded as a regional backwater, Abancay surprised me with a vibrancy that I'd found lacking in other Peruvian cities. I sensed a strong feeling of both national and regional pride, and attributed much of this to its large population of university students. I wondered if it was the same pride that had sparked the rebel communist movement in this part of Peru two decades earlier.

We had no problem finding a good clean *hostal* where we could stow our gear until we returned from Cachora to pick it up. And there was no shortage of exotic bakeries and cafes to wash the taste of campsite cooking right out of our mouths. Unfortunately, this willy-nilly stuffing of faces sent each of us back to revisit the hell of acute diarrhoea. As in Corire, we were unable to stay off the toilet for longer than ten minutes, and even the water we guzzled to stave off dehydration, passed straight through us.

Returning to Puente Cunyac by bus was an absolute

nightmare. I thought I'd explode. When we stopped in a hamlet to pick up passengers, I beelined for the nearest adobe cottage and pleaded for use of their outhouse. I was only half done when, after five minutes, the driver started honking his horn.

Arriving back at the bridge to begin the portage, my body felt drained of energy and fluid, yet heavy as lead. But part of me actually savoured the discomfort. After all, the likely alternative was to die slowly from asphyxiation and internal bleeding, deep in the hole at the base of a gigantic cataract.

The bitumen road climbed a few hundred metres above the level of the river then levelled off. Initially, the road cut into the left flank of the Apurimac Canyon, snaking its way around a series of gullies. Where a valley carved by an Apurimac tributary intersected, the road took the opportunity to veer away from the canyon before it became an abyss.

For the most part, we managed to stay out of trouble en route to Cachora. Our only brush with near disaster came in the form of a rockfall. It happened at a point where the road made a sharp elbow-turn to trace the indent made by a wide gully. A work team laboured to reconstruct the elbow, which had been swallowed by a landslide. The newly exposed gully fringe was still unstable. The workers had dug earthworks as a barrier against most of the tumbling debris – the important word here is 'most'.

As we passed, a mass of rocks loosened themselves from the fringe high above and clattered down the gully slope. The smaller rocks came to rest at the base of the slope, but one fragment, the size of a washing machine, breached the earthworks and tumbled across the road where we had been only seconds earlier.

The work crew fully identified with the awe and shock on our faces. 'There are rocks coming down all the time,' said one of them. 'We cannot turn our backs for a moment.'

I drove myself into the ground to reach the village of Curahuasi, 25 kilometres on from Puente Cunyac, and a soft bed. As we neared the village, a group of children started following us. They hurled insults from the other side of a stone fence. In no mood for cheek, we returned verbal fire. Doing so must have gained us some respect because their manner switched: they hopped the fence and offered to carry our backpacks for the rest of the way to the village. Mine was shouldered by a girl not much taller than the backpack itself. We treated the kids to sodas then checked ourselves into the Hostal Anis, so named because of Curahuasi's status as a major producer of aniseed.

During the night, my bowels relapsed, and by morning I was too ill to move beyond frequent crawls across the courtyard to reach the toilet. I improved enough for us to continue the next day. My body drew on the conditioning it had received during the coastal desert experience.

As it had done for much of the leg from Puente Cunyac to Curahuasi, the road wound its way uphill. By the time we reached a scattering of Inca ruins known as Saywuite, we were almost 1500 metres higher than the river. Saywuite was a ceremonial centre dedicated to the worship of water. It is home to one of the more curious artefacts from the Inca era. Among walls of perfectly fitted stones, there is a granite monolith. The rock is about five metres in diameter and the top half has been carved. The sculpture resembles an architectural model of a city, a metropolis where every structure is interconnected but at the same time blending into the naked rock. There are staircases, archways and terraces, merged together like something from the illusional artworks of M.C. Escher.

And when it rains, as it did while we were there, the water trickles through a network of tiny channels. It cascades into rectangular pools, overflows into more channels, and ultimately drains off the sculpture in a few select places. I wondered if this sculpture reflected a dream of the Incas. Was it an artist's impression of a mighty eco-city that their people might have eventually built, an idea snuffed out by the conquering Spanish?

Saywuite nestled just below a divide. Cresting this divide, the road then forked at a valley head. On the Apurimac Canyon's far side, I could see the high peaks of the Cordillera Vilcabamba – Facchac, Camas and Marcani. The valley descended quickly towards Cachora. The town seemed directly below us, as though we stood on a cliff overlooking it. To get there before nightfall, we used a steep pathway that traversed the gently sloped switchbacks.

As I watched the distant snowcaps be turned to gold by the setting sun, and the shadows of mountains creep across the Cachora Valley, the pain in my knees dulled. I plodded through the outskirts of town, well behind Colin and Scott. From the other side of a high plastered fence came the unmistakable din of wild partygoers. Curious, I paused for a moment to look through an open gate. Seconds later, a throng of revellers swarmed through the gate and crowded around me. Their ear-to-ear smiles and uninhibited back-slapping reeked of chicha, the homemade corn alcohol beverage that is almost as old as the mountains themselves.

The party was a wedding reception. A wooden bowl was filled with chicha out of a clay jug, then thrust into my hands. 'Drink!' they cried.

Caught up in the moment, I didn't think twice. The bowl was refilled and before I knew it I'd slurped this down too. I answered a few of their questions. Then I turned to answer a tap on my shoulder. Another bowl of chicha appeared right under my nose. My attempts to drink slowly this time met with a chorus of disapproval. I was sober. I had a lot of catching up to do.

'Where are the newlyweds?' I asked, hoping to divert the spotlight from myself.

'They went to bed at five o'clock,' one woman said with a wink. 'Now, drink.'

The Catholic religion dominates life in South America, especially in the rural areas. In this part of the world, 'no sex before marriage' is a decree obeyed more often than not. Who could blame a young married couple for making up for lost time?

Feeling the chicha turning my legs even mushier than before, I refused a fourth bowl and excused myself. I found my companions in the plaza, chatting with a moustached man who wore a bright yellow cap. Juan was of thin yet muscular build and aged about 40. Through him we could rent pack animals for lugging our gear the last fifteen kilometres down to the river. That night, we rented a room above a grocery store. My bed was so lumpy that I half expected to wake up with a dislocated spine.

A pre-dawn bus took us back to Abancay, where we collected our rafting equipment and bought enough food for three weeks. Our maps showed the next leg of the Apurimac to be especially remote and uninhabited. There was little hope of being able to resupply before we hit the village of Lechemayo, some 200 kilometres downstream. We were heading into one of the least known areas in South America.

Just how unknown was highlighted by Dayme, a civil engineer who we met on the bus returning to Cachora. He was in the process of overhauling the trail that linked Cachora to the long-lost Inca fortress of Choquequirau.

In 1534, the year following conquest, the Spanish had

installed a puppet emperor named Manco. His appointment was designed to quell unrest in the native population while the Conquistadores plundered the empire's riches. After three years of humiliation, Manco realised that the invaders had no intention of leaving, and so he planned rebellion. He laid seige to Cuzco for eight months and was only narrowly defeated. He retreated to Ollantaytambo and built a fortified city from which he commanded the Incan resistance movement for several years. Eventually, the Spanish defeated him there too and Manco fled to a rugged corner of the empire, a region called Vilcabamba. Here he built Choquequirau, a citadel that eluded the Spanish for decades. When the Spanish at last sacked Choquequirau in 1572, Manco's successor, Felipe Tupac Amaru, was captured and hauled off to Cuzco. His barbaric execution in the Plaza de Armas marked the end of the Incan Empire.

The Spanish exploited the resources of Vilcabamba for 200 years. When they were used up, Choquequirau was abandoned. Dense forest soon reclaimed the city and it remained buried until 1965, when an American archaeologist named Gene Savoy discovered the ruins. Only in the last decade have they been cleared of vegetation and readied for tourists.

The government expected a rise in the number of visitors and had commissioned the trail upgrade. Reaching the famous ruined citadel of Machu Picchu, 80 kilometres to the east, is an exercise no more strenuous than boarding a bus. The only way to get to Choquequirau is to hike cross-country for a day and a half.

'At the moment, it is common for people to fall off the track and die,' Dayme said.

It was a length of this same track that would return us to the Apurimac's banks.

Next day, our moustached friend Juan arrived at the store with the promised beasts of burden. This time, no donkeys were involved. Two horses and a mule would do the job. The mule seemed particularly strong and ill tempered. Juan put a hessian bag over its head while we secured the raft to the animal's back. 'Don't forget,' he warned, 'if he sees you behind him, he will kick.'

I looked at its twitching hind flank then down at the hooves. I could imagine them shattering my pelvis or breaking a dozen ribs. Juan removed the hessian. The mule flared its nostrils and pushed its ears back as if to say, 'Just give me that chance, amigo.'

As we set off, Juan explained that there were two trails, each leading to a bridge across the river. He recalled what he knew about a Swiss–French rafting crew that had launched their boats at one of the bridges five years earlier. Within half an hour, a raft had flipped and two men had drowned.

'Which bridge did they start from?' queried Colin.

Juan indicated that it was the upstream bridge.

'We're going to the other one,' I said quickly.

It soon became clear that, without a trail, going overland would have been impossible. The trail skirted a mountain with flanks sloping 45 degrees at their gentlest. Dayme's work team had levelled the existing path and widened it to just over a metre. Remembering my own experience in walking-trail construction, I was able to appreciate this as no small feat of earth moving. The path was firm and stable. Still, one step over the edge and we'd be tumbling to our deaths.

Over the first ten kilometres, we descended only a little. The slopes were coated in emerald-coloured heath and grasses, and sprinkled with wildflowers. The Apurimac came into view, still the better part of 1000 metres below us. It was dark green, flecked with white and looked deceptively at peace from this height. On the other side of the river, the chiselled crags of the Cordillera Vilcabamba stretched away towards a haze of cones.

I might have been in the Alps of Switzerland, except that the panorama here tugged at emotions far beyond a tourist's exhilaration and awe. A sense of mystery hung in the air. So much of this land – spires, chasms and caves – was virtually inaccessible to humans. Only by really exercising its problem-solving ingenuity could our species even get as far as we had. I felt like an intruder.

Our descent quickened. As the altitude dropped, the fertile heathland turned to bony scrub country. After reaching the end of the engineering team's efforts, the trail got rough, and Juan had a hard time coaxing the skittish mule around several washed-out sections. We arrived at the footbridge just before nightfall. The roaring Apurimac welcomed us back for the decider.

NINE
TRIAL BY WHITEWATER

24 October 1999 (day 42):
last stretch of the Acobamba Abyss,
6620 kilometres to the Atlantic

A family from Cuzco had also camped at the bridge. A man named José and his nine-year-old daughter Salina were returning from the ruins of Choquequirau. In the mid-morning heat, they and Juan helped us move our gear to the river's edge. All three waited expectantly as we organised the raft.

'Looks like they're keen to go for a spin,' noted Scott.

I looked at the river and nodded.

'The rapids don't start for 40-odd metres. We could whiz 'em across to the other side and back. Easy.'

Colin seemed less inclined. He only agreed to it when Scott, who was guiding us first up, spoke without any doubts: 'If we can't do this, then there's something very wrong with us.'

From the instant we pushed off from shore, I thought there was something wrong with us – or at least, there was something wrong with *Los Labios.* She was sluggish and

I could feel Scott using more effort than normal to turn her. The added weight meant that the boat sat lower in the water and caught more current. As we struggled to ferry across the river, it shocked me how much less responsive a few extra people on board made her. Scott called out encouragement.

'Come on, boys. Let's not show ourselves up. Dig in hard!'

The Peruvians chuckled nervously. It was Juan's first time in a boat.

We reached the other side.

'Shall we walk back over the bridge?' asked Juan, but you could tell he was hopeful of a return leg.

'No need,' I said.

There was still some 25 metres of water before the river turned ugly. When we were halfway across, with over fifteen metres of calm to spare, the current quickened. Scott responded. He angled further upstream, calling out, 'Harder forward! *Harder!*'

Colin and I paddled as hard and fast as we could. It wasn't enough, we were too heavy. Due to our sharper angle, more ground was lost in proportion to the distance ferried. Realising that our resistance was futile, Scott swivelled *Los Labios* to meet the whitewater head on.

We dipped into a slalom run of rapids. As far downriver as I could see, boulders littered the waterway like gate markers. Between them were chutes and cascades of all shapes and sizes. It was a question of picking out the safest, most direct route to reach an eddy by the left bank.

We charged over two falls without error. The nervous laughter of our guests ceased as a wave crashed over the boat and soaked José. The joyride was over. Above a third cascade, Scott changed his mind at the last minute and tried for the alternative chute.

'*Hard forward!*'

But we were destined for the cascade. I looked to my left. Oh, no – not side on! As the pontoon was sucked down and pulled backwards, Scott yelled out the obvious: 'We're going over, lads!'

For the few seconds I was trapped under the raft, my main feeling was embarrassment. As I surfaced, the gravity of the situation struck. Thanks to us, there were three Peruvians in a wild river and not one had a life jacket or a helmet. I saw only Juan and José hurtling downstream ahead of me.

'The girl!' I spluttered.

'I've got her!' It was Colin, hidden from view, on the other side of the raft.

He pushed Salina onto the upturned boat then clambered up after her. Juan doggy-paddled his way to the raft but poor José was struggling to keep his head above water. Scott was at the stricken man's side moments later and holding him afloat.

I pulled myself up. Salina was wailing hysterically. Colin tried his best to comfort her. He had his work cut out. Her father was sobbing too, whether from relief at seeing his daughter alive or from mortal fear, I couldn't tell. Our Cachoran mule driver seemed to be coping reasonably well. He was clinging to the perimeter rope.

'You okay, Juan?'

'Si, si.'

So what now? Our best option was to try manoeuvring into an eddy while still upside down. I searched in vain for a paddle. Colin and I had let go of ours in the flip. Each paddle had then become entangled in the strap of the other and were now stuck uselessly beneath the raft. Scott still had hold of his, but he was at the end of its line and hanging on to José with his other arm.

'We've got to right the boat!' I yelled.

Colin shook his head. 'No way. We'll lose the girl. It was a miracle she hung on when we flipped.'

This was a fair point. Salina might easily have been swept away and drowned but for her instinct to grab hold of the raft. Yet, with her on the upturned boat clinging to Colin, our hands were tied. We could do nothing except hope that the raft snagged before a cataract devoured us. I hated feeling so helpless.

I straightened up and craned my neck to peer down-river. The boulders made it hard to gauge the situation, but I saw water leaping somewhere ahead. My imagination did the rest.

'Look, I'll take care of her. She'll only be in for half a minute. We've got to –'

'No!' Colin was adamant. And as if clueing in to what I proposed, Salina tightened her grip on him. The last place she wanted to go was back into the jaws of a monster.

We dropped through a chain of closely spaced holes. I cursed them for not being big enough to keep hold of the boat. In the situation, recirculation might have given us time to organise and regroup. The irony was that when upside down, the raft was more stable. The four heavy dry bags acted like the lead ballast in the keel of a sailboat. Only a big hole would flip *Los Labios* back up the right way, and perhaps only for an instant.

I clawed at passing boulders, but all of them were too well rounded, with nothing on which to hook even a finger. Scott and José were now hanging on to the perimeter line. Scott held the rope on either side of José, using his body to shield the terrified man. I saw the brave South African stiffen his arms to brace for a boulder impact. He took the blow then looked up.

'Thank Christ for spongy life jackets,' he said, smiling ruefully.

I pulled José aboard and scanned downstream again. The jumping water was much closer now. Ooomph! Colin crashed into me, almost knocking me overboard. We were snagged. Below us, the cam-strapped bags pressed against a submerged boulder. How long before they slithered off it? The shore was only two boat-lengths away; an eddy-line was at one-and-a-half. Scott swam for it, got there, and heaved himself onto a dry boulder top. Meanwhile, Colin had unclipped the throwbag from the perimeter line. He hurled it like a gridiron football, the tightly coiled rope inside streaming out behind it. Scott caught the rope and pulled us into the eddy.

José and Salina scurried away back to their campsite, whimpering, but not before José had thanked us profusely for saving their lives. I felt ashamed. Juan's reaction was more what I expected.

'You are crazy gringos! You will die on this river!' Then he too disappeared back upriver. That was the last we saw of him.

I could hardly bear to watch as the raft was pulled over upright. In most flip scenarios, the boat is righted within the first two or three minutes. We had given the river almost fifteen to wreak havoc. Even the most tightly secured gear could be loosened by the relentless undercurrents and the scraping against submerged rocks.

There was a moment of relief as we quickly accounted for all the dry bags, both big and small. But that was all we could account for. The rest was gone. Everything that had been merely wedged or stuffed into some tight space, because it couldn't fit into the dry bags, was lost. We were furious with ourselves. That the dry bags had been full of food rations was no excuse. There were more secure methods of arranging the gear overflow and we had not bothered to practise these. Most of the lost items would not have stood much more of a chance even had the boat been righted immediately.

Why had we been so stupid? How could we have thought ourselves immune to flipping? Had we forgotten so quickly what we were up against? It was not the worst of it, admittedly, but this part of the river was still referred to as the Acobamba Abyss. While we made a tally of the missing items, each of us fumed over the extent of our complacency.

During our morning pack-up, the pile of cooking and eating utensils had escaped our notice. Rather than repack everything, we had put them in a plastic bag and tied this to a cam-strap. The knot had held, but a wide split down the side of the bag told a sad story. Pots, pans, knives, forks, plates – everything inside was gone. Everything we had to cook and eat our food with now lay at the bottom of the Apurimac.

There was a slim chance that we might retrieve the foam mattresses, the spare paddle and a wetsuit jacket, but the canister containing all our topographical maps was certain to leak and had probably already settled on the riverbed. Scott's sneakers were gone too, despite having been tied around one of the cam-straps. Somehow the river had managed to undo the laces.

We debated whether we should take time out to go get more pots and pans. The consensus was no. We were sick of hiking, and certainly, none of us wanted to face the citizens of Cachora once Juan's story got around. Much of our food was dry hard staples, but we were confident of being able to improvise means of preparing them. We might not eat well, but we wouldn't starve.

But there was more to our decision than that. Although it was never discussed openly, I knew that each of us, in our own way, was constantly haunted by the white-water. While it was there, we could not relax or feel secure. There'd been several close calls and luck seemed to have played too big a part in us getting this far. As soon as possible, we wanted to reach the end of the Apurimac and stop it tormenting us. No one wanted to put it off longer than was absolutely necessary.

There was no let-up in the drama. We finished the slalom only to be confronted by a seething class 5. 'Fucking hell! Leave us alone!' Colin shouted at the roiling waves.

We had made it through rapids as tough as these before the Cunyac Bridge, but right now our confidence was in tatters. The river churned for over 100 metres before levelling out into a calm expanse equally as long – the *plano*, as we lovingly referred to it. We decided to send the raft down unmanned, but the rocky shore made lining too difficult an option. Our plan instead involved Scott releasing *Los Labios* at the top of the rapids and letting her careen down alongside the left bank. As soon as she hit the *plano*, Colin would swim out, climb aboard, then toss the throwrope to where I waited, another 50 metres downstream. On any day but this, things might have gone off without a hitch.

A third of the way down, the raft was flipped by a hole. No problem. The way we'd cinched the gear in this time, nothing would budge. Three-quarters of the way, she was snared by an eddy. Now there *was* a problem. Poised by the water's edge, our views obstructed by boulder stacks, neither Colin nor I saw this happen. Eventually, we climbed on top of the stacks to chance a look. Scott was scrambling towards the boat, his progress slow over the slippery rocks. Colin and I began making our way to the raft as well.

The shore terrain was bad – it had taken us ten minutes to get from above the rapids to our positions on the *plano*. When Colin was just half-a-dozen metres away, the raft slipped from the eddy and back into the rapids. My eyes were fixed on where I could safely put my hands and feet, not on what unfolded upstream.

Over the whitewater crescendo, I heard a faint shout. I looked up to see Colin waving his arms and *Los Labios* making a charge for freedom. I was only five metres away from the water's edge, but separated from it by a jumble of greasy boulders. The raft slid over the *plano*. I slid over the rocks.

As she shot past only a few metres from shore, I turned a trip into a graceful lunge. I hit the water, and for a sickening moment, expected to feel my knees smash against a granite boulder just below the surface. It didn't happen. I snatched at the end of the excess perimeter line that was untied and trailing behind her, and looped it around my hand. Simultaneously, I managed to fix my leg between two submerged rocks – this raft wasn't going anywhere.

'Gotcha!'

For the remainder of that awful day, we rafted nothing easier than class 4 – we were given no chance to regain our composure.

As we skipped over the riverbank to scout yet another set of big rapids, Colin whooped in triumph. It was the first happy sound I'd heard that day. He reached down into a space between the rocks and yanked free a plastic jerry can, the type used for carrying fuel.

'Our new cooking pot,' he beamed.

'Huh?'

Colin explained that if you supplied a low, even heat underneath, it was possible to boil water in a plastic container. He told a story of how he'd once seen plastic bags full of water tossed onto a fire. Amazingly, the plastic hadn't melted, because the water inside had kept it cool.

The base of the can was cracked, so we cut it off and plugged the nozzle with a thick piece of cane. That evening, it successfully took the crunch out of a batch of rice.

Victory was short-lived, however. Next morning, I emerged from the tent to find a puddle of ash, sand and porridge, with Colin beside it examining a hole where the plastic had melted.

But the jerry can had inspired us. At every stop to scout, our eyes darted into each shadowy nook and cranny. Scott found a plastic teaspoon. I found a glass jar (that had somehow avoided being smashed to pieces). Colin found an old rusted shovel blade. Only the top half of the blade was intact and even one side of that was badly eaten away. Nevertheless, it was this acquisition that gave birth to the legend of Amazon Oatcakes.

Mixed with the right amounts of flour, sugar, oil, cinnamon and water, oats made a great dough. The shovel blade fried the flattened ball of dough mixture to perfection. A dollop of jam on top then put the finishing touch to a breakfast that we craved waking up for.

The need to improvise means of cooking our food distracted us from the challenges we faced on the river to some extent. Still, we felt both frustrated by the inconvenience of having no utensils, and relieved that there had not been more dire ramifications. The river could inflict much worse. There was a fine line between challenging and downright nightmarish. Given the seriousness of several incidents to date, we had a lot to feel grateful for.

If one of us broke a bone or needed any sort of medical attention, the only way to reach help was by continuing downriver. I didn't even want to imagine the kind of trauma something like that would cause – controlling the raft with three fit men was hard enough. A couple of weeks before leaving Canada, Colin and I had rented the cult river movie *Deliverance*. The powerful images of Burt Reynolds's broken leg never seemed too far from our own reality.

I wondered what Colin and Scott would do with my body if I died, if my body was even retrievable. Would they bundle me up and carry me out? Would they bury me on the shore? Or would they weight my corpse with rocks and send me to the riverbed? I always stopped short of asking them.

Our progress was slow. The river made us fight hard for every hundred metres. We had been reduced to ticking off distance in small increments. I had to go to the toilet every half an hour. Whether because of the continuous noise of running water or the anxiety generated by the rapids, I wasn't sure. Both theories made sense. I could almost feel my bladder filling up as we bounced through the loudest, most dangerous rapids.

There always seemed to be more coming out than I'd taken in, although I didn't count the plumes of spray that strained through the spaces between my gritted teeth. And when the urge hit, there was no holding it in.

The process I went through in order to relieve the pressure made me realise that my 'Farmer John overalls'–style wetsuit might not have been the most prudent choice. My groin was like a bank safe – strict procedure had to be followed to allow access within. I had to get my helmet off before I could get out of my life jacket. Then, only after unzipping my wetsuit from neck to waist and wriggling my torso free was

I able to pull it down far enough. At the bottom of several especially scary rapids, there simply wasn't enough time.

By the evening of the second day beyond Cachora Bridge, no suitable replacement for the jerry can had been found. I was on food duty during this overnight stop, and a meal was expected regardless.

I opened a big can of Ecuadorian pilchards, carefully leaving the lid attached to the rest of the can, and placed the fish inside the case of Scott's diving mask. I then bent the lid of the can back and folded it twice to make a handle for our new saucepan. Over the next three hours, I boiled six saucepans full of red kidney beans – just enough to muffle the growls of our stomachs.

Next morning, I collected water to make oatcakes and noticed that something was different about the river. It had changed colour. Instead of the usual green, it now resembled chocolate milk. The change was easily explained. Somewhere upstream the heavens had opened and washed many tonnes of topsoil into the river.

The change of colour was the first sure sign that the wet season was here. It meant that the Apurimac was rising. Overnight, its rapids would have increased their lethal power. I shivered. More than ever I felt like an intruder. We were a foreign object that needed expulsion, like a parasitic worm clinging to the walls of an intestine, and now the rains were infusing the Apurimac with poison whitewater to flush us out.

We came to a long stretch of whitewater that was split by a narrow island. The left-hand side was triple the width of the right. Although it also possessed the bigger drop-offs and holes, the left offered more room to weave around the turmoil. This is where we headed.

Under the whip, *Los Labios* surged down the entry tongue and ramped off the first standing wave. Ahead of me I saw Colin's and Scott's paddle blades take a stroke of fresh air.

As I looked down from the crest of a second wave, my blood ran cold. The water immediately in front of us pillowed off a semi-submerged rock before it fell down a one-metre-high cascade. This rock had not been visible when we scouted.

As one we cried, 'Aaaahhh!'

Fortunately, we hit the pillow's left edge, avoiding the possibility of being snagged on the rock. Most of our momentum was salvaged, but the starboard bow deflected upwards in a movement so violent that Colin and Scott tumbled over the side. Both lost hold of their paddles.

We all brushed the rim of the hole and kept going. Colin was nearest the raft. I jumped the bags, sprawled onto the pontoon and stretched my paddle out. He grabbed hold and I pulled him back on board. Meanwhile, the current pulled Scott further away from the raft, towards a vertical wall that formed the left bank.

The raft began to buck wildly. Colin and I gripped the nearest strap, stayed low and kept our eyes glued on the river ahead. We'd have to rendezvous with Scott at the base of the run. *Los Labios* spun out of control down the remainder of the rapids but managed to stay upright.

At the bottom we waited in an eddy, throwbag ready to toss at Scott when he floated past. Several minutes passed. No Scott.

'Last I saw, he was close enough to the cliff to touch it,' said Colin.

We secured the raft and scrambled back upstream. Sure enough, he was sitting on a ledge at the cliff base. When he saw us, he pointed at his leg then made a motion with his hands as though snapping a stick in half. My stomach sank.

'Oh, shit! His leg's broken.'

'Jesus!'

I sucked in my breath and looked ruefully at Colin. 'We're buggered now.' My mind was whirling. How would we get through the rest of the Apurimac with just two able-bodied men?

Colin was more optimistic. 'Could mean he's just banged it badly.'

Scott bowed his head, as though in great pain.

'He doesn't look very happy.'

'How do we get the poor bastard out of there?'

Yes. First things first. The wall of the cliff rose sheer for five metres above his head then became a thinly grassed slope, angled at 45 degrees. It would be possible to carry the raft up above the rapid, shoot across to an eddy on the other side, then climb up the bank ahead of where it became sheer. But then what? One of us was likely to slip and fall off either in the process of getting into position, or in the act of hauling Scott up on the end of a rope.

Getting any sort of rescue rope to him would be tough. The split river rejoined downstream of Scott's ledge. Without attempting a risky crossing to the sliver of land dividing the rapid, we could get no closer to him than about 80 metres. Even if we made it to the island, one of us would still have to toss the throwbag 40 metres to reach him. That was virtually impossible. The crescendo made it impossible to vocalise our assessment of rescue options. All we could do was mime, then shake our heads and cross our arms as a sign of 'can't be done'.

We could do nothing. Scott's only means of escape from that ledge was to swim.

The lower half of the rapid was much kinder than the top half. It was essentially a long train of waves. Although big and powerful, there was nothing that could capture and drown a swimmer. The ride would be rough, and painful in his condition, but there was no doubt he'd make it through to the bottom alive.

Colin and I made freestyle swimming motions. We swept the rapid with our hands then gave the thumbs-up signal. Scott shook his head and made the motion of tossing a throwbag.

'He's got no idea what's downriver from him,' I noted. 'It's no wonder he doesn't want to swim it.'

From the ledge, the only part of the rapid he could see were the boiling holes upstream and the thrashing white caps right in front of him. Below that, he could only take our word for it.

For fifteen minutes we tried to persuade Scott to swim. He insisted on either a rope down the cliff or the throwbag. To drive the message home that the ball was in his court, we lounged on a boulder top. The standoff continued for another half an hour. Finally the South African conceded.

'Quick, let's get the video camera,' said Colin. 'This'll be something he can show his grandchildren.'

First thing Scott did was show us what he thought of the decision to film his torment. He stood up on both feet, turned around, bent over and dropped his pants.

'I'd say that means his leg isn't busted.'

'Thank the river gods.'

He backed his way along a narrow extension of the ledge. Through the zoom, I saw him stare at the river, trying to master the terror that would not let him go back into a rapid that had already injured his body. Only later did I fully comprehend what he must have been going through. I'd been forced to swim rapids on a number of occasions but the difference was that when the raft flipped, or you were bucked overboard, everything happened so fast. There was never time to think about it. On this occasion, poor Scott had far too much time to think.

Five more minutes passed. Finally, he jumped. Initially, his head and shoulders bobbed along the surface. Then he was sucked down and out of sight. Ten metres downstream, his white helmet reappeared. Scott was still inside.

Wave after wave crashed over him. They pushed and punched and slapped. His head twisted left, then right, then left again, as the currents had their way with the rest of his body. It was like a very one-sided wrestling contest. One arm tore free and flailed, but only for an instant. Then it was back to just his head. A whitewater wall lined him up for a slam. Scott's neck whipped back as it hit and he was again dragged beneath the waves.

Seconds passed. I didn't know where to point the camera. I tracked down the last chute, assuming his speed remained constant. He surfaced at the base of the chute, sneaking into the left-hand side of the screen. Scott had done it. And it was all on film.

As Colin stood ready to help him from the water, his eyes saw something embedded in a mass of slime by the river's edge. He picked it up, scraped off the coating of muck, then gasped.

'Your shoes, Scott! It's your goddamn Nikes!'

We're being toyed with, I thought. *This bastard river really does know we're here*. They were the pair lost at the same time as the cooking gear – what were the chances of that?

Scott was in no mood to appreciate this uncanniness. The heavy blow to his thigh had bruised muscle and bone. Every movement brought tears to his eyes. For the remainder of the day, he hardly spoke, except to curse the pain in his leg. On top of being sore and badly shaken, he was angry. He was annoyed that Colin and I hadn't even bothered to attempt a rescue off the ledge, and that we'd seemed to make light of his ordeal by capturing the whole thing on film.

'Maybe we shouldn't have raved on about how good that footage is,' I whispered to Colin later.

'Hmm. I reckon he thinks we put him through it for the camera.'

'Nothing we could do,' I insisted.

'Nothing,' agreed Colin.

'Amazing footage, though.'

'Yeah!'

As far as we could see, whitewater thundered through a chasm whose walls plunged vertically into the water. It was one of our worst nightmares. Both sides rose to over 100 metres. Even before the chasm veered left, the whitewater had disappeared into gloomy shadow. We could not scout. And the only way to portage was by helicopter.

Colin grimaced. 'We'll be making this one up as we go.'

Scott groaned. His ordeal from the day before had stripped away any lingering shreds of the gung-ho attitude that he'd brought with him to raft the Apurimac. Now when he looked at the river, he knew only fear, pain and pessimism.

'And what if there's a 20-metre-high waterfall?' he asked.

'Then try not to do a bellyflop.'

The last was spoken without humour.

As we entered this stretch that not even the sunlight of early afternoon could penetrate, the air became eerily chilled.

We seemed tinier and more pathetic than ever. When not paddling, each of us stood to survey downstream as best we could.

'Whirlpool on the left!' shouted Colin. 'Hard forward!'

It was five metres in diameter and more than capable of slurping down even a very buoyant raft for several seconds. We skirted the edge harmlessly and then bobbed through a jumble of waves and chutes. A pillar of brightness appeared, marking the chasm exit. There must be holes in here too, I thought. There were, and our sequence of impromptu manoeuvres had put us on course to hit a big one.

'It's a frowner!' cried Colin.

I knew what this meant. We'd seen plenty of 'frowners' on the Apurimac so far, but had never gone through one. The 'frowner', or 'keeper hole', was something we had been desperate to avoid. They were the most persuasive reason for a portage if running the rapid meant having to deal with one.

The name 'frowner' comes from the shape of the lip of the cascade that creates it – where the river plunges over appears like a frown when you view it from upstream. The curve of churning, recirculating water at the base tends to move objects from the edges into the middle. Whereas 'smilers', holes curving the other way, would usually spit out a swimmer within a matter of seconds, frowners might hold on to them indefinitely (hence the alternative name 'keeper hole'). You could struggle as hard as you liked, but short of a rescue rope, drowning was a near certainty.

The method of evaluation was simple. Naturally, none of us were happy about where we were about to go.

'HARD FUCKING PADDLE!' screamed Colin.

The only way we'd beat a hole this big was by hitting it fast. For several metres above the lip, the river pushed and tugged at us, as though it also realised where it was headed and had begun to panic. It made Colin's job of keeping *Los Labios* on course a Herculean task. Just how straight we broke over that lip could also mean the difference between getting caught and charging to safety.

And then we were over the edge – and falling down. As we hit, the sudden deceleration made me lurch forwards. At that same moment, the front third of the raft bent at the forward thwart. For a split-second, the red hypalon rubber pinched my bum cheeks. It was long enough to hold me in place, and to make me think that *Los Labios* must be looking out for me.

'Hard forward!'

The hole started reeling us in. There was a brief moment, a half-lifetime, where we made no progress against it. Then we crawled forward. Colin grunted to keep us pointing downstream. He desperately wanted to paddle madly as well, but realised that might cause us to skew sideways and play into the hands of the keeper.

My arms burnt. My mind was filled with everything and nothing. And then we were free. Later I would wonder if the only thing I had known in those few seconds was the purest form of the fight-or-flight instinct.

There were signs of humanity not far downstream of the chasm. We pitched camp where a cable ran high over the river. It served as a means of crossing. Halfway up the cliff on the other side, at the end of a tortuous foot trail, a cable car waited. The car was nothing fancier than an open wooden box, designed to cope with no one bigger in stature than a Quechua person.

On our side of the river, the trail continued up a gully. Kane's book talked about a trail that led to Triunfo, an abandoned mill two kilometres from the river. Without maps, the only way we could estimate our time left in the whitewater was through his descriptions. Was this the Triunfo trail? We argued about it, though none of us had the energy to go and verify.

Shrubs and tall grasses covered either side of the gully and also extended around its margins onto the slopes of the canyon. And there, among dull hues of pea and olive, were the glossy green leaves of five banana palms. Someone had planted them and was no doubt waiting for the bunches to ripen. I didn't even think twice about raiding the patch. Bananas made easy eating and, driven by the niggling dissatisfaction of my belly, this was a chance to stuff my face. Besides, who would deny us comfort food after everything we'd been through?

Despite the size of each one, inside the fruit was green, and it tasted like cardboard. No big deal. I could wait a day or two until they ripened. Colin tried a bit, then smiled.

'Sorry to break this to you, mate, but these aren't bananas.'

'Eh?'

'They're plantains.'

Colin was our banana expert. Two months into his sailboat voyage across the Pacific, he'd arrived in French Polynesia completely broke. For several weeks, the only food he'd eaten were bananas, and a close relative of theirs – plantains.

'These will never be sweet,' he said.

I was a little deflated.

'We'll roast 'em in their skins and they'll be nice,' Colin continued. 'Trust me.'

They didn't taste too bad. Like a floury boiled potato.

Later, as we sipped coffee from glass jars, Colin talked at length about the many ways of cooking the plantains.

There were more than 50 left on the bunch and he had no shortage of recipe ideas.

'Too bad they're not bananas,' I moaned.

While tying the plantains to the raft pontoon the following morning, I looked around and took conscious note of the speed and efficiency with which we were breaking camp. It was similar to the way we set up camp at the end of each day, and it extended to our attitude of diligently maintaining equipment and trying to cook interesting meals. It struck me then that perhaps these were the only times when we could exercise a sense of feeling in absolute control, a feeling denied us while we sat in the raft paddling downriver.

Through dire necessity, our skills had developed in quick time. I had learnt to read many of the river's moods – not all of them, but many. I had learnt how to survey white-water for the safest route and take the raft down that route. But there were subtleties to every set of rapids that might escape the notice of even the world's most experienced rafter. All the perfectly executed manoeuvres and everything I had learnt could never muffle the voice that said: 'Only one small mistake, one error of judgment, separates you from death.' Drowning or receiving a fatal headwound was still very possible despite every rapid we tackled successfully.

In another way, experience only counted for so much. The river was rising with snowmelt and rain, and progressively commanded the flow of more and more tributaries. As the volume grew and its nature changed, our knowledge became obsolete and possibly our physical ability would become unequal to the task.

I slapped my shin for the umpteenth time that morning, then flicked away the splattered remains of an insect. The bloodsucking flies – the moskies – had plagued us since day 1, when we were on the Camaná Valley trail. Since the start of rafting, mornings and evenings onshore had proven the worst times for us because moskies rarely ventured out over the water. Maybe they too could take some of the credit for our speedy breaking of camp.

But for all my visions of calamity on the river, the biggest scare for me that day came while I was *off* it. It happened during a routine scout, as I worked my way from boulder to boulder. As I leapt on top of a regular car-sized rock, the thing decided to flout convention by moving, and with a sickening grind, it kept toppling over, towards the river. Eyes bulging, bladder loosened, I back-pedalled to stay on the highest point. I knew that if I lost my footing, I might be crushed. Just before it started sliding also, I flung my body sideways at an adjacent boulder, and landed sprawling but unhurt.

An afternoon of mainly *plano* nurtured the idea that the Apurimac had run out of evil intent and decided to be nice to us from now on. Typically, our notion was blown to pieces when we rounded a sharp bend and beheld the sort of rapid that doesn't even bear thinking about except for a shudder at the destructive forces contained within. As we had done several times in the past, we chose to make camp and divide the lugging between evening and the following morning. Portages sucked a lot of energy from us. At every campsite, the boat was normally unloaded anyway.

Pitching camp always put me in a good, positive mood – and not just because I knew that my death was at least put on hold until the next day. Rarely could our campsites be described as anything other than cosy beach havens. As with this entire canyon, they seemed to exist outside the boundaries of territory or real estate. Many were unlikely ever to have known the tread of human feet before. Some would never know it again. Invariably, huge chunks of granite littered the beaches, as though having fallen from the sky as a shower of meteorites.

Starting fires was as easy as harvesting a few blades of dry cane grass and putting a match to them. Enough driftwood could be gathered from the riverside rocks in a few minutes to keep the smokeless fire going all evening. I enjoyed lying back on the cool sand and burying my feet in its softness. The prospect of more deadly whitewater was dulled by keeping a tally of shooting stars.

Our latest campsite was in a league of its own.

From Pilpinto, our luck with the fishing rod had been extremely bad. None of us could remember even having had a bite. The rare fishermen we'd seen back upriver were always empty-handed too. Discouraged and doubtful, we had not bothered casting a line in the river since departing Cachora Bridge.

Here, though, there was no mistaking the fact that fish lived in the Apurimac. Hundreds of *trucha* were jumping up through a chain of pools that flowed beside the rapid. I guessed it was part of a mass migration upstream, coinciding with some sort of mating or feeding behaviour. Flinging themselves up to two metres through the air was obviously an easier alternative to swimming through the rapid. For us, catching them was no more difficult than plucking fruit from a tree. We spread some mosquito netting between two sticks and held it in front of a one-metre-high cascade. The unwitting *trucha* literally jumped into the net.

In all we snared fifteen fish, to roast in the fire alongside a plantain. For the first time in five days, my belly felt satisfied. And at long last, I looked at rafting the Apurimac as something more than simply hanging on as tightly and tenaciously as I was able to. Here now was the opportunity to live completely off the land. For all the skin it stripped, the blood it drew and the nerve it sucked out of us, the Apurimac Canyon provided the means for self-sufficiency. There were moments when we stood our ground against this river.

We were on the lookout for the first of two sizeable tributaries that would, between them, double the volume of the Apurimac in the space of 20 kilometres.

On a section of calm, just before the confluence of the Apurimac and the Pachachaca, we met our first curious resident since leaving the Cachora Bridge. He swam to within a couple of metres of the boat and fixed us with a beady stare. The slick brown otter then spun around and cruised back to shore.

The Pachachaca River looked like an enormous aqueduct. On both sides, smooth vertical walls met the water at a perfect 90-degree angle. And like a stormwater drain boosting the flow of a suburban creek after heavy rain, so the Pachachaca swelled the Apurimac.

The wave train just below the confluence bucked and tossed us with more power than anything upstream. It felt like we were caught up in some kind of wrestling match, as though the two rivers weren't happy about having to share the same turf and so now had to contend for dominance. The fact that the river here is still called the Apurimac means that geographers at least think they know the winner.

Beyond the Pachachaca confluence, we entered cactus country again. They were the only form of vegetation to be seen, standing tall and straight, like mute sentinels who seemed aware of our passing. Not for the first time on the journey, I felt closer to the Wild West of North America than the Amazon. This place could have been on a postcard of the Grand Canyon.

Midway between the Pachachaca and the Pampas confluences, we came across the first people in six days. They were workers on a half-completed steel bridge. When complete, the bridge would link a road between Ayacucho and Cuzco. All the men were from Ayacucho, but they had lived at a compound above the river for the past six months. The foreman was delighted to see us, as we were to see him when he promptly issued an invitation to lunch.

The workers' compound felt like an army base. Four young women ran the kitchen and mess area. We sat at a long table while the giggling cooks took it in turns to serve the soup and main dish then collect our plates. When the foreman excused himself, the two higher-ranking cooks came out to chat. The other two women regularly peeked through the service hatch.

The head cook was flirtatious and blushing simultaneously. Her second-in-command didn't say much, but fixed on each of us, one by one, an intense gaze. Both radiated plenty of sexual energy. I couldn't help but wonder what sort of dynamics existed between four women and 40 men in a remote work camp.

I steered the conversation in a direction that might get us something we wanted. 'There's one thing we haven't been able to do for a while.'

'What is that?' the head cook smiled.

'Cook ourselves a good meal,' I announced. 'You see, all of our pots sank a week ago.'

We explained about the flip and whined about how tough it had been to prepare food since.

The head cook went to the kitchen and returned minutes later holding a large black pot. It was covered in dents and a layer of hardened soot, but the sight of that pot thrilled us. I gave it a nickname there and then: 'the Cauldron'.

The bridge workers spoke of a very bad rapid around the next bend. They knew their stuff all right. Over 100 metres, the river was compressed into a quarter of its width. Then it fell into a cataract so demented that looking at it gave me a headache. Even as we portaged, I didn't feel safe. I half expected the monster to reach out an enormous watery paw and yank me in.

The junction of the Apurimac and Pampas rivers marked a former boundary of 'the Red Zone'. During the 1980s and early '90s, the Red Zone had been the guerrilla stronghold of the *Sendero Luminoso.* Under martial law throughout this period, it had spanned the remaining length of the Apurimac Canyon, between the confluence of the Pampas and where the Apurimac at last unites with the Mantaro River to form the Ene.

Founded in Ayacucho by Abimáel Guzmán Reynoso, a philosophy professor at the University of Huamanga, the *Sendero Luminoso* (or 'Shining Path') blends the ideas of Marxism, Leninism and Maoism with those of José Carlos Mariátegui, Peru's major Marxist theoretician. They are considered to be amongst the most elusive, secretive and brutal guerrilla organisations of the last century.

From 1980, the insurgency gained international notoriety for its policy of terror and targeting of almost every Peruvian institution. Through car-bombings, military strikes and execution murders across the country, they tried to topple the central government. Between 1980 and 1995, a total of 30,000 people died and 600,000 more were displaced nationwide. More than half of the victims came from Ayacucho.

The core of the movement's popularity is resentment. Lima has always bled resources from the peasant rural areas, deepening the divide between the 'haves' and the 'have-nots'. Imbalances in economic development and social conditions were, and still are, massive. The Shining Path claimed to fight the people's war. It spread across dozens of impoverished villages and had no trouble recruiting members. Counter-insurgency techniques, often applied indiscriminately by the armed forces, resulted in severe human rights violations against the civilian population and only created more recruits for the Senderistas.

In 1993, Reynoso and several other leaders were captured, sending the activities of the movement into sharp decline. Most important from our point of view was that the government had regained control of the Red Zone. People we had consulted before arriving in Peru claimed that the residual elements of the *Sendero Luminoso* would be no threat to us. I hoped it was true. I'd read that one of Reynoso's ultimate aims was to rid Peru of all foreign influences. There were many cases of foreign nationals having been attacked and killed over the past two decades.

The Red Zone was no more, yet Scott's discovery of footprints in the sand near our campsite still made each of us a little jittery. In 1986, at the height of the insurgency, the Chmielinski–Kane team had encountered a band of Senderistas not far from here. We were camped on a wide-open beach opposite the mouth of the Pampas River and our tents stood out like dog's balls. For any remnants of the guerrilla forces that had once held on to this region, we were an easy target.

Before the river had claimed our maps, my attention had been drawn to large blank areas in the former Red Zone region. Inside each of these blanks, were printed the words '*Informacion no suficiente*'. Those particular maps had dated back to the mid 1980s, but as the wind caused my skin to break out in goosebumps, they seemed eerily up to date.

Under the influence of the Pampas, the canyon lost its claustrophobic air. Instead of seeming to be about to topple on our heads, the walls now leant back.

The river itself became easier to handle. Very few rocks poked above the surface. Its power increased, yet we could place less emphasis on manoeuvring the raft from left to right across her width. Rafting became less a matter of looking for the friendliest chutes and cutting turns precisely on the edge of a nasty hole. The holes were bigger and more potent, but easily avoided.

Rapids came mainly in the form of wave trains. Big wave trains. They posed little threat if the bow was pointed into them. Keeping the bow pointed in that direction was the hard part. As we launched off the crest of some waves, half of *Los Labios* flew through the air before crashing down into the next trough.

Other waves were angled across our path. When we struck the crest of these, the bow deflected left or right as though it had been punched. If we copped a couple of hooks in quick succession, the raft could end up in that dreaded sideways position. In waves this tall, the subsequent risk of flipping was as great as heading side-on into a hole.

Beyond the Pampas, we flipped three times in two days, more than doubling our total for the three weeks prior to that. Each time, the cause was a rogue wave. The consequences of flipping in a wave train weren't anything more serious than getting soaked and swallowing a few mouthfuls of water. They were relaxed experiences compared with the moments of wide-eyed terror that flipping had induced upriver. At the base of the run, we would casually right the raft and keep on paddling.

Dark greenery began to appear in the gullies. The air started filling with the smell of plant life and the chirping of birds. We were excited by this. The Kane book claimed that a transition from arid canyon to moist highlands coincided with the ending of the rapids.

In the space of a few hours, the vegetation had transformed from cactus to forest. The rugged cliffs softened into a panorama of lushly carpeted hills. This new landscape went by the term 'cloud forest'. Cloud forest separates the grassed plateaus and dry valleys of the high Andes from the *selva*, the true jungle of the Amazon lowlands.

'Shssh.' Scott's face split into a grin. 'Can you hear that?'

'That insect buzzing?'

'No, mate. That's no insect,' he said, his smile broadening. 'It's an engine.'

He was right and he knew the significance of this sound. For the first time since bidding farewell to the Instinct rafts, we shared the river with another boat. But it wasn't this fact alone that made Scott so happy. This was a *motorboat,* and motorboats had no place in big whitewater. Its appearance confirmed that the Apurimac had indeed delivered its worst.

Minutes later, a long, narrow-hulled craft rounded the bend and sped past us. The locals referred to the boats as 'Johnsons' because of the predominating brand of outboard motor that powered them. For all of the noise it made, the passage of that Johnson was a glorious sight. If we were to die at the hands of the Amazon River, its rapids would not be the cause.

We reached Lechemayo by day's end. Solitude had become a tough habit to break: instead of landing at the village, we decided to camp on the opposite shore and celebrate our achievement in private. The villagers didn't feel snubbed; about ten of them swam the width of the river to pay us a visit.

A man named Alfredo invited us to breakfast at his house. We declined, citing our desire to reach the much larger town of San Francisco by the following evening. But Alfredo was insistent. His wife was a wonderful cook and it wouldn't take more than eight hours to reach San Francisco anyway. We agreed to come and Alfredo swam back to Lechemayo.

Next morning, our host greeted us enthusiastically at the bank as we pulled in. He shepherded us to a lopsided plank cottage and sat us down at a table. His wife and eight-year-old daughter emerged briefly from a dank scullery to introduce themselves. We ate chicken, rice and fresh bananas, washed down with delicious orange cordial. As we got up to thank our hosts and leave, Alfredo motioned that it was time to pay. Colin, Scott and I looked at each other. There was no doubt about it – we were back in the civilised world once again.

Our spirits were high. The riffles continued, but their noise was music compared with the mind-numbing crescendo back upstream. Nothing could wipe the smiles from our faces. Each of us felt our new leases on life had been signed. It was like going back to the doctor who had given you only days to live, and being told that the fatal disease has gone into complete remission. We talked about things we would do when we got home, things people rarely mention because they are so mundane. But we discussed them as if they were to be the highlights of our future.

Before those weeks in the whitewater, I had regarded my death as something that would happen so far into the future that seriously contemplating it was out of the question. With youth came a sense of immortality but the Apurimac had erased it. Still, it was only now that death had crept so close that I felt a real longing to savour the beauty of experience.

TEN
THE GUERRILLAS

2 November 1999 (day 51): on the edge of the New Red Zone, 6400 kilometres to the Atlantic

San Francisco is home to 10,000 people, by far the largest town on the Apurimac, and linked to Ayacucho via a sealed road. A steel bridge spans the Apurimac, linking the two halves of the town. This bridge is the first after the crossing near Cachora and the last before the Atlantic.

San Francisco is a splattering of concrete without charm or beauty. The buildings resemble boxes stacked on top of each other. Hundreds of metal spikes, the ends of concrete reinforcement rods, poke from the flat rooftops. They are successful at lending every building the appearance of still being under construction (Peruvian law states that tax is paid only on a house that is completed).

Less than 1000 metres above sea level, and only 10 degrees south of the Equator, the town swelters in tropical heat. The smells of third-world decay and rot are strong. Pigs and vultures wade through garbage piles that fill the ditches between riverside tenements. These same ditches also drain raw sewage into the river.

But to us, it was a wondrous place. There were restaurants, an ice-cream parlour, and grocery stores selling all our favourite chocolate bars. For the very first time, I drank a refrigerated bottle of Inca Kola. I was able to call my parents in Adelaide for the first time since leaving the Pacific coast.

We found replacements for most of the items either lost, damaged or simply used up over recent weeks. Buying a new set of kitchen utensils was cheap and easy, but our hunt for a portable stove proved fruitless. We did invest in a kerosene lantern as a cheaper alternative to running torches and picked up a shortwave radio to help stifle the faint murmurings of homesickness.

I left San Francisco feeling restored, convinced that the only things between us and our goal were legions of mosquitoes and many long days of rowing.

Our plan for beyond the whitewater had always been to stop paddling and start rowing. The long continuous paddle from Lechemayo to San Francisco had left our shoulder, neck and back muscles extremely stiff and sore. Bad posture was more to blame than the workout itself. We knew that plans to build a rowing frame had to be put into practice as soon as possible.

No one in San Francisco sold bamboo, but several people had claimed that there was a stand growing wild on the riverbank not far out of town.

'Do you know how far?' we'd asked on each occasion.

Of course they knew. We concluded that the stand was somewhere between five and 50 kilometres away, and would be on either the left-hand or the right-hand side of the river.

Three hours went by without any sign of the bamboo. An old man watched us from where he stood at the edge of a small clearing. Behind him, a track led into a thick stand of cane grass while on the bank were stacks of the cut cane. We knew the cane was too thin and flexible for our needs but thought he might also harvest bamboo.

'I have no bamboo,' the old man said with a single shake of his head. I was tempted to ask after its whereabouts but checked myself. 'But I have balsa,' he added.

One thing came to mind when I heard the word 'balsa' – crap model aeroplanes. I remembered how, as a child, I had never once finished making one without snapping at least one of the pieces while sticking it on. And if the plane lasted more than a week before it either lost a wing or got totally crushed, then nothing short of a miracle had taken place. Balsawood, as I pictured it, seemed a long way off what we needed.

Colin and Scott followed the old man up the track to his house for a look anyway. Maybe there were other materials he was prepared to sell. They returned carrying four thick logs, one on each shoulder.

'Balsa logs,' Colin announced, the initial surprise still evident on his face.

'Balsa *what*?'

'Logs,' confirmed Scott. 'Should do the job, I reckon.'

I was speechless. They were anything but flimsy wafers of wood that might break if you sneezed. Each was about three metres long and roughly 20 centimetres in diameter. They were, however, true to the most famous characteristic of balsawood: none of the four pieces weighed more than ten kilograms.

The logs created instant inspiration for a rowing-frame design. The thwarts were removed from the raft and a log laid widthways over the space where each thwart had been so that half a metre of balsa overhung the pontoon on each side.

The other two logs were rested lengthwise above the port and starboard pontoons. The arrangement of the logs was thus similar to a noughts-and-crosses grid. The cam-straps, which had held the thwarts in place, were reappropriated as means of securing the logs to the D-rings embedded in the pontoon fabric. In less than ten minutes, the rowing frame was ready.

We bought two-dozen lengths of the harvested cane, and laid these on top of the overhanging sections of balsa to create grill platforms. Each platform, or 'wing', was sturdy enough to take the weight of two big dry bags. Stowing the bulk of our gear on these wings meant we instantly doubled the room on board available for us to move around in.

Our mood was energised, back-slappingly so. I could hardly believe how quickly and painlessly the new set-up had come together. Beyond Apurimac whitewater, the world seemed a relatively easy place. Either that or the survival luck from those days had translated into good fortune of a new kind.

We only needed to paddle another kilometre downriver before the fabled stand of bamboo came into view and we could add the final crucial element to our set-up – the oars. The concept was simple enough: why not recycle two perfectly good whitewater paddles? A piece of bamboo roughly a metre-and-a-half long was to act as an extension of the paddle shaft.

Colin applied his knowledge of sailing knots to join them where they overlapped. The knots needed to be very tight because, with every stroke, the force on the paddle blade would be transferred as heavy strain on the overlap. A copious amount of duct tape ensured the join wouldn't budge. Lastly, we fashioned a couple of oar-locks by tying nylon strapping around the ends of the upper two balsa logs and making a loop about twice as big as the oar shaft's diameter.

And then we were rowing. The oarsman sat at the tip of the bow, grinning childishly at his two companions, who looked back at him with expressions of idiotic delight. The ocean was still more than 6000 kilometres away. But all of a sudden, that didn't seem very far.

The township of Surimena provided an opportunity to buy more hardware supplies. Now that we had propulsion, it was time to get comfortable. A table was next on the list of raft renovations.

Colin was keen to indulge his affinity for woodworking. 'My dream is to build a log cabin in the forest,' he had often told me. This went hand in hand with his desire to buy an old salmon fishing boat, completely refit it then spend his time sailing the fjords and islands of the Canadian west coast. To him, the world was a place with endless potential for him to realise his ideas.

Colin had dropped out of university after a year. He had planted trees for a British Columbian forestry giant and harvested forest mushrooms for Japanese restaurants to finance his sailing voyage. Although quick-witted, he preferred setting his hands rather than his brain to a task. Interacting with the physical world, merging his physical self with the elements, was his consuming passion. He always seemed to know, as a cat knows, where his body was in relation to everything else. The Amazon was there to be made the most of, and installing a picnic table in *Los Labios* was a serious and sacred event.

While he and Scott did the necessary shopping, I guarded the boat and chatted with a growing contingent of townsfolk.

'*Donde se van*?' came the query – every local arriving on the scene wanting to know where we were headed.

ABOVE: On the floor of his tiny Canmore apartment, Colin Angus toasts the long-awaited arrival of our brand-new raft, just three weeks before we flew to Peru (17 August 1999).

BELOW: Colin (left), Scott Borthwick (middle) and I stand fresh-faced and excited on the beach at La Punta, bidding farewell to the Pacific Ocean on day 1 of the journey (13 September).

ABOVE: Myself (nearest camera) and Scott on day 2, following the Camaná River deeper into the dry foothills of the Andes (14 September).

BELOW: Scott (right) crosses the fast-flowing Majes River via a rickety footbridge – day 4 (16 September).

ABOVE: The dry desert valley between Corire and a tiny oasis. Colin (right), Scott (middle) and I pose for photographic posterity in case our short supply of water should prove a fatal error (21 September).

BELOW: A Quechua woman and boy lead donkeys laden with our backpacks along a trail zigzagging its way down into the Colca Canyon (24 September).

ABOVE: Five thousand metres above sea level, at the Continental Divide, Willy (left) re-balances each donkey's load while I brace myself against an icy wind (26 September).

BELOW: Mount Mismi – the ultimate source of the Amazon.

ABOVE: At the summit of Mount Mismi I celebrate reaching the end of the first leg of a long journey. It is 27 September 1999, two weeks after we left the Pacific coast.

BELOW: On the banks of the Apurimac River in Pilpinto, moments before Colin (left), Scott (right) and I launched the raft and pitted ourselves against the Amazon's deadly whitewater (6 October).

ABOVE: Temporarily snagged on a submerged rock in the middle of a class 4 rapid, Colin (right) and I are able to briefly tear our gaze away from the wild river ahead and pose for a photo (8 October).

BELOW: Scott (guiding at the stern) and I charge down a small chute after having steered *Los Labios* through another boulder garden (9 October).

ABOVE: After a nerve-shattering day of rafting rapids, we set up camp on another pristine sandy beach in the Apurimac canyon. Scott (left), Colin (middle) and me (10 October).

BELOW: Lining the raft down a rapid on the middle Apurimac. Colin (right) releases rope steadily, gently easing *Los Labios* downriver while I paddle to manoeuvre her into an eddy by the shore (11 October).

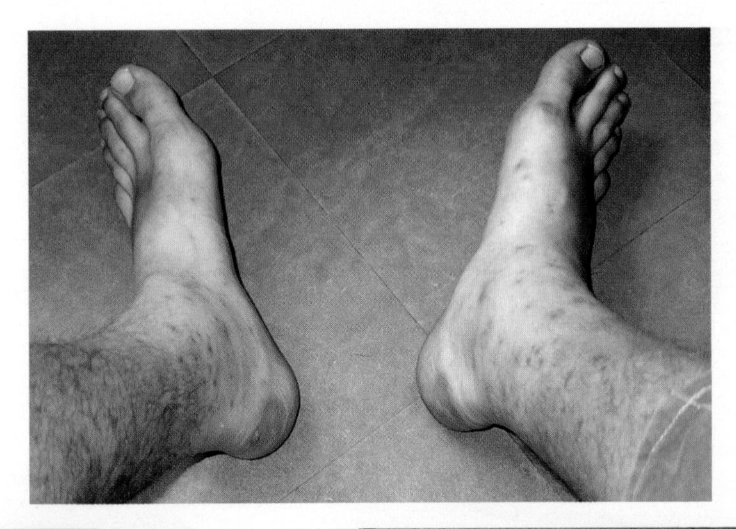

ABOVE: A particularly bad onslaught of the blood-sucking 'moskies' at the Cunyac Bridge caused my legs and feet to swell up by the time we reached Abancay (15 October).

BELOW: Besieged by an army of wedding guests on the outskirts of Cachora, I am lavished with copious amounts of chicha – the home-brewed alcoholic drink made from corn (21 October).

LEFT: The motley collection of implements we substituted for the utensils which sank to the bottom of the Apurimac near Cachora Bridge. From bottom: rusty shovel blade frying pan, glass jar coffee cup, stick spoons and pilchard can saucepan (26 October).

BELOW: Near the Triunfo cable crossing and the boat is pointing back upriver. Colin (left) and Scott are still in awe of the brute power of the now-distant rapid at the base of those sheer canyon walls and bemused by the fact that we somehow managed to keep the boat upright coming through it (27 October).

ABOVE: Near the Pachachaka River confluence. I get to bathe in a crystal clear pool that is fed by one of the many tributaries spilling down the steep sides of the Apurimac canyon (28 October).

BELOW: *Los Labios* after her transformation into a rowboat on the lower Apurimac. The 'wings' carried the bulk of our gear, creating more living space for the three-and-a-half month journey ahead (3 November).

ABOVE: Colin (far right) and I (second from left) pose with members of a military patrol on the Ene River, a day after our brush with communist guerrillas. These men sent us on our way with Colombian army rations (7 November).

BELOW: Before the erection of a bimini, we got baked by the tropical sun on the upper Ucayali River. Here, Colin rows past some of the last vestiges of the Andes (13 November).

ABOVE: An officer from Peru's *Policia Narcotica* (left) is assisted by Colin during a mid-river inspection of the raft near the town of Contamana (22 November).

BELOW: While it is Colin's turn to keep rowing along the flat expanse of the Amazon, Scott (left) and I have locked horns in another bout of chess (26 November).

ABOVE: Many houses in the Iquitos market district of Belen are built on high stilts as protection against the Amazon's yearly cycle of flooding. This laneway would be completely submerged in a few months (4 December).

BELOW: Scott takes a 'used' dugout canoe for a test drive on the river halfway between Iquitos and the Peru–Brazil border. We bought the dugout for $10 (10 December).

ABOVE: I am rowing up one of the thousands of small tributaries that feed into the wide Amazon, while Scott is soaking up the rainforest's beauty. When the channel became too narrow for the raft, we continued exploring in the dugout canoe (24 December).

BELOW: A sodden rat is being eaten alive by hundreds of vicious ants. Moments earlier, a massive section of the riverbank had toppled, throwing all sorts of plant and animal life into the murky brown river. It was a few days after Christmas and we were near the geographic heart of the South American continent (28 December).

ABOVE: Looking like a salty sea dog, Scott rows us into a fast-approaching squall during our race to reach the Brazilian city of Manaus by New Year's Eve (28 December).

BELOW: Near the start of the Amazon delta, Colin runs around on the largest floating island we saw (15 January 2000).

ABOVE: The Pará River was so immense, the far shore lay over the horizon. Here, I battle sea-like conditions as we try to cover the final 20 kilometres of our journey before the weather turns nasty (7 February).

BELOW: We celebrate our arrival at the Atlantic Ocean on 8 February 2000 with $2 bottles of champagne. From left: Colin, Scott and me.

'*Vamos Atlantico*,' I said, delighting in the cynical smirks and disbelieving pouts.

Our handiwork with the balsa and cane triggered a number of questions. When I demonstrated the oars, several heads nodded in approval, as though the use of natural materials suddenly lent a certain validity to my claims.

'You are not worried about the *Sendero Luminoso*?' asked one man.

'No, we heard there were no more problems now.'

Another man threw back his head and laughed. 'No, no, señor. The Senderistas are still here.'

'They are on the river below the Rio Mantaro,' somebody else said.

'On the Ene?'

'Si, amigo. Be careful there.'

As we rowed away from Surimena, I shared the warnings with my two companions. The locals back at the town were the first people who'd suggested that anything more than a few terrorist stragglers occupied the region ahead.

The morning before, as we had prepared to leave San Francisco, a curious youth had said that the *Sendero Luminoso* lived in town. I had assumed he referred to now-retired members of the movement who were trying to avoid recognition and punishment for their past actions. Prior to that, Cuzco had been the last place where the name of the organisation was mentioned in conversation between us and Peruvians. The warnings from the folk of Surimena seemed to fly in the face of a general silence on the issue. The *Sendero Luminoso* were done, the country had moved on.

'Stories from the past,' Colin said dismissively. 'Someone probably got killed around here a few years ago.'

Scott agreed. 'Remember all that talk of *banditos* back on the hike? It was just talk.'

That's the way I felt about it too, thinking the beliefs must have been a legacy kept alive by residual guerrilla elements that perpetrated the occasional incident. Violence and bloodshed can remain in a community's psyche for many years.

Nevertheless, it was food for thought. I believed I would feel at ease when we reached Atalaya. There, we knew the riffles came to an absolute end and the cloud forest made way for the jungle. I didn't want us to be victims of an 'occasional incident'.

That evening, Colin made the table, Scott made adjustments to the rowing frame, and I cooked up a big pot of my specialty – chilli con carne. As we ate, we listened to the BBC World Service. Of particular interest to me was a discussion about the upcoming referendum on whether Australia should become a republic.

The announcer's voice was abruptly drowned out by the clatter of an approaching helicopter. Obviously spying our red raft, the pilot adjusted his course to pass low over our campsite. I'd seen enough *Rambo* movies to recognise a gunship, and I didn't have to know much about missiles to know this one was armed to the hilt.

'Must be on a routine peacekeeping patrol,' Scott deduced.

It was the logical conclusion, but the cold-steel proof that this region was no stranger to conflict brought little peace to any of us.

Dusk bled to night, but on a hillside several kilometres to the west, the front of a raging forest fire cast the low clouds in a red copper glow.

Rowing was something I'd not done for almost a decade. In my first year at university, the rowing club had lured me to its ranks with claims that my height, muscle–fat ratio and greenness made me ideal for moulding into a champion. I endured three weeks of 5.30 a.m. starts. I finally realised it wasn't for me when, at the end of a chilly winter morning session, I got out of my boat and couldn't stand up because both legs were completely numb.

Now I tried to dredge up what had been instilled in me during those few weeks. I don't know why I bothered. About the only thing our lumbering craft shared in common with a narrow, sleek scull was that both floated. Instead of an ergonomically moulded seat, moving on rails, my backside slid around on the shiny hypalon. Instead of perfectly balanced oars, pivoting at the end of rigid mounts, we had crooked bamboo hybrids that slowly wore through the nylon loops and chewed the balsa. Both twisted in the hand with each draw. Each blade was predisposed to enter the water at any angle except for the one that would give power.

Every stroke required teeth-clenching concentration so that equal amounts of power came from the left and right, and the boat travelled in something close to a straight line. Muscles that had not moved throughout weeks of paddling were called into action. At the end of an hour-long shift, forearms burnt and fingers had set into a leper's claw.

We worked out quickly that the alignment of the two non-rowers made all the difference in terms of maintaining a crucial symmetry with the oar pivot points. In other words, whenever the other blokes moved around too much, rowing became bloody difficult.

The emerald waters of the Mantaro River flowed in from the west. At the junction, we bid farewell to the Apurimac and greeted the Ene. We entered a region known as the Gran Pajonal. The forest looked less penetrable. The river's width increased only marginally, but its colour changed and it moved faster. A few kilometres past the confluence, two men appeared on the bank. They wore the camouflage uniforms of soldiers.

To be honest, the army made us more nervous than the prospect of a few leftover terrorists. We were conscious of the bad press surrounding the Peruvian military. South America in general has never been short of juntas and military regimes prepared to throw their weight around. The number of 'disappearances' under the Pinochet regime in Chile was appalling. Argentina had known a similar scale of brutality during the late '70s and early '80s.

Democratic government had returned to Peru in 1980, but reports of corruption and abuse of authority by the military continued. An incident five years earlier made us particularly wary. It involved the slaying of two Japanese travellers by a pair of soldiers on the Amazon, near Iquitos. The subsequent investigation revealed that the soldiers' commanding officer had ordered the shooting, then divided up a bounty of money and electronic equipment three ways.

I recalled the advice that one of the Surimena men had given to me: 'Don't stop for anyone. Uniform or no uniform. Do not stop.' The soldiers we were now seeing seemed more dumbstruck than anything else. They returned our waves, spoke among themselves, but said nothing to us. So far, so good.

We saw no one else until the evening, when a fisherman in his dugout canoe arrived at the beach we had selected to camp at. Since Lechemayo, we'd seen quite a few people in canoes, often catching fish with handthrown nets. What set this fisherman apart was the shotgun slung over his shoulder.

He stayed long enough to ask where we were from and where we were going, then paddled away.

An hour later, he returned from somewhere overland with three others. The newcomers all had shotguns too. This time the guns weren't slung over their shoulders, but carried in both hands, at the ready. Battle helicopters and armed fishermen. Something was definitely amiss in these parts.

One of the newcomers, a middle-aged man with a sour face, interrogated us. He wanted to know everything. The fisherman and two adolescents looked on, lobbing in the occasional question. The inquisition lasted an hour. Eventually, the sour-faced man left with the fisherman, but the two adolescents put their guns down and made themselves comfortable.

Colin made soup. Even before we could make a grudging offer, one of the upstart Peruvians gestured that we should serve them a bowl each too. They stayed until it got completely dark. I suspected they had been stationed there to watch us. Every question we asked yielded shrugs or one-word answers. They spoke only to ask if they could look at something. Their lack of interest in making conversation created an awkward atmosphere. When our camp chores were done, we faked yawns and excused ourselves.

One of the duo pointed at my head-torch.

'Can we borrow that to get back to our village?'

'I'm sorry, no. I need it.'

'Amigo, we will bring it back tomorrow.'

The gall of these men. They had come waving guns under our noses, invited themselves to dinner and shown no inclination to do anything except study our every movement. Now they expected a *favour*. I figured the chances of me seeing either man again were slim and I was very fond of that torch. I'd often wondered why I'd only ever bought hand-held torches in the past.

'No.'

One of the men raised his voice. 'It is dark, amigo! We cannot see.'

I lost my temper. 'Look! You want to sit and stare at us all evening. It's not *my* problem how you get back. *Adios!*'

And with that I crawled inside my tent and zipped it closed behind me. Seconds later, the heavens opened. 'Cop that, *amigos*,' I smiled to myself.

A kilometre downstream, we passed an army base. On the riverbank, a group of four soldiers were washing their faces and brushing their teeth. A couple of them made half-hearted attempts to call us in. Our agreed response to anyone beckoning to us from shore was to smile, wave and pretend not to understand. Their bemusement was plain to see.

A short time later, more soldiers appeared on a spit where a small tributary came in. Set back ten metres or so from the river edge, in the scrub, was a makeshift shelter. These men whistled and made animated motions for us to go to shore. Two of the soldiers held their weapons in both hands, pointed at the sky. Our refusal to obey made them agitated. Ignoring the shouts of armed men is easier said than done. We reviewed the prudence of our strategy. What if the instructions given to these men were to shoot anyone who failed to comply with their demands to stop?

The soldiers did not become any more insistent. During those moments of indecision, the current had swept us into a position from which we could no longer get to shore. The decision seemed to have been made for us. Shouts followed, but the guns remained pointing up.

'What sort of guns are those?' I asked.

'Probably rifles,' Scott said. He had noticed that soldiers in the cities carried rifles.

The South African was no stranger to guns. As a teenager, he had spent part of the school holidays at a friend's property helping with the antelope harvest. Guns are a fact of life in the savannah. If you go bushwalking, it is crazy not to arm yourself against the threat of animal attack.

'Could they hit us from here?' asked Colin.

'How far away are we now?'

'About 300 metres.'

'Yep, they could hit us for sure,' nodded Scott.

He explained that shotguns were accurate only over a few dozen metres, at best. A rifle bullet, on the other hand, could hit you between the eyes from a much greater distance.

Around midday, we approached a clearing on the left bank. In the centre of the clearing stood a rundown hut. It had a pronounced tilt, and half the thatch was missing from the roof. It looked abandoned, until four men filed out of a doorless entrance. They lined up in a row between the hut and the carved riverbank edge. All wore plain clothes. The man on each end held a gun. The tallest of the four, a wide man with a potbelly, waved us in.

'*Hola*,' we called out, returning the wave.

'Beautiful day, isn't it?' cried Scott.

At the oars, I tried to discreetly quicken my strokes.

Our response initiated a frenzy of shouting. Even from the middle of the river, the potbellied man looked as though he would explode from rage. We held course.

'*Desculpe. No entiende!*' I yelled. I couldn't understand their jabbering, although the demands were clear enough anyway.

We drew level with the hut and were kept moving swiftly downstream by the strong current, as had been the case earlier with the soldiers on the spit. About 50 metres separated us from the hut now. The potbellied individual barked a command to the armed man next to him. The gunman scurried down to the water's edge and levelled his weapon. *Crack.*

In that instant, and only for an instant, something hot and bitter rose from my gut to singe the back of my throat. The sensation was completely new to me. Not surprising, I suppose, considering that I had never been shot at before. I figured this must be the 'bile' that writers talk about when describing victims of sudden, intense shocks.

Crack. A second gunshot rang out, the noise a cross between the lashing of a whip and a Chinese firework. More bile, but this bullet also had missed. At least, I couldn't hear the hissing of a ruptured pontoon or feel warm blood trickling over my skin. Scott and Colin had dropped to the floor of the boat, not because they were hit, but to hide.

I was torn between joining them, leaping overboard, surrendering and rowing like mad to get out of range.

Option one was out. Both my colleagues were in the front of the raft with me, having squeezed themselves under the balsa log and wriggled forward – there was no room for me to duck out of view. Jumping overboard could well allow the gunman a better opportunity to pick me off – not a good idea. And if our attackers were Senderistas, then surrender would probably mean a bullet in the head from close range. The rowing option would be difficult now since the shifting of body weight in the raft had caused the oar-locks to dip lower so that the oar shafts were hindered by the pontoon.

My deliberation probably lasted just a matter of seconds, and the last option seemed the pick of a bad bunch. It left me a sitting duck, a fact I was sickeningly aware of.

I knew that even now, the gunman might be taking careful aim, about to blow my head off. The distance to the hut was 70 metres. I bit my lip and squinted, willing the next bullet to bend around me.

Every oar stroke was a tussle. After only two days at it, rowing was still far from being a natural movement. The delicate weight balance needed for my novice technique to have any impact was in tatters.

Colin's eyes were like a rabbit's.

'Ben, get us out of here,' he stammered.

'You're in the fucking way,' I grunted. 'Both of you. Move!'

Scott shook his head. 'I'm not sticking my head up there.'

'Faster, mate!' croaked Colin, his body frozen.

My mind was screaming. The frustration would kill me before anything else did.

'For Christ's sake, give me some room,' I pleaded.

They slid back. It made all the difference.

A hundred metres from the hut, and no more shots fired. The other armed guerrilla ran along the bank. We passed the border between forest and clearing. Dense foliage prevented the gunman from going any further. I watched him raise the butt to his shoulder. He took aim. Then the barrel dropped, as he realised the current had pulled us beyond the range of his shotgun. Moments later, we'd rounded enough of a bend to lose sight of the men altogether.

For some time afterwards, our pulses and minds raced. Did they have a boat? Did they have comrades waiting to intercept us downriver? In the space of a minute, our world had fallen apart. The realisation hit: we were in big trouble. We had stumbled into a war zone.

The warning signs had been there yet we had kept daring to write off the *Sendero Luminoso* as a modest threat. I don't think we really believed the worst could happen, especially after we had been through so much hardship in the whitewater.

A new perspective was fast taking root. The Ene was the *new* Red Zone. The leadership was in jail, defections were common, but that didn't mean everyone had laid down quietly. The rugged cloud forest of the Gran Pajonal allowed a residual element of terrorists to elude capture and to launch modest strikes. Those remaining were fugitives, desperate and dangerous whether or not they were still loyal to the organisation's ideals. Some would know little else but a culture of violence.

Effectively, the rebels here were under seige. There might be villages sympathetic to their fight, but no doubt the military cut supply routes wherever possible. We had money. We had equipment. We had food. And we were foreigners. The only thing that might persuade them to leave us alone was the colour of our boat – communist red.

And once they had taken everything, what then? If they lived by the Shining Path ideals, killing us satisfied two of these: the removal of foreign influence in Peru, and striking a blow to the government through attacking the institution of tourism. I also considered what they would do with us from a practical perspective. By choosing to let us go, rebels risked authorities being provided with information on their whereabouts. The *Sendero Luminoso* had always been a notoriously secretive group.

By mid-afternoon, we were still in deep discussion, speculating on what we had got ourselves into. We rowed through a largish settlement occupying both sides of the river. The Peruvian flag flew. Several people on the near bank watched us quietly.

But just when it looked like this village was safe territory, a gunshot echoed. It had been fired from some distance away. Like a starter's gun on an Olympic rowing lake, it was our cue to start moving. Colin was in the hot seat this time.

We reached the edge of town, hearts thumping, but no sign of pursuit.

'No one coming?' puffed Colin hopefully.

'Sorry, mate, I think the SWAT team is on their way.'

Two hundred metres behind us, six figures ran to the riverside, jumped into a motorboat and began speeding in our direction. I turned to Colin. 'Stop rowing. We won't get away from them.'

'I think it's the army,' said Scott.

Colin shipped the oars. His brow was deeply furrowed. 'I goddamn hope so!'

As he finished speaking, there came a clap like thunder. The shell fizzed the air above our heads, then clattered through the forest.

'That came from a rifle,' Scott remarked.

Another shot – more fizzing. And again. And again. It was obvious that this shooting was deliberately directed over our heads. Oddly, a feeling of relative comfort came with this knowledge. But how many warning shots did we need?

'Fucking hell!' yelped Colin. 'Can't they see we've stopped rowing?'

'Maybe they can't.'

'Maybe they think we're Senderistas.'

Still the gunfire continued. Were the people chasing us indeed soldiers? Every few seconds there was another shot. The burning bitterness in my throat came back with each bullet, as though it was some kind of programmed reflex.

At a range of just 50 metres, the bullets still flew. Why? Now it must be plain to see that we were only drifting. Any short-lived feelings of comfort had degenerated into plain fear, and were fast approaching pure terror. We had nowhere to hide. The only thing we could do was jump overboard and stall the inevitable. Perhaps going overboard was the act of submission they wanted to see.

We slipped into the Ene and hung on to the perimeter rope. Ten or so metres from us, the boat's engine cut. Predictably, a couple of its occupants were shouting at us. I hardly dared to look up at them – as with a vicious dog, this might be considered a threat. The fellow doing all the shooting had a high-cut black boot planted on the gunnel. He was leaning forward, his rifle aimed squarely at my forehead. 'MILITARIA PERUANO' was emblazoned across his T-shirt. That it said this, and not 'SENDERO LUMINOSO', might have eased my mind, but for the menacing stance of the wearer.

'Swim to the shore!' he bellowed.

We swam to the shore and we crawled onto land. There we stood, dripping, pathetic. As I put my hands in the air, I noticed the faces of several of the soldiers. So young. Apart from the leader and two others, the rest were no older than sixteen. I shuddered. Good guys or not, it was a disturbingly feasible scenario that a fifteen-year-old soldier, ignorant of the world outside this troubled region, could panic in the heat of the moment and put a bullet through one of us.

The SWAT team leader, a big-nosed, barrel-chested man in his mid-twenties, picked us for the harmless gringos that we were.

'*Turistas?*'

'Yes.'

He nodded at *Los Labios*. 'No motor?'

'No.' I squeezed one of my biceps. 'Here is the motor.'

The SWAT leader shook his head but his smile was one

of genuine friendliness. 'When you did not stop, we thought you were drug smugglers,' he said apologetically.

The initial gunshot had been fired from the hill as a warning for us to stop for inspection. Our response of rowing faster had been interpreted as guilty men making a break for it. *Thank God for outboard motors, or we might have got away*, I thought sarcastically.

'There is a major Control base here. Everyone must stop.'

We boarded the army boat for the ride back to Control headquarters. *Los Labios* was towed. The SWAT leader did a good job of putting our thumping hearts at ease. He was from Arequipa, Peru's second-largest city, and oozed a worldliness that we had rarely come across during the past two months.

We explained our failure to stop by describing what had happened a few hours before. The SWAT leader's eyes flickered.

'What did these men look like?' he asked.

We described them as best as our terrifying memories would allow.

'You say one of them was a little fat?' he queried.

'Yes.'

'This one was also the tallest?'

'Yes.'

The SWAT leader turned to his deputy for a brief discussion. They nodded.

'I think we know these men. Bad men.'

The Control base occupied the highest point for many kilometres, with superb views of the river and surrounding terrain. A stockade surrounded it. Circling this was a ditch, or dry moat. The SWAT leader led us across a gangway spanning the ditch and into a structure that looked like a rotunda. A bench ran around the inside edge. A dome made from dead palm leaves kept the sun off. Here we were to wait for an audience with the base commander.

First to greet us was the second-in-command, one Officer Remondo. He was tall and thin, about 30 years old, with an aristocratic face that suggested an elite education and civilised upbringing. He had the look of a man who wondered how he'd managed to find himself where he was.

As with the other higher-ranking soldiers, Remondo was relaxed and listened with great interest to our story.

'Do you want a drink?' he asked. We nodded, and off he went.

While he was gone, I looked out from the rotunda into the compound where five young recruits milled, smoking cigarettes, waiting for a Senderista attack, watching us. When I caught their gaze, eyes were quickly averted and they casually moved to a new vantage point.

Remondo returned with three glasses of cordial.

'The commander is busy but will meet you soon. I must warn that he is not happy you are here.' He explained that it was wrong to have believed the *Sendero Luminoso* were no longer a threat. Although the situation became relatively quiet after the 1993 capture of Reynoso, strikes had continued under the leadership of Oscar Ramirez Durand (aka Comrade Feliciano). In recent times, there had been a sharp increase in Senderista activity.

Four weeks earlier, for instance, in the nearby town of Satipo, nine soldiers had been ambushed and slaughtered. Since then, skirmishes between the terrorists and military had become an almost daily occurrence. But despite President Fujimori's government sending 3000 more troops to the region, a month of all-out assault on rebel positions had failed to capture one Senderista fighter.

I felt ashamed of our ignorance, and sickened that

through this ignorance, we had exchanged one deadly situation for another. Except now it was worse. In the whitewater, I had at least felt like I had some say in my fate (despite the Apurimac's frequent reminders that it was master). When conscious beings are against you, it doesn't matter how much you grit your teeth or how hard you concentrate – time-outs don't exist. People are much harder to predict. They are active, not passive, aggressors. And we were sitting ducks. To continue was not courage, but a death wish.

The base commander's face was as hard as stone. Understandably, he had a lot on his mind, and the last thing he wanted was the scrutiny created by the deaths of three foolish westerners.

'The men you saw upstream are men we are looking for,' he said.

'*Sendero Luminoso*?'

He nodded. 'You were very lucky to get past them.'

I already knew the answer but I asked anyway: 'Is it better downstream from here?'

Every soldier in the rotunda shook their head and said, 'No.'

It was true. We were in the middle of a war zone.

'I cannot guarantee your safety from here,' the commander stated. To ram home the message that the terrorists meant business in these parts, he ran his forefinger across his throat.

All thought of continuing our journey melted away with the motion of that finger.

'Can you fly us out?'

He shook his head.

'Ask him if they can give us an escort to Atalaya,' said Scott, referring to the town some 160 kilometres distant that marks the end of the rapids.

I asked. No go, either. They had only two boats and both were needed for patrols. The commander's expression showed scant regret as he explained that resources were already less than minimal. His hands were tied.

'You may stay here tonight,' he offered, pointing to a small parade ground where we could pitch our tents. 'Tomorrow I will radio the next Control base to let them know you are coming.'

We all knew that it was a token gesture. If the next base didn't hear from us, it meant we were probably dead. Senderista rebels were not noted for taking prisoners.

The parade ground was hard-packed dirt into which we couldn't even push a tent peg. We left the tent freestanding and weighted it down with other gear. The commander didn't want us wandering around outside of that part of the compound so there wasn't much to do except wait for nightfall and ponder what fate lay beyond the relative safety of this military post.

No fire meant no way of cooking but none of us felt hungry anyway. After dark, Officer Remondo stopped by with some fried fish and a jug of grape juice. The last meal of the condemned, I thought to myself.

Exhaustion overcame worry. My last conscious thoughts were severely lacking in optimism. Given the recent attack and the warnings from hardened soldiers, I resigned myself to a 50–50 chance of making it through the next day alive.

ELEVEN
THE MILITIAS

7 November 1999 (day 56):
up sh*t creek

We left before dawn. The darkness hid us at first. Then, as daylight kicked in, a low-hanging mist became our ally. We hoped to cover as much distance as possible in the hours when human activity was generally at its least. The only sounds were the oar blades shattering the river's surface of glass.

It was Sunday. I tried lifting the sombre mood that hung over us: 'Maybe the rebels have been out all night getting pissed and will have rotten hangovers.'

Colin shot me down. 'Or maybe Saturday night is gun-polishing night.'

'If they're religious, Sunday might be the day of rest, and no killing,' Scott suggested.

'Communism *is* their religion,' I said. 'Yell out "We love Mao" and they might let us go.'

Nothing could soothe our nerves like peace and quiet. Four gunshot-free hours of forest slid by. The tension was just beginning to ebb when soldiers emerged from the wall of green and beckoned us over to a muddy beach. They were camped nearby as part of a routine patrol. Unlike with the last lot of troops, this time there were smiles all round, even from the commanding officer. We posed for photographs and were sent on our way with two packets of Colombian-made army rations.

The Ene was funnelled through a gorge. Sheer walls of rock rose out of the canopy, reminiscent of the escarpment country of Kakadu National Park in northern Australia. Because of conflict and ruggedness, there are large tracts of pristine cloud forest in this region of Peru. I was hard-pressed to appreciate the beauty. All I could think was, 'What else is in there?' The occasional riverside dwelling got our pulses up. As we passed, none of us even dared whisper, and a supreme effort was put into dipping the oar blades as quietly as possible.

We reached the next Control base by early afternoon. It occupied a similar position to the last, on a hilltop overlooking a village. To avoid any misunderstandings this time around, we landed on the upstream boundary of the village.

For its size, there were few people around. The first man we met was tiny and smiling. He wore only a pair of shorts and had a streak of ochre running diagonally across each cheek. If the red face paint didn't give it away that he was indigenous, the bow and arrow he carried left us in no doubt.

Scott was mesmerised by the bow. He had already confirmed his interest in firearms over the previous two days. On a few occasions, he'd asked to look at the guns carried by those who'd questioned or detained us. Each time, Colin and I had felt uncomfortable because, firstly, it flew in the face of how much we despised those weapons, and secondly, most of the gun owners regarded his requests with suspicion. Not surprisingly, no one had been willing to indulge the South African.

As he asked if he could take a look at the little Indian's bow, Scott reached out a hand to touch it. The Indian's smile vanished and he sprang back. As he did so, he drew the arrow and aimed it at us for several seconds while babbling angrily in his native tongue. Then he let out a strange laugh and ran off.

'Jesus, Scott!'

'Sorry, lads. Can't help myself sometimes.'

'Yeah, well, try to help it,' Colin fumed. 'These guys think you're trying to grab their weapon and shoot them.'

The riddle of the missing villagers was answered by the base commander himself. We bumped into him before even getting halfway to the base. He and several officers were on their way to watch the weekly football game between the Asháninka Indian and Army teams. Commander Rodriguez invited us to sit with him.

It was in stark contrast to the recent craziness we'd witnessed. Unlike his counterpart upriver, Rodriguez knew how to smile. He was very laidback and spoke candidly about the impact of this base on the original Asháninka settlement. When the army first set up shop here, the village had had very little contact with people of European descent. Resentment and animosity were rampant on both sides. Rodriquez seemed to understand the importance of maintaining respect for Asháninka traditions and belief. The Asháninka had a long history of aversion to assimilation. They had been one of the few tribes with the foresight to slaughter every Christian missionary who came to their region. The commander was no missionary. He saw reconciliation as an important means of countering the problem of terrorist rebels. There was a long way to go, but the football pitch had already become the ultimate level playing field.

We returned to the raft and got underway again. Nothing on board looked out of place, but Colin sensed something was amiss. He was right. The video camera had been stolen. It had been inside a case within a small dry bag, which in turn was inside a large dry bag. Obviously hoping we wouldn't notice until we were much further downriver, the thief had taken the time to close and replace each bag. A knife was also gone.

We knew the prospect of ever seeing the camera again was virtually nil. Still, Colin and I wandered the village in the hope of catching the culprit admiring his prize. The Asháninka were standoffish. Some threw us mocking looks, as if to say 'We know what you're trying to find but forget it.' The rest wore unreadable masks that made me feel I had absolutely nothing in common with these people.

We hiked up to the army base. In the meeting rotunda, Rodriguez listened sympathetically. He felt responsible. Before the football match, a soldier had been posted to guard our boat. 'We will try to get your camera back,' he promised.

The first thing Rodriguez did was summon the inept guard and yell at him. Then he assembled a search party. The squad of eight descended into the village. From the rotunda, we watched them move from hut to hut, making inquiries. The commander was confident, but I didn't fancy our chances. The camera could be anywhere, and after the cool treatment we'd received, I doubted a bunch of soldiers could extract willing cooperation from the villagers. Why would the thief come forward and risk being punished?

We chatted with a few of Rodriguez's officers. One was a self-declared tennis fanatic who relished the chance to talk with an Australian.

'Wally Masur and John Fitzgerald, they are very good. Also Paul McNamee.'

These were all players from the 1980s, and even back then had been relatively obscure names on the international scene. I quoted some more recent names: 'What do you think of Pat Rafter and Mark Philippoussis?'

Both men were in the world's top-ten ranked players but he had heard of neither. Rafter had won the US Open only a few months earlier.

Half an hour later, the search party returned, and with them, our first reason to smile in days – they had the video camera! By some miracle, they had stumbled across it in a patch of long grass on the edge of the village. I was left to wonder yet again whether the river gods were pulling all the strings, toying with our emotions.

Commander Rodriguez had claimed that the Perené River marked the boundary of the current Red Zone. This river joined with the Ene to create the Tambo.

Several kilometres before the Perené confluence, the forest peeled back to make way for a lush grassland. An aggregation of simple wood shacks denoted the village of Puerto Prado. I wondered if the clear felling was meant to deny the Senderistas their element of surprise. The vertical bands of the Peruvian flag – two red, one white – fluttered on a rise behind the settlement.

A whistle drew our attention to the shore. There a man stood, shotgun over shoulder, gesturing downstream towards an eddy where several Johnsons were moored. Another three armed men waited beside the boats, one beckoning with his hand. There was no angry shouting or flourishing of weapons. That in itself made us wary.

They were Asháninka men, not military personnel. Unlike the traditionally dressed and face-painted residents of the last Asháninka village, these men wore T-shirts and trousers. They could speak Spanish and had seen blond-haired people on television. The leader, despite his less than formal attire, dealt with us in a purposeful, comfortingly officious manner. He checked passports, asked about guns and drugs, then had one of his men make a brief inspection of our big dry bags. He even found cause to laugh when we explained our reasons for being on the Ene.

It seemed clear what was happening. The Peruvian Army had created militias in each village below the new Red Zone. Rather than deploy its own men and resources to police this region, it armed an indigenous population keen to make sure the trouble upriver stayed out of their back yard.

The Perené met the Ene at right angles. Given the similarities in both size and speed, there was plenty of justification for warnings of whirlpool activity – where the waters collided was *chaos.* Whirlpools drifted like submerged tornadoes, appearing and disappearing without warning. Twice *Los Labios* was sucked down to the point of having water flood in over the pontoon.

Conversely, enormous boils pushed us upwards. Equally impossible to predict, they erupted with a fearful snarl as though heralding the arrival of a monster from the depths.

The Tambo, as the river now became known, was noted for its cliff slams. At a few tight chicanes, the fastest part of the current got funnelled into a wave train that proceeded to smash head-on into a vertical rock face. The unwary could find themselves pummelled against such a wall. Our balsa and cane extensions certainly would not cope with a solid hit. And being flipped right over was a real possibility as well.

The next people we saw were two men in a dugout

canoe. They waved. It was unmistakably a wave of welcome. They were the first people we'd seen without scowls for quite a while. Emboldened, we rowed to where they drifted in a slow part of the current. As we came alongside, one of the men reached down. Instead of a shotgun, he lifted up a fish.

Another man appeared on the shore, yelling something I could not understand. The men in the dugout turned to listen. Abruptly the smiles disappeared, replaced by expressions of military purpose. One fisherman grabbed hold of our perimeter line. His colleague pointed at shore, jabbering away in an Indian dialect. Then he picked up a wooden paddle and began the task of towing us to shore. I groaned. Everyone was in on this militia thing.

We were fed up with being stopped. Men with guns could demand our cooperation and get it. But going through the rigmarole of another passport check for a few unarmed vigilante fishermen was ridiculous. In the space of four days, I'd had my passport examined more times than during an entire year of backpacking around Europe.

'We've been cleared already,' I growled in Spanish.

I rowed downstream, dragging their dugout, the power of two oars no match for a single paddle. The man holding the rope tightened his grip. Both started shouting and continued to point to the riverbank. Colin tried prising the man's fingers off the rope. 'Fucking let go,' he said through clenched teeth.

A group had gathered onshore. All were yelling. Cleverly, the fishermen moved their dugout to obstruct my right oar. There was more chattering and more pointing at the bank. Finally, their stubbornness won out and we relented.

At the bank, we thrust our passports at several members of the group, impatient to be on our way as soon as possible. Each man looked, but without interest. Clearly their role was as watchdogs and detainers only. These men either had no authority or lacked the literacy skills to clear us. They looked around as though waiting for a spokesman to arrive. The shore was a muddy strip at the base of a high bank. I saw no sign of a settlement, yet more and more men came trotting onto the scene from each direction. Most carried either a shotgun or a bow. All were shabbily dressed. The two fishermen kept hold of the perimeter rope to ensure we didn't make a break for it.

Eventually, a spokesman did arrive to hear our story and examine our passports. He was stern-faced and incredulous: 'Where are your "Certificates of Authorisation"?'

'Our *what*?'

'To travel here, you must have permission from the government in Lima.'

It was the first we'd heard of it. The certificates had probably been in use during a time when the *Sendero Luminoso* was holding the entire nation to ransom. We explained that none of the army bases and Control checkpoints upriver had asked for such a document. That did not matter. He would not let us pass without the 'required permission'. He shoved our passports into his pocket.

The militia leader pointed upstream, saying we must go back to the last military base and get written permission there.

'It's impossible. We have no motor.'

For the first time, his brusque attitude faltered. He hesitated, unsure what to do with us. For our part, we lounged in the raft and twiddled our thumbs, highlighting the fact that a stalemate had been reached.

The standoff continued for an hour. Finally, the leader backed down. He gave back our passports, reprimanded us again for not having the certificate and said we could go. As we were about to push off, he asked whether we could donate some money so that his men might buy more guns.

We travelled unmolested for another half-hour while a blanket of thick, dark clouds amassed overhead. We spied a hamlet in the distance and routinely hugged the opposite side of the river. Men waved their arms, demanding us to stop. We pretended not to notice.

A dugout canoe launched and gave chase. I doubled the speed of my strokes. Although the canoe sliced through the water, I had the mechanical advantage of oars. I thought if I could maintain my break on them, surely they would give up the pursuit and go home.

The sky broke. For the first time since our arrival in South America, we were caught in the rain. More specifically, it was a tropical downpour. The river surface fizzed. Colin and Scott took cover beneath the large sheet of plastic that was yet to be attached to the bimini frame.

In a deluge, even the most ruthless city parking inspector is unlikely to give you a ticket. The militia men of the Gran Pajonal weren't so easily put off, patrolling the Tambo with tenacity. The occupants of this dugout proved as stubborn as the last.

I maintained the gap, but was so intent on staying ahead I didn't see another two canoes arrive to intercept us.

'Halt, amigo.'

And, like squad cars, they escorted *Los Labios* to the nearest bank.

Our interceptors had come from a different village to that of the initial pursuers. It was agreed that I would take all our passports and accompany them to meet with their militia commander. They marched me inland several hundred metres to the banks of a small river. There, a long, sleek and very shallow dugout waited to ferry us to the other bank. I knelt in the front, fearful that the slightest movement would tip it over. All the while, the rain came down hard.

The opposite bank was a wall of red clay into which had been carved a crude set of steps. At the top of the staircase, the village of Nerana did a good job of blending into the forest. Every hut was on stilts and roofed with a matting of palm leaves. The only things connecting it to the modern world were T-shirt logos, a basketball hoop and a laminated desk underneath the militia chief's hut. Even the guns looked like they could have dated back to Spanish conquest.

As though he dealt with my sort every day, the village chief shook my hand, took the passports and asked me to wait while he wrote down the necessary details in a ledger. This relaxed approach was not shared by one of the armed men nearby. He was middle-aged with skinny legs, a fat belly and a major chip on his shoulder. His expression showed an unsettling mix of fear and mistrust. The barrel of his shotgun pointed at my feet, as though he expected at any moment to have a reason for blowing me away.

If this wasn't enough to have me sweating, he also had a severe nervous twitch that regularly spread through his body as a spasm-like shudder. At a distance of five metres he could hardly have missed hitting me. I stood rock-still, avoiding his almost rabid gaze and paranoid that any sudden movement would set him off. If I slipped and fell over on the wet clay, I'd probably be full of holes before I hit the ground.

Colin, Scott and I were so far outside the realm of experience of most people in this region, it was small wonder that some militia men fingered triggers and nocked arrows just in case. To a few, like this fat-bellied Indian, we must have seemed an alien species.

Similarly, much of what I'd been party to in the last few weeks had been alien to me. To see a finger on a shotgun trigger and know that you are the sole reason for it being there is a truly chilling experience.

I was very relieved when the village chief had completed the necessary formalities and sent me on my way. I'm sure the villagers, as a whole, felt the same way too.

The downpour continued. In the failing light, we searched for high ground on which to make camp. For all we knew, the river could rise metres overnight. Neither bank offered anything secure. Ultimately, we decided on a sand island with a highest point of about two metres above the river level. We erected only one tent, tied the raft to it and left everything else on board, ready to go, against the possibility of the island being submerged as we slept.

In the morning, we emerged from the tent and came face to face with yet another bunch of militia men. They made no demands for passports or documents. Although no words were spoken to this effect, I could tell that the only thing they required was for us to leave as soon as possible. Terrorists, cocaine smugglers, crazy gringo tourists on a red raft. They did not want any of these things corrupting their efforts to live simply and peacefully.

We had grown used to this attitude, the only one we'd known since farewelling the Apurimac. Our presence on their patch of river had made the residents of the Ene and Tambo uneasy. While the Senderistas may have viewed us as a plump game bird (one they missed the opportunity to pluck), no one else had been happy to see us.

We knew the barely disguised suspicion and contempt were not intended as any reflection on us as men. These attitudes had been instilled through long exposure to fear and the culture of violence. Still, when someone threatens your life or is directly responsible for the sort of stress and strain we felt, it is hard not to feel strong dislike for them in return.

There are only a few small pockets of South America where protracted conflict exists. We had just come through arguably the worst of them. Our nerves were flayed raw – the sight of guns made us feel ill. We couldn't get to Atalaya fast enough. There, we understood, all the madness would finally come to an end.

TWELVE
THE UCAYALI

11 November 1999 (day 60):
5850 kilometres to the Atlantic

Atalaya marks the absolute end of the Amazon's rapids. For deep-hulled vessels, the *lanchas*, this town is as far as they can travel upriver. Upstream of Atalaya is the realm of Johnsons and the occasional gringo-powered raft.

For the better part of a week we had lived in a state of constant anxiety. On a positive note, it had taken my mind off my blisters. A year of digging holes to plant trees, slashing weeds and building trails had not prepared me for rowing. In quick time, blisters had formed at the base of most of my fingers and in the middle of each palm. They had burst, and stung for days. Now the weeping sores had healed and the new skin was that little bit tougher. Calluses were on their way.

As the second wave of euphoria receded, our minds turned towards time factors and what sort of effort was needed from this point on. It was mid November. Not only were our money reserves unlikely to cover more than a few months' worth of supplies, but there was a time limit on our flights out of South America. In line with our slim budget, we'd bought flights with a maximum of just six months in which to use the return ticket. That meant we had until early March 2000 to complete our journey and get down to Rio de Janeiro. Otherwise, we faced the prospect of being stuck in South America, penniless. It was a scenario more daunting than the Amazon voyage itself.

We had always thought about it, but now the question was raised in earnest: how fast does the flat Amazon flow? As well as the influences of geology and the time of year on a river's rate of flow, there was no doubt that the Amazon moved at a different speed depending on where you were along its length. If we could figure out the average current then we could determine what was required of us.

Our best conservative estimate was between two and three kilometres per hour, based mainly on what we knew from Kane's account. This didn't take into account the variable current over the river's width – water travels faster on the outside of curves than on the inside. In terms of our own input, *Los Labios* could not be rowed any faster than three kilometres per hour. She was a star in whitewater but certainly not made for long-distance travel. For economy of stroke, it was hard to do worse: she didn't slice through the water and she caught a lot of headwind.

So we worked out our expected average speed between Atalaya and the Atlantic to be about five kilometres per hour. Combining this with a daily regimen of twelve hours' rowing, then plugging the result into the estimated 5800 remaining kilometres, generated a total of almost 100 days. That was frighteningly close to our outside limit, and didn't allow for any days off. Even without the threat of losing time to sickness and bad weather, we were cutting it close. Over the next three-and-a-half months we faced the equivalent of rowing from Sydney to Perth and halfway back again.

A few kilometres past Atalaya, the river again changes its name. The Urubamba, having run alongside the Amazon for 700 kilometres, at last greets it. Their meeting is that of two lost lovers who have wandered the Andes in search of each other. They embrace and intertwine, united as the Ucayali. At 400 metres across, the Ucayali is twice as wide as the Tambo. It was also considerably faster than any length of the river since the Apurimac Canyon. Relatively speaking, our rowing contributed less to our forward progress, the impetus we needed to put aside concerns about time constraints.

What was left of the Andes became lighter and increasingly grey; the mountains sank further and further into the horizon. We had crossed into the lowlands. My first glimpse of Amazon jungle was far from inspiring. Gone was the undisturbed rainforest that had hugged the banks of the lower Apurimac, the Ene and the Tambo. Here, the vegetation was low and straggly. A clue as to why chugged past in the form of a *lancha* and its barge laden with fat tree logs.

Late on that first day out of Atalaya, the river began to do something it had never done before – it forked. The two channels split apart at right angles to each other. Before selecting a campsite, we had to choose between left and right. Without detailed maps there was no way to know which was the shortest route. Potentially, one route might be ten times longer than the other. We knew from the Kane account that further downriver, between the port cities of Pucallpa and Iquitos, a channel known as the Puinahua Canal sprouted off the main river and did not rejoin with it for 150 kilometres and that water flow in the Puinahua dropped to almost nothing.

It was an evening for firsts. We were attacked by mosquitoes for the first time. And after dark, caimans lurked at the edge of camp. Their eyes reflected back my torch beam as eerie yellow circles. Even spookier was the noise they made – their high-pitched croaks sound like a bird on helium gas. Though they don't grow as big as their cousins, the Australian saltwater crocodile, caimans are still regarded as man-eaters. The frequency of attacks is much lower these days because of hunting, the older, bigger reptiles having been all but wiped out. Now a huge population of the stuffed variety inhabits the interior of dingy restaurants and bars down the length of the Amazon.

More intriguing wildlife emerged the next day. It started as a series of unexplained splashes, which we attributed to jumping fish, big jumping fish. Occasionally, we saw a flash of grey or pink out of the corner of our eyes. Scott cast a line, hopeful that the first fish our rod caught would make up for all of its previous failures.

Later, the source of the splashes revealed itself. I was rowing, bored, my eyes following the wake of tiny whirlpools made by the left oar blade as I levered it through the water. Up through the swirls came a dolphin. It was pink and plump, with tiny eyes and a squashed nose, but definitely a dolphin. The creature lunged skywards, out of the water right up to its tail, then flopped back in and disappeared. I had heard of the Amazon dolphin but never really expected to see one. And I certainly hadn't expected one to perform for me. This was the jungle, not Sea World.

Typically, these dolphins are much shyer than their ocean-going relatives. They are about the same size but look much more primitive, like a cross between a porpoise and a seawater dolphin. A second Amazon species is similar in shape and colour to the seawater variety but rarely grows more than a metre in length. Through research on Amazon dolphins, scientists confirmed that at one time the Amazon flowed the *other* way, emptying into the Pacific Ocean before the Andes rose. Genetic comparisons revealed a closer link between pink dolphins and the ones living there than to Atlantic populations.

The Ucayali itself took on the form of a gigantic snake, meandering through the jungle in never-ending curves. Several times, we rowed hard for a few kilometres, only to find that the river had almost completely bent around on itself. The actual distance we had gone was closer to zero.

For all of the river's twisting and turning on a small scale, the broad-scale maps showed the Ucayali heading north in a direct fashion. Although 1000 kilometres still separated us from the Equator, the sun already packed quite a punch. Wide-brimmed hats only kept our heads cooler. I worried that the tan I'd sport by the time we reached the Atlantic would at best age me 20 years and at the likely worst condemn me to death by skin cancer.

We wore sunscreen on our faces, but strict rationing forbade our spreading the stuff all over exposed limbs. Our original supply was dwindling, and the average Peruvian pharmacy sold bottles of sunscreen for the equivalent of $45 (Australian). Our best alternative was to create some shade on *Los Labios.* No easy task. The solution we hit on generated a sense of satisfaction rivalling that we'd felt regarding our makeshift rowing frame and oars.

We raided one of the tent kits for its carbon-fibre poles and the outer sheet, or fly. The tents had cost $100 (Canadian) each at the local supermarket back in Canmore. On two sides, the waterproof fly did not come right to the ground; instead, a horizontally fixed pole allowed the fly on these opposite sides to overhang as a sort of verandah.

Initially, this had been viewed as their major weakness. Now it seemed to be a design feature uncannily tailor-made for the raft.

We gouged four holes into the balsa to make the corner points of a square, then we bent the two tent poles as criss-crossing arcs, inserting their ends into the holes. The resulting frame was identical in shape to the specified arrangement of poles used to erect the tent. Finally, the fly was draped over the frame and secured firmly in place by hooking the elastic loops on each corner.

Colin said that we had in effect constructed a 'bimini'. This is the name given to a shade awning on pleasure yachts. As I reclined on the pontoon beneath it and opened a book, I couldn't argue with such a label.

The third camp out of Atalaya was our last.

Dense vine thickets on both sides of the river made pitching a tent impossible. With dusk appeared a large sand island. It was bare except for grass patches, a few low shrubs and the skeleton of a long-dead tree. As far as having clear, flat ground and access to dry firewood, the camp was equal to the best we'd come across.

I heard a hum, not in my ears, but in the air all around – the collective hum made by millions of tiny insects. Then came the mosquitoes.

Swatting was futile. Hundreds were on us at once and biting in unison. We scampered for the tents, and armoured ourselves in trousers, long-sleeved tops, socks and shoes. We donned caps with specially designed mesh netting and coated our hands in repellent. Only then did we dare venture back outside to make a fire and cook food.

But the bloodfest continued. Mosquitoes needled us

through the fabric of our clothing and found ways through the mesh. Many of them were so frenzied they ignored the repellent on our hands. I put on extra layers, but these made the humidity almost unbearable.

We sat in the path of the wafting smoke and pleaded for the fire to belch out more. Smoke was the only thing that made them think twice. When the food was ready, we fled to the tents, meticulously annihilated the mosquitoes which entered with us, then ate. All night they pattered against the tent fabric. We did not emerge until the morning heat had chased them away.

Scott shook his head. 'I'll go crazy if we have another night like that.'

'I was busting for a piss but couldn't bring myself to go out there,' said Colin.

I flinched at the thought of my genitals covered in biting mosquitoes.

'And that was an island! Can you imagine what it's like in the forest?'

Colin had an idea. 'Maybe we should start going around the clock. If we stay in the middle of the river, perhaps the bastards won't find us.'

No one offered any resistance to the suggestion. There seemed no reason why we couldn't just keep rowing. The river was flat, we couldn't fall over a waterfall, and with our style of boat, there was no risk in running aground. It would mean an uncomfortable bed and interrupted sleep patterns, but it might avoid the misery we now associated with camping.

Anyhow, there were other good reasons to stop camping. The night before had rekindled my anxiety over the threat of malaria. We had been taking preventative medicine for three weeks, but I knew it was no guarantee of not contracting the disease. Malaria is caused by a parasite carried in the gut of some mosquitoes, and the chance of being injected with the parasite of course rises with the number of bites you get. Even the strongest antimalarial drug, mefloquine, which can cause madness as one of its side effects, is not 100 per cent effective in staving off malaria – a disease which can kill you within days.

Scott had brought a supply of mefloquine with him from England. Colin and I were taking our chances with a cheaper drug we'd bought in Cuzco. It wasn't mentioned in our tourist guidebook, but several pharmacists wearing white lab coats had sworn by it.

The other advantage of a 24-hour rowing regimen was the time gain. The extra distance we covered each day would take the pressure off trying to meet an impossible deadline. That night we gave it a trial run. We held our breath as dusk settled. There was the occasional lone mosquito, that probably just happened to be buzzing by as we passed, but no horde. We tested Colin's theory. Within 30 metres of the bank, they swarmed us. As long as we stayed in the middle of the river, it seemed we were too far away for mosquitoes to pick up our scent and fly out from shore.

We established a nightly system of three rowing shifts, each lasting three hours. Over three nights a full rotation of shifts would occur. The man on duty was not expected to row solidly for three hours, however he *was* expected to stay awake. More important than keeping the raft away from shore was the responsibility of making sure *Los Labios* didn't collide with a *lancha*. As a safety back-up against the possibility of the rower dozing off, we suspended the kerosene lantern from the bimini frame.

When darkness fell on our fifth night out of Atalaya, the moon was ringed by a distinct halo, and there was a glow across part of the downstream horizon. The glow was Pucallpa but the halo was a mystery.

At dawn we rowed into the inlet serving as the city's port. Pucallpa is the only river settlement below San Francisco that is linked by road to Lima. As a result, it is the gateway for trade between the Amazon and the Pacific. The jungle is a formidable barrier to development and the road link was established only in recent times. In no time at all, the sleepy village exploded into a sprawling city. Over 200,000 people now call it home and Pucallpa remains the fastest-growing jungle settlement in the country. It was the perfect place to find a kerosene stove.

Cargo boats and fuel barges blocked the water's edge. They lined up for over a kilometre in front of the waterfront precinct, making it impossible for us to land. Opposite what looked like a market, we pulled alongside a refuelling pontoon and convinced the operator to let us tie up. I drew the short straw and stayed behind while the stove hunt began.

The waterfront was hideous. An expanse of sunbaked mud served as the delivery/pick-up bay for trucks. Teams of bare-chested men moved backwards and forwards between the trucks and *lancha* decks, up and down sagging ramps. All were bent double under heavy sacks, regardless of whether they loaded or unloaded a boat. Chickens scratched around in rubbish piles. But the most striking element in this organised chaos and filth were the vultures, a few of which squabbled for rotting food scraps. Dozens more perched on the rooftops, like stone gargoyles, waiting in silence for something or someone to die. They are one of the few creatures that has thrived on the relentless encroachment of humans into the rainforest.

A man looked down at me from the lower deck of the *lancha* moored next to the fuel barge. He was short and wiry, with squinting eyes.

'You look like you need a shower,' he laughed. I had not washed properly in over a week and it must have showed. 'Tie your strange-looking boat to ours and come aboard,' he said.

Destructor II was one of a fleet of ships that shunted goods between Pucallpa and the larger port city of Iquitos (ocean-going freighters are able to travel upriver as far as Iquitos, some 4500 kilometres away from the Atlantic). I didn't ask what had happened to the original *Destructor*.

The wiry man's name was Roy. He was a deckhand on the boat, and judging by his larrikin nature, also its resident comedian. Everything that came out of his mouth was a wisecrack.

I had a shower, then ate a meal of fried fish with Roy and several other crew members. The fish was delightful. Unlike *trucha*, with which choking on slender bones was almost unavoidable, the flesh of this species melted in my mouth.

'Wonderful,' I commented. 'Where do you catch these?'

'Here,' said Roy.

As he spoke, I noticed a woman on the neighbouring *lancha* tip a bucket of used engine oil over the side.

Later on, I went looking for a bank at which to replenish our cash reserves. Away from the waterfront, the allure of Pucallpa did not increase. The buildings had been hastily erected and few roads were paved. The streets were filled with the drone of two-stroke engines, which belonged to the chief form of people movers: motorcycles with a canopy-covered seat situated behind the driver, that up to three paying customers squeezed into. In Thailand they are known as tuk-tuks. In Pucallpa they made up the vast majority of traffic. As I walked, a group of motorcycle taxis clattered by, kicking up clouds of choking red dust. I staggered blindly, rubbing my eyes clear just in time to dodge the fully laden truck rumbling straight towards me. Madness.

That night, we sat around drinking rum with *Destructor II*'s captain and chief engineer. Roy was there also, as usual, playing the fool. Egged on by the captain and the engineer, he sang a repertoire of songs about life on a riverboat.

By the time he'd finished, it was late and the rum bottles empty. The captain and the engineer departed for bed, saying we were welcome to sleep anywhere on deck. Roy suggested that we go and buy more rum. Neither Colin, Scott nor I was keen to drink more. Hearing this, the good-natured smile vanished. Roy insisted. We refused. The little man's nostrils flared, his eyes narrowed and he began making demands. 'You owe me for my singing,' he said angrily.

We remained defiant. Finally, the wiry deckhand stormed off in disgust.

While looking for a space to sleep, I spied Roy sitting on a hammock. He was injecting the contents of a syringe into his arm. I realised that a cocaine habit explained much about this strange little man.

A kerosene stove cost us 40 soles ($20). With its installation, *Los Labios* became a fully self-contained vessel. From that moment, the only thing that would force us into shore was either a shortage of fuel or food.

As a unit, the stove was one of those mass-produced backyard welding jobs. We had seen stoves with the same design being sold by a number of vendors in Pucallpa. The only universal part was the burner itself. We were excited by the purchase. The stove could not have been more ideally suited to us: the three dimensions of the metal frame were equal, giving it an open cube shape; four legs gave it excellent stability as it stood on the floor of the raft behind the second balsa cross-log; and the height of the stovetop proved ergonomically perfect for a person cooking while he sat on the pontoon.

Best of all, it was beautiful in its simplicity. A cylinder that held the fuel was pressurised by pumping air through a one-way valve; after manual priming, the vapourised kerosene passed through the jet of the burner. There was no chance of a repeat of what had happened to our stove in the Camaná Valley. Now when impurities or carbon soot blocked the flow of vapourised fuel, maintenance was as easy as pricking the tiny opening of the jet with a wire filament.

No effort was spared in organising the galley. Ultimately, the cook had everything he needed to hand. As it had done since Pilpinto, the designated food dry bag held the bulk of our supplies. It lay on a balsa-wing platform over the cook's shoulder, at arm's length. Vegetables and fruit occupied plastic net sacks. A rectangular board, suspended underneath the table by string, functioned as a spice and condiment rack. The table itself (when cleared of books, sunglasses, tubes of sunscreen and countless other odds and ends) was used less for dining and more as a food-preparation bench.

From a logistical perspective, we considered ourselves invincible. Everything had continued to come together so quickly and easily – the oars, the bimini, the stove. There seemed no limit to our ingenuity, nor to the resources offered by the river. In quick time, we had engineered a platform that we felt confident would survive to the Atlantic.

Questions remained, however. From both a physical and mental point of view, were we up to the task? Leaving aside the threats of disease and running out of money, did we have enough fuel left in the tank to last the distance? Whether we were prepared to admit it to ourselves or not, the events of the first two-and-a-half months had already sapped a good portion of our inner strength. And as beings of flesh and reason, we had access only to limited reserves.

I now saw not disease, not wildlife, not spear-wielding natives, not cocaine runners, but the around-the-clock rowing regimen as the greatest threat to us. Colin, Scott and I had lived together in close quarters for 70 days. Now we faced the prospect of spending a similar amount of time virtually in each other's pockets – 24 hours a day, seven days a week.

None of us were strangers to a lack of seclusion and privacy – whether it be through sharing a bedroom with a sibling or, more recently, living in share houses and over-crowded youth-hostel dormitories. But in those situations, if you need time to cool down or be alone, you just walk away and get it. In the same way, when we were back upstream and setting up camp every night, morning and evening were times when as individuals we could wander off and forget we were part of an inseparable trio.

There was no such luxury now. Aboard a four-metre-long raft and several hundred metres from either shore, where could we escape to if one of us just plain got sick of the sight of the others? I had no idea if anyone had ever formulated an actual theory, but I wondered if there was a minimum personal space needed by a human being for a given period of time. If for a span of two months it was calculated to be less than two-and-a-half square metres, then there was trouble ahead for us.

Rowing around the clock also demanded adaptation by the body. Our workload was greater. We each hauled on the oars for between five and eight hours every day and we slept less. Night shifts started at 9 p.m., 12 a.m. and 3 a.m. Doing either the first or the third nightshift afforded us six hours of sleep time; the middle shift allowed a mere four-and-a-half hours between rowing stints. From the outset of the new rowing regimen, this was the shift we all despised. The last thing our bodies needed after five hours of daytime rowing was to have a three-hour session driven like a wedge right through the middle of their slumber.

It's important to mention here the difference between the time that was 'available' for sleeping and the 'actual' time spent in the land of nod. In a nutshell, inflatable rafts are not designed to be slept in. The only places to lie down were along either side of the pontoon, between the bow and stern, and the raft floor was far from the soft, spongy air mattress that you might imagine. Stretched taut under high pressure, the rubber tubing felt more like a concrete pipe. If you've ever tried to sleep on a trampoline . . . well, it was much worse than that.

Only the wings on either side stopped us rolling off the pontoon and into the river as we slept.

Another frustrating thing was that we could not lie completely flat. The other two logs, the ones extending widthways across the pontoon, made sure of that. It was possible to make one of the logs into a sort of pillow, with the help of a life jacket. The other log, however, you just had to put up with.

Exposure to the elements was the other thing that made sleeping difficult. As the wet season progressed, the weather was becoming more unstable. Showers were beginning to hit us at any time, day or night, and sudden strong headwinds turned the smooth river into a choppy mess. The threat of a tropical squall played on my mind as I lay there trying to doze off.

Our bimini was designed for shade, not protection from the heavens. It couldn't cope with anything heavier than a light drizzle. And, anyway, if the wind started blowing, we had to take it down before it got ripped away. When the rain came, staying dry took precedence over sleeping, of course. We would retreat under sheets of blue plastic and sit through the loud thwacking of raindrops. Rowing around the clock certainly took some getting used to.

The body that regulates international shipping has established uniform guidelines in order to prevent collisions between large vessels. One of these concerns 'navigation lights', the display of which must conform to a worldwide standard so that there can be no confusion by sailors. In narrow channels, like a river, they are very important.

Navigation lights are a fixed arrangement of red, green and white lights. Carefully aligned blinkers mean that the way in which you see the lights is determined by your orientation with respect to the other vessel. They can tell you if that vessel is travelling upstream or downstream, and confirm the course it is taking – in other words, whether it is heading straight for you or angled to miss you.

As we found since beginning our night shifts, these rules are policed very loosely on the Peruvian Amazon. Not one ship displayed the correct configuration of lights. Scott and I didn't know any better but the conscientious and dutiful seaman in Colin got angry every time he saw the rules flouted.

From a safety perspective, the lack of navigation lights meant that instead of rowing out of a boat's way, we might in fact be rowing into its path. Normally, the outline of the ship could only be seen when it was almost too late to do anything else. We shone torch lights to alert others to our presence and most times the boats veered away. But on the long, straight stretches of river, we reckoned that more than a few helmsmen had probably locked the steering wheel and gone off to do something else.

At about 1 a.m. on our third day out of Pucallpa, I sat on the bow, watching the stars. They were about the only things visible in the inky black of that moonless night. I was only an hour into my shift, but the oars had been shipped for the past 20 minutes. I was dog-tired and struggling to keep my eyes open. Staying awake was even tougher when the night was so peaceful. I decided that the only way to keep sleep at bay was to start rowing again.

First I needed to regain my bearings. Once you stopped rowing, the raft would quietly spin around on gently swirling surface currents. In four nights of travel so far, each of us had found himself rowing upstream on at least one occasion. On the first night out of Pucallpa, half an hour passed before I had twigged that something was amiss.

From the middle of the river, each shore appeared only as a dark, fuzzy band. (Remembering the orientation of the moon and certain stars was the best way to clarify which direction was downstream. Failing that, you simply had to row in close to shore, stop, then watch to see if the shore moved left to right or right to left. It quickly became customary to ask 'Which way is downriver?' when you got woken up to start a shift.)

I found the Southern Cross, yawned again and resumed rowing. Then something disturbed the peace.

A low rumble, like the purring of a cat, reached my ears from somewhere downriver. It was the trademark rumble made by a barge and the tugboat that pushed it. I turned around and scanned the darkness ahead but saw no lights. This was not unusual. I'd already noticed that the river had some peculiar acoustic qualities at night – the engine of a boat was sometimes audible for up to half an hour before it passed by. The snaking bends of the Ucayali meant that an approaching boat could be out of our line of sight until it was only a few hundred metres away.

Ten minutes went by. No lights. Another five minutes passed and the rumbling sounded near, I guessed no more than half a kilometre away. Still there was no light to indicate the barge's whereabouts. I strained my eyes to follow the vague outline of the rainforest canopy fringing both sides of the river. Nothing indicated that there was a tight bend up ahead.

It was not uncommon for a vessel to display a minimum of navigation lighting, namely one white light, but this one showed nothing at all. For several moments, I thought I must have confused the noise with that of a generator or some other stationary motor located on the riverbank. Then I realised the rumble was increasing in pitch faster than we drifted with the current.

My heart began to pound. I couldn't pinpoint where the rumble came from. Such was the tone of the reverberations and the way they echoed off the forest wall that the barge seemed to occupy half the width of the river.

'Guys, wake up! Help me look for this bastard.'

Colin raised his head. 'What's up?' he asked with a sleepy lack of interest.

'We're about to get mown over by a fucking barge!' I shouted.

Both the Canadian and the South African sat bolt upright. Getting hit by a barge was the fear foremost in our minds.

We had talked in depth about the dangers of collision and discussed how the consequences would vary depending on what type of boat ploughed into us. It all came down to a matter of hull shape. If we collided with a boat which had a hull that was pointed at the bow and V-shaped in cross-section, the raft would be deflected off to the side and out of further harm. A barge, on the other hand, was flat-bottomed and potentially much more dangerous. Instead of being pushed out to the side, *Los Labios* was more likely to be run over by it. After being scraped along the underside of the barge's hull, she, and us, could then be sucked into and minced up by the tugboat's powerful propeller.

Colin grabbed the lantern and held it aloft while Scott pointed a torch into the gloom. Neither of these two light sources was expected to illuminate the barge. We simply hoped that they would draw the attention of the tugboat's helmsman. Maybe they had, and the barge was at that very moment veering away from us – we had no way of knowing. Surely, though, even if the tug's electrical system was completely down, the driver would have some kind of device to shine back at us, we thought.

Going one way seemed better than waiting; having some momentum was important. Yet I hesitated, acutely aware that by rowing blindly, I might very well put us directly into its path.

'Where the fuck is it?' I yelled, giving voice to the one hysterical thought filling each of our brains. Soprano notes of splashing water were suddenly mixed with the engine's tenor rumblings. Their origin was easier for the ears to pinpoint.

'There!' said Scott, jabbing a finger at the darkness.

'What's his course?' I demanded.

Scott shook his head. 'Can't tell. Fuck!!'

And then we were given the vital clue. For once, whitewater proved the ally, not the enemy. As the barge bulldozed a path through the river, it piled water up in front of the bow. This water was churned white. It glowed faintly, enough to be visible, enough to warn me. Above that dim line of white, a black wall of iron was bearing down on top of us.

The icy shiver that had preceded many a rapid washed over me again. For an instant I felt tied to a horrible fate, stalled on the tracks in front of a speeding train. A single image flashed across my mind: a broken mast and rigging tangled up on the bow of a giant container ship. Colin had spoken of incidents where freighters had smashed into sailboats out in the middle of the ocean. The freighter crew would know nothing about it until they reached port and found wreckage hooked onto the ship's bow.

My body went onto automatic pilot. The oars flailed. Moments later, the barge cruised past, missing us by just two raft-lengths.

In the morning, another boat headed straight for us. It was smaller than the barge the previous night, but much, much faster. Such was the power of its outboard motors that it tilted back on a 45-degree angle. As it approached us, the only thing visible was the front half of its shiny black hull rearing out of the water.

At a marginally respectable distance, the boat's engines were cut. We steadied loose items on the table as a large wave rocked *Los Labios.* Simultaneously, the front of the motorboat lowered to reveal six men. All wore dark grey fatigues. Their smiles were genuine enough.

'*Policia Narcotica*,' one of them announced.

I recalled the tin runabout used by the Ene military patrol to apprehend us and how its engine had stalled a dozen times as they towed us back to the army base. At first glance, the Peruvian Government's spending seemed a trifle misplaced: while there were boats in a war zone struggling to make it between point A and point B, this vessel seemed the height of overkill. Not only that, but all six men had the look of highly trained, seasoned campaigners. There were no fifteen year olds here.

The explanation was simple enough. Indirectly, these men were on the US Government's payroll. In their 'muscle boat' they patrolled the river between Iquitos and Pucallpa, looking for those trying to smuggle drugs north.

The *selva*'s major export was coca paste. The paste got shipped by boat or plane to Colombia, where it was refined into cocaine. Understandably, most people living in the region (and probably most officials in Lima) had few qualms about a drug industry that brought in dollars and created jobs. Those involved could earn three or four times the amount they made in any other line of work. But Peru received pressure and money from the United States to do something about it.

Scott and I traded places with an officer who had been given the task of performing a cursory inspection. Colin remained on board the raft to show him around. The mood in the muscle boat was relaxed and informal. Scott and I talked about the journey so far and about our ultimate goal.

'What about women? Don't you miss women?' asked a tall, handsome officer.

'Not really,' I said honestly. 'There's been too much else to think about.'

'You don't like Peruvian girls?' he queried.

'Yes.'

'Amigos,' chimed in another, 'Iquitos has the finest girls in Peru.' He moved his hands down around some imaginary curves to reinforce his point.

I had the impression that these men regarded themselves as the pin-up boys of the river. Three of them wore stylish sunglasses and I could smell aftershave.

'Are you from Iquitos or Pucallpa?' I asked.

'Iquitos, of course.' They dismissed Pucallpa as a rat-infested sewer.

Iquitos. I knew only two things about the place: it was the birthplace of rubber and the largest city in the world that could only be reached by plane or boat. No roads led to Iquitos.

'How long does it take you to travel between Pucallpa and Iquitos?' I asked.

'We can do it in eight hours,' the chief officer said proudly.

If *Los Labios* managed to do it in ten days, we would be pleased.

On the fifth morning out of Pucallpa, a single red sore had appeared on the bottom of my heel. The skin was gone, exposing the raw flesh beneath. I noticed it not because of how big it was (at the size of a freckle, it was barely visible), but for the disproportionate amount of pain it caused me.

The origin of the sore had me stumped. I couldn't recall hurting myself. It looked like no insect bite I'd ever seen, unless there was some Amazon beastie that could bite off chunks of flesh without the victim knowing. And we'd not touched land for three days, which ruled out the possibility of my having trodden on something.

By the following day, the sore had multiplied. There were ten scattered over the sole of my left foot, and two on the inside arch of my right foot. The pain was worse. I lathered both feet in antiseptic cream, and wept three times that day, after each application of Dettol. Those tears were in vain. The seventh morning revealed another tenfold increase in the number of sores, more than I cared to count. By day 8, the bottom of each foot was as much raw flesh as skin. It appeared that my soles were gradually being eaten away.

It was not until we stopped at the town of Requena that some light was shed on the mysterious sores and I could feel convinced my feet would recover. I hobbled and winced my way along the pier to a riverside 'menu' bar, where a local asked what my problem was. I showed him. His face screwed up in disgust, disgust borne out of a similar personal experience.

'You must keep your feet dry,' he advised. 'This problem happens if your feet are always wet.'

I realised then that the sores must have been the work of a fungus. Indeed, the best way to tackle the infection, apart from using an antifungal cream, was to deprive it of moisture. Since departing Pucallpa, I could not remember a time when my feet had stayed dry for more than a couple of hours. If they weren't dangling over the side of *Los Labios*, then every time I stepped on and pushed down the floor of the boat, water rushed in through the self-bailing holes and soaked them. This had been going on around the clock.

After this revelation, I became obsessed with keeping my feet dry. I continued to disdain shoes, partly because in the Amazon Basin shoes seemed inappropriate outside the larger settlements, and partly because I worried they would make my feet sweat.

After only one day of following the advice given by the man in Requena, I noticed a change for the better. No more new sores appeared. When I was not rowing, I aimed the soles of my feet at the sun. This hurt, but I was correct in thinking that the fungus, like vampires, hated sunlight. Starved of moisture, the sores began to harden and heal.

On the tenth day out of Pucallpa, we reached the Ucayali's confluence with the Marañón. The Marañón was for a long time recognised as the longest tributary of the Amazon. After the Ucayali–Apurimac system claimed its rightful place in textbooks, the Marañón was relegated to being the largest of the Amazon's Peruvian tributaries. The Marañón is considerably larger than the Ucayali and usurps it as bearer of the Amazon's operating name between where the rivers meet and the Brazilian border.

But all this information didn't interest us very much. The joining of these two rivers meant something more significant: the width of the Amazon now exceeded one kilometre.

THIRTEEN
IQUITOS

30 November 1999 (day 79):
4500 kilometres to the Atlantic

Iquitos hummed in the sticky sunlight of late November. The place looked and sounded big. Our sense of expectation had grown through the night as the city's glow gradually spread across more and more of the horizon. Now we could barely sit still thinking about the fix of urban living that was almost in our grasp. I felt like a lost explorer stumbling back into civilisation after years in the wilderness. In appearance and odour at least, I probably looked like one too.

Beyond some much needed R and R, we had pencilled in Iquitos as the staging point for the battle to get ourselves financially solvent once again. The sums had each of us worried. If Brazil ended up being as pricey as people claimed, then we might be living completely off the land before journey's end. Worse still, we'd have next to no money for emergency situations, bribes or even a celebratory bottle of champagne at the Atlantic.

The plan was simple. Iquitos had Internet access. We'd relaunch our drive for sponsorship in earnest. People we'd approached had written us off as no-hopers a few months ago, maybe now we could be taken a little more seriously. (Perhaps now we might actually get some replies.)

Iquitos had once been incredibly rich. As we approached, I noted the prominence of ornate towers and spires. The native rubber tree had supplied all such opulence. Before synthetics existed, the world craved its latex sap, and Iquitos was the hub of production and export. The wealth must have seemed without end – until someone smuggled a few young plants over to South-East Asia and the South American rubber trade fell flat on its face.

We rowed up a small tributary, flanked by communities that seemed never to have known prosperity. The all-wood dwellings were floating affairs, which crowded the tributary's edge and squatted in the festering muds that bordered on the heavily polluted water.

Eventually we found a modest stretch of free bank and landed. What next? How to get everything packed up and moved to a *hostal*? A welcome party gathered to gawk and giggle. We asked one youngster (the one who looked the least flabbergasted) what our options were. He ran off. Twenty minutes passed, then one option spluttered and clattered onto the scene – a flatbed Dodge truck that was the oldest, rustiest moving vehicle I'd ever seen. A short, rotund man eased himself from the driver's seat, smiled broadly at us and patted the tray top suggestively. Colin, Scott and I looked at each other, then shrugged our shoulders – no better offers were forthcoming.

We started disassembling the raft. A dozen children jumped to attention, taking it on themselves to haul our bits and pieces up and onto the Dodge. It was pure bedlam and impossible to keep track of what got stacked where. The kids could have just walked off down the street with half the gear, for all we knew. We rushed about frantically, calling to each other above the confusion: 'Have you seen the . . . ?', 'Where's the . . . !'

But very soon everything was deflated, loaded and accounted for. '*Muchas gracias*,' we chorused. As if on cue, twelve hands were instantly thrust out, palms facing upwards. 'Ah, the joys of being "rich" foreigners,' Colin said in defeat.

The fat driver took over. He knew a decent and cheap *hostal.* Colin and Scott rode in the tray. I took my chances upfront. The passenger side had no door, a fact I must have looked a tad perturbed by.

'Wait one moment,' bid our driver.

He whisked out a loose door from the space behind the cab. I was motioned to get in. Then he deftly slotted in the hinges and slammed the latch home. Inside, the dashboard boasted not a single dial or gauge. The fat driver reached into a nest of wires, picked out two and crossed their exposed tips. The Dodge barked like a seal for half a minute then rumbled to life. Our shore leave began.

The market throbbed. Belen was known as the poor quarter of Iquitos and I could easily see why. Lame men and mange-ridden dogs begged for half-rotten slabs of beef. Vendors shooed both away as nonchalantly as they did the hordes of flies laying siege to the meat. For the latter, no doubt there were at least a couple of days left of exposure to the warm, moist air before shoppers might turn up their noses.

Down one alley a girl of about eight years old squatted on the hard-packed ground, overseeing a dozen fish. They were arranged neatly on a piece of cloth. Bored with trying to catch the eye of would-be customers, she instead pried the dirt from under her toenails with a large knife. A more enthusiastic fishmonger across the laneway rushed over to wave a piranha in our faces. I was unsure whether he wanted to shock a few tourists with the fish's razor-sharp teeth or if it was his way of demonstrating their freshness. Even in death, the man-eating fish looked menacing.

'There is no fish that tastes better,' he claimed. The rows of glistening white gnashers certainly put the fishmonger's handful of yellow teeth to shame. But, when it came to pirahnas, part of me liked the idea of humans giving back as good as they got.

We pressed deeper into the market, wending our way through a maze of bustling streets back towards the waterfront. High-stilted houses leant over to cast the stalls in gloom. Each looked as if the slightest gust of wind would blow it down. We nibbled on bananas and papayas, then stepped into a bar occupying the ground floor of one especially rickety-looking structure. A roomful of glazed eyes instantly turned our way. We shuffled over to a wonky table. The buxom owner pounced.

'Foreigners?' she asked rhetorically, and with a sly grin. 'You want a drink?'

'Sure. Three beers, please.'

'No beers here.'

The grin broadened. I looked over to the bar for some display of the alternatives. Several unlabelled flagons crowded together on a sagging shelf. That was all.

'Umm, what do you recommend?'

The grin spread from ear to ear. 'I will make for you.'

She spun on her heels and left. Colin and Scott looked at me and then at each other. Make? Around the room, men sipped from small glass tumblers and hardly spoke. They looked more hypnotised than drunk. At the bar, our host busied herself with the flagons. Some were full, others almost empty. The mysterious fluids inside ranged in colour from dark brown to cloudy grey. A few green-tinted bottles disguised their contents entirely.

Shots from five different flagons were funnelled into one plastic bottle. Meanwhile, I surveyed the decor. There were no windows, instead light filtered in through the door and cracks between the wall planks. The ceiling was strangely high, at some four metres above our heads. A trapdoor was cut into its centre. Given the ladder-like staircase already leading up to the first floor, this trapdoor seemed quite pointless. Returning with our drinks, the barmaid noticed my interest in it.

'We open it to collect water,' she offered matter-of-factly.

'To collect *what*?' I asked, thinking I must have misheard.

'Water. Each year during the flood season.'

And only then did the light of realisation flash in my head. I looked high up on the wall and saw a distinct watermark, just half a metre below the ceiling. My mouth fell open. In a couple of months, this bar would be underwater. Half of the Belen district would be inundated. My mind could barely grapple with the concept of an Amazon River six metres higher than I'd already seen.

'Come. Drink,' said the barmaid impatiently.

Our 'cocktails' were served and a verdict was expected. I sipped mine. It was delightfully sweet, but bore no resemblance to anything I'd tasted before.

'Well?'

'Mmmm – very good,' I confessed.

There was no way to tell how strong this stuff was. Delicate sips seemed the way to go.

From above the ceiling came the muffled giggles of several girls. Less innocent sounds followed. Colin, Scott and I again shot each other glances. Our host smiled more devilishly than ever. Her title seemed a little more clearly defined now, as did the nature of the establishment.

The madam pulled up a seat. An old man sitting across the other side of the room called for another bottle of potion. She turned and let him know in no uncertain terms that she was busy and that he could jolly well wait a few minutes. The old man sat down sheepishly. The madam turned to us, her face a mask of almost motherly tenderness.

'Have you seen the Iquitos Zoo?' she asked.

'No.'

'We have all the famous jungle animals here.' She rattled off a list that included cougars, tapirs, sloths and anacondas. 'We also sell them to zoos in other countries. It is good business.'

'You've worked there?' queried Colin.

'No, no, but I like animals and how they behave.'

She paused and then continued.

'I would like to show you.' Her double meaning wasn't lost on me, especially considering the proximity of her leg to my own.

'The zoo?' I clarified hoarsely.

'*Si.*'

But the prospect of seeing once proud beasts of the Amazon boxed into cages barely larger than themselves was not appealing. As two men at an adjacent table fixed us with beady stares and several curious heads poked through the ceiling trapdoor, I felt like a caged animal myself. The madam leant closer, eyes fluttering and breasts about to spill from a low-cut blouse.

'It will be good fun,' she crooned.

I felt like cougar meat. 'I'm afraid we don't have enough time,' I lied.

We excused ourselves and fled back into the wilds of the marketplace.

A rotten stench filled the waterfront air. And yet, I liked what it stood for. The Belen poor quarter fascinated me. From the cigarette merchant who rolled his smokes at a finger-blistering ten per minute, to barefoot, dirt-streaked urchins kicking a wornout football through the legs of angry policemen, every turn revealed another spectacle. In an odd way, the dog carcasses, smoking garbage piles and runnels of human effluent seemed an integral part of the whole Belen collage. Without them, any appeal might disappear. Local Belenese went about their business without batting an eyelid at the filth. The concepts of hygiene and sanitation seemed to be given short shrift. Perhaps this was due to the knowledge that the flooding Amazon would soon come through and rinse the place off anyway.

Two months earlier, these scenes might have repulsed me. But whether I was becoming attuned to the way of things in third-world Peru or whether I was simply finding comfort in the similarity to the feral conditions aboard *Los Labios*, I now felt desensitised to it all.

Hot meals were sold at countless streetside stalls, with little variation in both the menu and the quality of food being served. Without exception, it was all simple, greasy and super cheap. I doubted whether many citizens bothered cooking at home. The prevalence of these roadside kitchens meant that whenever and wherever the urge to eat struck, it could be satisfied in seconds. Even with our ailing finances, the prices were low enough for a bit of regular indulgence by us.

We would sit on a line of stools, arranged around the cook like punters at a casino blackjack table. On one occasion the cook was a broad-shouldered woman with muscular arms that glistened in the humid evening air. A stained tank top clung to her sweaty torso. One by one, she pointed at the variety of dishes laid out in front of her; one by one, the three of us shook or nodded our heads. A mix of dollops and portions was dealt out in bowls before each of us.

We ate hungrily. A couple of minutes passed. As I bent my head low over the bowl and shovelled in some oily rice, I noticed with a sideways glance that Scott had put down his fork and stopped eating. Head still bowed, I lifted my eyes to follow his gaze. The rice caught in my throat. Our cook was in the process of dealing one final card. Her left hand reached skyward, exposing a moist, bristly armpit. With her right hand, she used a carving knife to shave off the short, unruly hairs. Then in a seasoned, fluid motion, she switched the knife's attention to the other armpit. My appetite disappeared. I almost gagged. Quite obviously, I still had a way to go before being able to match the locals' contempt for hygiene. I doffed my hat to the folk of Belen; they were indeed in a league of their own.

We met Alfonso patrolling the front of his shop in a more exclusive part of the market precinct. He'd been harassing passers-by with his wares but no one seemed to take any notice of the small vials he flourished between thumb and forefinger. As we walked by, looking anything but Peruvian, Al's face lit up. He stuffed the vials into his pocket and cranked over some rusty English.

'Hello, Americans!'

'We're not American,' I intoned and kept walking.

'Do you have any sickness?' he asked hopefully.

'Umm, why do you ask?'

'Because I can cure with jungle medicine,' came the almost cocky reply.

Now he had my attention. I stopped and looked over at his corner-store bazaar. Bundles of dried plants hung from a low, crooked verandah. Several urns contained either pieces of gnarled tree root or strips of bark. Al herded us closer with the slickness of a born salesman, but I, for one, needed little convincing. Here, perhaps, the very essence of the Amazon sat bottled.

Three flickering oil lanterns illuminated the interior. Their flames cast dancing shadows across a wall of shelves. Vessels of all shapes, sizes and colours huddled close together as if trying to escape notice. Snakeskins and panther skulls adorned the ceiling supports. The air was soaked with hybrid fragrances that stirred a heady mix of sensations.

I selected a longnecked bottle at random. Al materialised by my side as if by magic.

'It is for toothaches,' he said, flashing a set of perfect teeth.

From the top rack I pulled down a corked flask. It contained small red leaves suspended in a glutinous liquid. The handwritten label meant nothing to me. The short, sprightly medicine man again interpreted.

'This one is good if you have an itchy skin. Ahh, how you say . . . '

'A rash?' I supplied.

His eyes twinkled at the opportunity for a sale. 'You have one?'

'Err . . . no.' But I mentioned the foot fungus infection that only recently had cleared up.

In a lightning-fast movement, he retrieved a bunch of

twigs from behind the counter. They were reddish-brown and tied together by coarse twine.

'Put these ones in water for three days, then take them out and put your feet in the water.' Al said this in the same tone my Australian doctor used when writing me out a prescription. And who knows? I thought. If the same fleshy sores ever struck back at home, the prescribed treatment might well be based on whatever leaches out of those twigs.

Looking around at the array of balms and concoctions, I realised that in fact there wasn't a big difference between Al's jungle-juice emporium and the typical Aussie pharmacy dispensing its plethora of brightly coloured tablets. Let's face it, a good proportion of modern drugs have their origins in the rainforests of South America.

'How do you get the plants for these medicines?' I asked.

'Some I collect myself. Others I buy from old men who live in the forest. They are very wise men.' My mind summoned up the image of a barefoot, face-painted Indian elder skipping silently and stealthily through a tangle of undergrowth.

'They have cure for everything except puma biting off your head,' he added with a chuckle.

'Do pumas often attack people?'

'Last week, one of my business competitors goes to forest. Now he is no more my business competitor,' came Al's disturbingly frank reply.

Our conversation was drifting too far away from the matter of trade for Al's liking.

'Here, try this,' he said, handing each of us a glass and pouring shots from what looked like a bottle of white wine.

I sipped. It was anything but a reisling. The only thing it had in common with wine was a slight alcoholic kick. My tastebuds hummed with delight – the flavour was divine, exotic, and yet familiar in an odd way. It left a lingering tingle on the tongue. Al saw the pleasure in our faces. Two full bottles appeared and the price for one was quoted. A discount was available if we took a second. We bought two.

Now that a transaction had taken place, Al became less businesslike.

'Do you know of Huyawaska?' he asked quietly, as if we had now been invited into some kind of brotherhood. We shook our heads.

'You want to try?'

'What is it?'

'It is drug that will let you see jungle spirits,' he claimed, again in the prescribing tone of my family doctor.

'Now?'

'No, it is taken at shaman ceremony,' he explained. 'Shaman calls to spirits in the forest. They come.'

The ceremonies were conducted every Wednesday night out in the suburbs of Iquitos (the Peruvian equivalent of quiz night at the local RSL?). I was intrigued. So, too, were Colin and Scott. So far, we'd noticed very little that diverged from the staunchly Catholic; the tribal beliefs seemed to have been all but snuffed out. Al was delighted by our interest.

'Meet me here tomorrow evening.'

As we headed off, purchases in hand, I looked forward to another drink.

'By the way, is this stuff good for anything?' I asked, confounded by the illegible Spanish words on the bottles' labels.

Al's face split into an impish grin. 'Maybe you need to find some local girls. This drink, it is my best aphrodisiac.'

Two motorcycle taxis sped noisily through the outer districts of the city. As the headlamp lit up a crater-like pothole, I swallowed involuntarily and clutched the seat even tighter. Our driver swerved hard, just managed to avoid catastrophe, then straightened up and decided to accelerate. Colin and Al rode in the lead taxi. Scott was squashed in next to me.

'These blokes have got bloody good reflexes!' he yelled, probably trying to convince himself more than me. I wondered how many of these blokes with good reflexes swerved a fraction too late.

We pulled into a muddy alley as it started to rain again. The fare was triple what Al had promised it would be but, as the heavens opened, I was in no position to argue. I handed over the cash and we made a splashy sprint for shaman headquarters. Our medicine man associate led the way. He ducked down a narrow lane, then sidestepped into a mired courtyard. Whitewashed walls were illuminated faintly by a perfect half-moon, crouching low in the sky. Medieval-style hovels edged the courtyard. In one corner, Al held open a door and waved for us to enter. We were feeling more like part of a brotherhood than ever.

Thatched roofing muffled the downpour outside and a melody of waterdrips whispered seductively through the hovel's interior. One low-wattage light bulb dangled at eye level, its cord disappearing into the gloominess of a loft. The floor was of the hard-packed dirt variety. Benches nestled against the coarse-cut slats of a sloppily erected partition. Two single beds and a table skirted the opposite wall. The shaman's wife, a middle-aged woman with long grey hair and tanned face, sat cross-legged on one of the sagging mattresses.

The shaman himself looked exactly as I had imagined someone with that title. There was an agelessness about the man. He may have been 50, he may have been 100. Despite the dim lighting, I saw his eyes blazing with fiery intensity. His slight frame reclined in a low seat that almost resembled a baby bouncer, and yet, I could tell that this shaman was anything but frail. We were greeted as though he had anticipated our arrival. Of course, this may have been due to nothing more psychic than a phone call from Alfonso, but I liked to think that the Huyawaska had supplied such knowledge ahead of time.

Without further ado, an old soda bottle full of dark liquid appeared from the shadows. Not quite the smoking crystal decanter I'd envisaged, but still, a shiver of nervous excitement passed through me at the sight of the mysterious hallucinogen. The shaman uttered something in a language completely unknown to me. Al interpreted.

'Shaman says that for Huyawaska you must pay 40 soles.'

Twenty dollars each for half a glass of jungle juice! The evening budget had suddenly blown right out. Oh well, what the hell! No one ever said that entry into the brotherhood came free. Cold hard cash was password enough in these parts nowadays, and besides, I was convinced that, like it or not, we would never shirk our mantle of 'rich western tourists'. In truth, the stereotyping went both ways.

Money changed hands. The evening continued.

One dirty cup went to each of our lips in turn. The shaman waved his hand as if we should gulp it down quickly – no sipping was allowed. I drank. My tongue recoiled and I fought the urge to bring the liquid straight back up. A few seconds passed and my repulsion fled. I was left with a strange fruity aftertaste in my mouth that reminded me of burnt figs.

'How long before we should feel something?' Scott asked, his tone unable to hide a twinge of misgiving.

Al knocked back a draught of Huyawaska, wiped his mouth on a sleeve then jerked his head with a grunt of distaste. 'During ceremony, you will see the forest spirits,' he coughed. 'Come, sit. It is time.'

Moments later the light bulb was switched off and the world turned to inky blackness. I made a quick scan in all directions for possible early-bird spirits. Nothing. Outside, the rain abated. The shaman took a deep breath, filling the expectant silence. Then he sang.

At first it was a sort of crooning. I imagined the lyrics acting as a beacon for those entities from another dimension, roaming phantoms summoned to this modest hovel by the archaic and powerful words. The singing rose in pitch. Long, wavering notes made my neck hairs prickle. Then the shaman's wife joined in with her own wailing, their voices blending into a kind of mystical harmony. There was a few minutes of this and then silence fell once again like a sharp axe.

My leg itched but I dared not move a muscle. The shaman began to intone. His chanting caressed the darkness. Occasionally, more harshly spoken words punctured the otherwise silky-smooth delivery. I wondered if these were designed to snap any dozing punters back to attention. There was certainly a hypnotic feel to the whole business. From the void of black beside me came a steady nasal rasping. I knew that sound well – Scott had nodded off.

For half an hour, stints of song and chant alternated without pause. I willed the Huyawaska into every neuron, but to my eyes at least, it seemed the spirits weren't yet in the mood to make an appearance. A smattering of vaguely familiar words mingled with the indigenous dialect. Maybe it was a form of old Spanish. After a time, through wavering consciousness, I noticed that two words in particular were being repeated over and over. One was 'Cristo', the other 'Maria'. It took a fraction longer for the penny to drop finally. I was not privy to some age-old tribal ritual – this was some odd kind of Catholic Church sermon!

I felt duped. My chance to gain insight into Amazon culture now seemed to be little more than a history lesson on the exploits of South America's Christian missionaries. Not only had these missionaries gone about ruthlessly obliterating native beliefs and legends, but it appeared that they had also made strange hybrid religions of what little remained. I quickly lost interest in proceedings after that. Foggy, indistinct illusions evaporated and I was left waiting for the farce to be over.

When at last the lights came back on, I could barely keep my eyes open. The Huyawaska, however, intended supplying me a vivid take-home message of its own. Throughout the ride back to our *hostal*, it was all I could do not to cry out in panic and terror. The hallucinogen gave every object a trail of successive snapshot images as we sped by. Each perfectly spaced image faded to nothing in a matter of moments like some special effect produced by a movie camera. Trails merged and blended. My lucid mind cringed, my body shied as we collided with the lingering traces of cars, pedestrians and other motorcycle taxis. I expected death at every bend in the road. And the part of my brain that simply waved it away as drug-induced mania instead recalled the innate recklessness of Iquitos drivers.

We rowed out of the former rubber capital three days later, well-fed, rejuvenated, eager, yet poorer than ever. Our bombardment of sponsorship requests had yielded a lone reply. His name was Monty. Monty was the bored ten-year-old son of an executive with a sports sunglasses firm. He'd figured he might as well take a peek at his dad's emails while 'the old guy' was in a meeting. Monty didn't know where the Amazon River was but it sounded like a 'cool' trip to him and, if he could, he'd send a few pairs of his favourite 'shades' to us.

In the grotty markets of Belen before our departure, our haggling for food supplies had taken on a more ruthless and impassioned edge.

FOURTEEN
HEADING FOR BRAZIL

12 December 1999 (day 91):
250 kilometres from the
Brazilian border, 4200 kilometres
from the Atlantic

We nervously joked about our approach to Pebas. It was at this town, roughly halfway between Iquitos and the Brazilian border, that two Japanese adventurers had met a shocking end. The incident highlighted the corruption that goes hand in hand with police and military operations in South America. In the aftermath of international outrage, the three perpetrators had been brought to justice and were now serving hefty jail terms. For us, there was comfort in the logical notion that the Peruvian army chiefs would probably want to ensure something like that never happened again.

Our contact with the army on the Ene had, on the whole, left us with a good impression of the military so far. But as we tied up to a dock and I gathered up all our passports for the obligatory check-in with the local base commander, there were doubts in my mind.

Since leaving Iquitos, Pebas had been occupying the

majority of our thoughts. The incident involving the unfortunate Japanese men seemed frighteningly close to home. Our disquiet was compounded by the recollection of a phone call that Colin had received on the day before we left Canada. The caller had been a man named Luis, who was originally from Iquitos but now lived in Calgary. Although Luis thought well of our plan to raft the Amazon, he had been deeply afraid for us. He had felt it his duty to warn us about the extent of violent crime in the region where he grew up. 'It is a beautiful part of Peru, but there are people who would happily kill you to take your money,' he had told Colin.

A long staircase, cut into the side of the riverbank, led up to a cluster of hastily assembled and poorly maintained buildings. Soldiers lounged on the grassy slopes either side of the staircase. Their smiles were sly and mocking. Unlike its counterparts back upriver, an air of poor discipline surrounded this base.

The base commander did not deal with me personally. That task was for one of his deputies, sitting patiently at his desk beneath an open marquee. Back on the Ene River, the sight of uniformed fifteen year olds wielding semi-automatic weapons had shocked me enough. Here at Pebas, I was processed by a boy not much older. He was quietly spoken, of a slim, almost prepubescent, build, and obviously held in some contempt by a few of the other soldiers who in their boredom hung around. All of them were older than him by at least a couple of years. Their laughter was cruel, emphasising to me the absurdity of such misplaced authority.

The young man's composure was admirable: despite the jibes of his fellow soldiers, he remained polite, and went about the necessary paperwork dutifully. Only when I asked for official stamps – so that we might avoid any future militia distrust – did he become uncertain. Suddenly, the boy in him emerged. He raced off to one of the buildings, returning several minutes later to say that his commander had advised that there was no stamp to give us. We could keep going. I returned to the raft, wondering if there had been any need to stop at this place.

With Pebas behind us and still no obvious signs of threat from the local inhabitants, we shed a great deal of our morbid outlook. On the whole, river life agreed with us. The Amazon no longer seemed impossibly huge. Since Atalaya, we had covered over 1500 kilometres and done so in good time. But the last thing we wanted was for our journey to be a mad dash for the Atlantic.

Tunnel vision was something that we had sought to avoid from the very beginning but experience had demonstrated that this was easier said than done. When the going gets tough (or indeed life-threatening), the last thing on your mind is to indulge in some cultural interaction or wilderness sightseeing. Moving forward as quickly as possible becomes the only important thing. Similarly, we had been blinkered by the equation of time and the vast distance that remained.

But our viewpoint was changing. Perhaps for the first time since departing Camaná, we had at least created the illusion of being in control. Our minds embraced the concept of slowing things down, taking time out to investigate the countryside around us. Moreover, we felt a need to experience how the other half lived. Partly, we liked the stir that our passage caused among onlookers, and partly, we were fed up with sticking out like a sore thumb. As she looked now, *Los Labios* would be a unique sight no matter where we were in the world. I suspected that the shiny red rubber immediately distanced us from the local people. The balsa logs only partially redeemed us.

In this part of the world, there was only one form of non-motorised river transport: the dugout canoe. Dugouts harked back to another age. People cast nets from them, speared fish from them and loaded them full of jungle produce for a trip to the nearest market. I was sure that some of the bare-chested folk I saw in them were simply out for a lazy Sunday paddle, that dugouts were the Volkswagens of the jungle.

There was something about a dugout canoe that seemed far more appropriate to the Amazon than our inflatable rubber raft did. While we had no intention at all of replacing *Los Labios*, we yearnt to at least experience the tradition of river travel in a wooden canoe. It was a case of 'When in Rome . . .'. We wanted a dugout of our own.

There is no category for 'used dugouts' in a *Trading Post*. In the Amazon's backwaters, there is no *Trading Post* to begin with. Nevertheless, we had no trouble finding a willing seller. It proved as straightforward as stopping on a beach where three canoes were pulled up and telling the occupants of a cane hut that we were in the market to buy. Five minutes and $10 later, we were the proud owners of one of what is widely regarded as the world's first true boat.

It was impossible to know whether we had bought a lemon, as none of us knew the first thing about such craft. We each had one past dugout experience to call on. Scott's had come when he was a youngster on safari in Africa, Colin's was during a sailing visit to Papua New Guinea, and mine had been just three weeks earlier while en route to a Tambo River militia passport check.

The science of a dugout seemed basic enough. It was a hollowed-out tree trunk, one solid piece of wood. The only things that could go wrong with it were splitting or rot. Our dugout measured about three metres in length and just over half-a-metre wide in the middle. It tapered symmetrically to a point at each end so that the bow and stern became arbitrary fixtures. Two planks were wedged in sideways, functioning as seats. The wood was two-and-a-half centimetres thick all over and very waterlogged. On land the dugout was too heavy even for two men to lift, yet it sliced through the water like a torpedo. Leisurely paddle strokes got it moving quicker than *Los Labios* did under full whip.

In all, our acquisition was perfect for exploring the narrow tributaries that fed into the Marañón. And that was exactly where we went. Most of the time, however, there was no need to paddle a dugout up some obscure little tributary for a dose of jungle intimacy. Just rowing *Los Labios* down the guts of the Amazon itself made for cosy interludes with the surrounding land.

The river continued to fork. Since Atalaya, it had rarely been confined to one single channel. There always seemed to be at least some small conduit, somewhere off to one side, separated from the main body of the river. We could only guess at how much of the total flow we were seeing at any one time. The river, as we saw it, might split into more or less equal halves at one point. Then, the half we chose to follow might be divided into two channels again, one of which was two-thirds of our half. If we took this two-thirds route, then at some point downstream it might meet up again with, say, a tenth of the flow that had been separated at the initial forking, and with the other nine-tenths at a point further downriver.

Days could pass before the true left bank or true right bank came back into view. And even then, we had no way of being sure if it was the mainland or not. In simple riverine terminology, the Amazon was 'braided', but it was braided on a massive scale.

The braiding is a result of the sheer flatness of the Amazon basin. Over millions of square kilometres, it has a featureless topography that sits no higher than a metre or two above the average river level. Most years, the river bursts its banks and temporarily inundates immense tracts of rainforest. At bends in the river, the faster-moving water is too impatient to conform with the curves and simply rushes overland, carving out new channels in the process.

To label the bed of the Amazon 'dynamic' is an understatement. Every year, the Peruvian and Brazilian governments have to dispatch survey crews to update the charts that are essential for shipping. New waterways and islands must be added, depths must be changed. But what is a nuisance for mapmakers is vital for some wildlife. Many Amazon fish species rely on the regular floods for their spawning and so that they can take advantage of the jungle floor's rich store of food.

Whenever the river forked, we always opted for the widest channel. Through reading the Kane account, we had become conscious of unwittingly slipping into the sluggish Puinahua Canal. We dreaded crawling along for days or weeks in this or other, similar, channels. Also on our minds was the knowledge that a number of these smaller branches never actually returned to the main river, but instead fed a maze of stagnating swamps.

Initially, our river logic had dictated that the fastest currents and shortest routes coincided with where most of the water flowed. This was flawed logic, of course. There was nothing at all to stop the main channel from meandering about in a haphazard fashion for many kilometres and its modest companion from carrying faster-flowing water only a fraction of the distance before the two of them rejoined.

This fact was driven home to us on one particularly humid afternoon. The river split between a channel 50 metres wide and one that was ten times this. A short distance down the narrow option, there appeared a quaint village. As per usual, we didn't hesitate to ignore the slimmer channel. Three hours and a lot of sweating later, it flowed back in. Normally, we would not have remembered or been able to recognise a channel reuniting after that length of time but we looked back up the narrow channel and saw the same quaint village from three hours earlier.

Choosing which way to go fell to the rower, who was expected to heed his gut feeling. At night, though, our rule of thumb was still to keep to the main body of flow. We did so, firstly, to avoid mosquitoes, and secondly, because if we were to end up getting lost in a swamp, it seemed best to do so by the light of day.

We were roughly 100 kilometres from the Colombian border as I rowed down the narrower of two channels. The sky was pale, the air still and hazy with mist. In the pre-dawn light, there was no movement from the rainforest that crowded in on both sides. An insect symphony was playing and the tang of 10,000 plant species swirled through my nostrils with each long breath I drew. This was the way I had always pictured it to be on the Amazon. Growing up reading Paddington Bear books, this was what I had imagined 'darkest Peru' to be like.

I had also spent many a rainy weekend sifting through my dad's collection of atlases and *National Geographic* magazines. For me, some of the first, and indeed probably the most lasting, images of the Amazon were the aerial photographs of her lowlands. Usually they showed an emerald-green carpet through which curled watercourses that were the colour of every variety of olive.

I remember thinking how impenetratable that landcape looked, how it seemed to harbour a thousand mysteries, none of which would ever be solved. But here I was now, right smack bang in the middle of it and, in my drowsy state, feeling like it all made sense.

Rrroooaaaaaarrrrrrrr.

With that, one of those mysteries proceeded to challenge my presumption.

Rrrooooooaaaaaaaaaaaaaaaaarrrrrrr.

Challenge acknowledged. I was no longer drowsy, and definitely no longer thinking that I had this place even remotely figured out.

I'd never heard anything like it before. Each roar was drawn out and agonised, a hoarse, rasping and spine-chilling sound, erupting from somewhere behind the jungle fringe. I thought that if any noise belonged to a creature from outside the span of scientific knowledge, then here it was.

Colin and Scott still slept. Blood drummed a primeval beat in my ears. I was gripped by a mixture of unease and curiosity. My curiosity briefly won out and I rowed closer to the shore to peer through the trees.

Rrrooooaaaarrrr.

I saw nothing, but I assumed that the creature was eyeing me from some treetop lair. I couldn't help but believe that there must be man-eating predators in the Amazon jungle so ferocious that no one who had encountered them had ever escaped from their clutches. That notion didn't require much imagination. The Amazon basin covers an area greater than that occupied by Australia, and biologists estimate that they have not yet identified even half of all the lifeforms that make their homes in its jungles.

I woke the others. If the thing rushed us, our chances were better if everybody was ready to defend.

Rrroooaaaaaarrrrr.

But nothing happened. The source of the roars did not come any closer, nor did it move further away. The roars continued at regular intervals, still reaching our ears after we had rowed several kilometres downstream.

We were to hear roars intermittently for weeks to come, always around dawn. And each time, our pulses would quicken and our imaginations run wild. On one occasion, we'd stopped at a tiny village to buy food when the roars started up.

'Listen!' I gasped. 'Do you hear that? What animal is that?'

One of the villagers smiled. '*Mono,*' he said. A monkey! Monkeys!

It would be later still that we would find out exactly what type of monkey it was. 'Howler monkeys' are a strictly vegetarian species of primate, growing to less than a metre in height and about five kilograms in weight. Their howling is simply a territory-marking exercise, to ward off other howler monkeys. From where I stood, it was a technique that worked on at least one other primate species as well.

In actual fact, howler monkeys lay claim to the title of loudest land animal. All up, only the blue whale is a louder creature.

Just beyond the settlement of San Pablo de Loreto, a banana boat sped from the opposite shore to intercept us. Laden with green bunches of fruit, the hull cut a wide swathe through the glassy water. The water was level with the boat's gunnels.

On board with the owner and his family, stood an unarmed soldier. Broad-shouldered and tall, he had an imposing presence. But like so many other young officials we had encountered, he appeared shy, and clearly unsure how to handle us. The overenthusiastic smiles and friendly greetings we had developed for just such occasions probably threw him off-balance even more.

'You must come back with me,' he stated, barely audible above the clatter of the banana boat's engine.

'What for?' I asked.

I knew full well what this was all about and sensed it was going to be another one of those days. He motioned towards the distant shore and the receding tenements of San Pablo.

'Control,' came the reply, but his tone was one of embarrassment.

Control! I was fast learning to hate the word. Here in Peru it implied the opposite. 'Hindrance', 'torment', 'circus', 'pointless' were some words I readily substituted for it.

'We have no motor,' Colin said flatly.

I enjoyed the added perplexity that this caused the soldier. But Scott was already fishing around for a rope. Within minutes, we were being towed upriver by the banana boat, choking on the smoke that billowed from its wheezing engine.

In truth, I felt sorry for the young soldier. His superiors had sent him to intercept and bring back a rubber boat and its crew of odd-looking tourists. There was no fuel for the military speedboat so he'd been left with no choice but to commandeer the nearest civilian vessel. Detainment by shambling banana boat! In his situation, I'd be feeling somewhat sheepish too.

We eventually pulled into shore at San Pablo. Colin and I ambled up the slippery bank. The owner of the banana boat gave pursuit.

'Oh God, here we go,' groaned Colin.

'You must pay for my fuel!' he demanded. It seemed such an obvious scenario now that it was happening. I narrowed my eyes and stared at the quiet soldier. He only shrugged in response and I knew it was pointless arguing.

'Twenty soles,' the boat owner continued.

Ten dollars! Ludicrous. I shoved six soles into his hand and stormed off, answering his complaints with my own that even this amount was too much.

The duty sergeant was a short, fat man. He seemed a little put out by our arrival as he rummaged around for the necessary papers. But after the tall, shy soldier had given him a brief description of *Los Labios*, he suddenly became intrigued. When we told him that Brazil was our destination, he even raised an eyebrow.

'Colombia is close to here,' he declared melodramatically. 'There are many dangers. You must stay on this side of the river, and you should not travel at night.'

It sounded like good advice, but I couldn't tell if it reflected real concern for our safety or some instilled military contempt for Peru's neighbour. Either way, Colin and I filed these warnings right alongside all our media-fed images of ferocious Colombian drug barons and the country's culture of violence.

On the wall, a small-scale map detailed the length of the Amazon over which Colombia and Peru warily eye each other. After pressing home his warnings, the chubby sergeant asked where we would be going beyond the large Brazilian border town of Tabatinga. Were we flying to Rio de Janeiro or Sao Paulo, or taking a *lancha* down to the city of Manaus?

'No, no, we're rowing to the Atlantic Ocean,' Colin said proudly.

The sergeant blinked, obviously confounded. Then he

began to smile at the absurdity of what he was hearing. It was the standard response, and Colin and I launched into our standard defence. We briefly recounted the mountains, the rapids, the guerrillas and the voyage from Atalaya to here. Plainly, though, all this didn't impress him much. This was a man who probably regarded the distant Atlantic as one of the ends of the earth.

'Where is your boat?' he asked. 'I want to see what you are talking about.'

We pointed the way. He returned our passports and scurried off quickly.

Colin and I left the building and walked along a wobbly raised walkway that linked many of San Pablo's buildings together. We sniffed out the local store, intent on getting some benefit from the interruption to our carefree morning drift down the river. Fittingly armed with a bunch of bananas, we picked our way between the mud puddles and protesting pigs back to the boat.

Four older men, in camouflage uniform and shin-high black boots, stood with the duty sergeant high on the bank overlooking *Los Labios.* Arms folded, they were chattering among themselves, taking turns to point out the host of odd features in our raft set-up. They appeared to be highly ranked men. The sergeant noticed our approach and turned to fire a mocking broadside: 'Where did you say you were going in that?'

'The end of this river,' Colin repeated.

At this, the sergeant snorted and made exaggerated rowing motions. His bulk made it a ridiculous spectacle, but he looked around at the faces of his fellow officers, searching for applause.

My smile was pleasant yet contemptuous. I decided to indulge them further.

'*Los gringos loco*,' I supplied.

They all erupted in laughter. '*Si, si. Gringos muy loco*.'

I was fast tiring of these Peruvians, and perhaps of the country altogether. I hoped the people living in Brazil had better things to do than unashamedly gawk at and poke fun at a few honest, adventure-seeking westerners.

At the Brazilian border, the river becomes known as the Solimões. Early in the morning of our first full day on the Solimões, a motorboat, travelling at high speed, approached us from the opposite shore. We were used to this type of directness. Maybe in Brazil, it was a sign of curiosity.

The engine cut at a respectable distance from us and one of three men on board began giving a loud speech. On paper, Portuguese looks very similar to Spanish but the spoken form is a different story. None of us had much idea of what was being said.

There were, however, two very telling clues. One was the speaker's insistent pointing back in the direction his boat had sped from. The other was the man at the bow, nursing an automatic rifle, 'POLICIA FEDERAL' emblazoned on his T-shirt. We were being hauled in by the cops again. For the third time, *Los Labios* was towed upriver.

As we neared a large floating pier, tethered by the shore, the reason for our being detained became clear. Without realising it, we had snubbed a customs check, one that applied to every river-going vessel, from the biggest cargo ship to the humblest dugout.

The procedure was straightforward. We lined up before an open-air desk, showed passports to the customs officer, then followed him to the raft. It was obvious that he had no desire to step aboard to make a close inspection. We supplied a brief description of our possessions and were allowed to leave. There was no fuss, no suspicious gazes. We were just another border statistic.

In the afternoon, one of the aforementioned cargo ships passed us. It was a Norwegian freighter, a monster more than 100 metres long. The Atlantic was still 3500 kilometres away. This freighter had crossed an ocean, and now it was halfway across a continent.

Seeing the mass of water pushed up by its hull – the bow wave – struck me with awe. It struck the raft with power. We rose higher than a metre as the first swell passed. The calm river quickly turned into a writhing mass of choppy water. Bow waves reflected off either bank and collided with each other. They half merged, half intertwined, forming a jumbled array of spikes, dips and king waves. There was no cadence. All we could do was point ourselves into whichever direction the most threatening crests came from. Now I know how a rubber duck feels when it's in a bathtub with a splashing baby.

It took a quarter of an hour before the surface settled down again to something that could be rowed on.

Next morning, we planned to get some footage of us rowing the Amazon in Brazil.

'Ben, have you seen the video-camera bag?'

'Should be where it normally is.'

'Scott?'

'Last saw it where you are, in that pile of stuff up the back.'

But it wasn't there. It was nowhere on board. And, ironically, the reason for this went right back to the previous occasion on which we had lost the camera. When we'd stopped for the customs inspection the previous day, and all filed off to meet the official, a well-drilled Colin had remembered to bring the video-camera bag along for safekeeping. Unfortunately, because of the shock of our being cleared so swiftly and minus any drama, he had left it behind.

'I leant it up against a pole near that guy's desk,' he said sheepishly.

So began the debate on whether we should bother going back for it.

Hopes were slim that by the time one of us managed to get there, anyone would know anything about it. The authorities got paid peanuts in this part of the world; you couldn't blame them for supplementing their income wherever possible. Then again, if their honesty matched their efficiency, our chances of finding the camera seemed good.

As it usually did, money entered the debate. The passenger fares to get back upriver and down again would decimate our reserves of cash. The next ATM was in the city of Manaus, over 1000 kilometres away. I liked the idea of starving even less than I liked the idea of saying goodbye to the camera.

The discussion was still in progress that evening as we rowed a short way up a tributary called the Amatura and docked at a town of the same name. A shopkeeper, although unable to sell us any concilliatory Sublimes, said that the weekly passenger boat to Tabatinga was due in the morning. Colin insisted that this good timing meant something. Ultimately, the need for closure won out. It would be nice to know for certain what had happened to the camera.

Colin was gone three days. Each morning, Scott and I tied up to a snag in the middle of the Amatura River, from where we kept vigil on the wharf and avoided the staring townsfolk. In the evening, we rowed against the slow current to where the river forked. On the flat, grassy 'V' of land, we camped beneath a statue of the Virgin Mary.

When Colin at last returned, he *had* the video camera. The accompanying story was itself worth the wait. He had reached the customs checkpoint the day after leaving Amatura, a total of three days after leaving behind the camera. The same official was on duty but, he was sorry to say, he knew nothing about the bag. Together, Colin and he had searched the pier, then carefully checked the storeroom where lost and unclaimed goods ended up. Nothing. The other officers on duty likewise didn't know anything about it. They had said that a passing crewman must have taken it.

Dejected, Colin had sat on the pier to wait for the next boat. He hoped that he might talk the captain into dropping him off in Amatura. He waited all day. It had started raining, but he just sat there, getting drenched.

Finally, the official seated at the desk had taken pity on him and said that they would go up to the barracks, on the hill behind the checkpoint, to look for the video camera. While the off-duty staff watched TV in the common room, the desk official led Colin to the dormitory. There he told the Canadian to look in the dufflebags that were next to each bunk. Inside the third bag he examined, Colin found the camera.

FIFTEEN
THE RACE FOR THE NEW MILLENNIUM

25 December 1999 (day 104): somewhere in the middle of South America

Christmas arrived as just another day to burn up more kilometres. Resupplying in the village of Fonte Boa had cleaned out the last of our pennies. Save for considering the unlikely scenario of our receiving an invitation to dinner as we floated downriver, we didn't bother much about trying to celebrate. We baulked at the idea of imposing ourselves on a random riverside family. Past experience had made us cynics. Even here, along this densely jungled, sparsely populated length of the Amazon, and on this festive day, the unexpected foreigners would be expected to splash their money around.

It hardly felt like Christmas anyway. But we couldn't let the day pass without going to some effort. We had indulged during our last shopping excursion. I made pumpkin soup for a first course and our main course was a selection of three colourful salads. Dessert consisted of an assortment of fruits. As we took time out from rowing for a couple of hours to drift, eat and relax, our only guests were the pink and grey dolphins, and a monkey who screeched at us from an overhanging tree limb.

It all seemed a far cry from our long-talked-about vision of landing at a small village, buying a wild pig, spitting it over a fire, then inviting all the villagers along for a feast. 'That,' said Scott, 'would have been a Christmas to remember.'

We agreed to make up for our quiet Christmas a week later at New Year. We vowed to reach the city of Manaus by 31 December. The year 2000 might not officially be the start of the new millennium, but the world seemed to be treating it as such. Celebrations around the globe would be massive. Every year, as far back as I could remember, TV news reports in Australia had shown footage of wild street-partying as Brazilians welcomed in the New Year. This year's promised to be the mother of all street parties. Here was the ultimate chance to be a part of the action and really let our hair down.

The race for New Year was on.

I started out of my fitful sleep. As usual, my dreaming had been brought to an end by a single prod on the foot. In my dream, I had been running along a windswept beach, playfully dodging the foamy salt water that streamed over the sand with every breaking wave. The dreamscape faded slowly; images of glistening seaweed lingered in my thoughts. I drew a long, cool breath of Amazon air, searching it for the faintest hint of Atlantic saltiness. Of course it wasn't there, we were still some 3000 kilometres from the ocean. But 3 a.m. bleariness, our proximity to either bank, and the boat's gentle rocking to a sea-like swell conspired to make me wonder.

Scott was working overtime. My three-hour shift at the oars had officially begun four minutes earlier. He gave an irritated yawn as I slowly prepared to trade places with him.

'Which way is downstream?' I mumbled, slotting a line of calluses into a groove on the oar handle. He gestured.

The light breeze gusted momentarily, sending a shudder through me with its chill. Behind, I saw distant lightning strikes, and soon thick black clouds engulfed the moonlight. Minutes passed, and my hopes of the storm missing us disappeared as the raft began to dip and prop in white-capped waves that had been whipped up by the now howling wind. My misplaced optimism meant that the bimini was almost ripped apart before I could unfasten and gather it in from its frame.

Scott and Colin awoke in spite of their exhaustion. The three of us assumed action stations, readying ourselves for imminent battle. In truth, it would be a one-sided affair: Mother Nature would attack, and all we could do was defend. As the first marble-sized drops of bruising downpour hit, we hurriedly tightened straps, sealed dry bags and shoved bits and pieces of equipment anywhere they might fit.

The boat pitched violently in the angry waves. I lurched with it, then suddenly found myself sprawled ungracefully and painfully across our makeshift table. It collapsed.

Satisfied that nothing was in a position to tumble overboard, we each took refuge under three large plastic sheets. All up, it was a system at which we were grudgingly becoming adept. The reality is that four-metre inflatable rafts provide no shelter whatsoever. Wrapping up in leaky, clammy plastic merely delayed an inevitable scenario: we knew that our ultimate fate on nights like these was to lie as sodden, shivering wretches.

The groans coming from our balsa-log rowing frame gave me cause for new concern. Our large dry bags hung over either side of the raft. They squatted on cane platforms, which in turn relied on the strength of the balsa. With every exaggerated rocking motion, the platforms slammed heavily into the water. Each time, I was beset by visions of those bags floating off helplessly into the night amid the echo of splintering timbers.

Twenty minutes crawled by. Everything was holding up well. I folded up a corner of plastic and chanced a look in the direction the wind was blowing us. Straining to catch a glimpse of the shore, only an inky blackness greeted my eyes.

'How close are we?' Colin yelled above the wind and deluge.

I was about to say that I had no bloody idea, when a lightning flash answered the question. A high vertical bank rose just 50 metres away, looming fast as the wind relentlessly pushed us on.

'Holy shit, she's close!' I bellowed.

Even without waves pounding against them, such banks were dangerous places to be near. Always on the outside curve of a bend in the river, they experience massive erosion forces. The shallow roots of precariously perched rainforest trees provide little resistance for the soft soil. In daylight we had seen 20-metre-high trees topple into the river as the bank literally disintegrated beneath them. Even from a long way offshore, the collapse of many tonnes of riverbank rung out like thunder. In a punishing tropical storm, it was the last place on the river we wanted to be.

'Still your shift, mate!' shouted Colin. 'Get us the fuck out of here!'

I was already scrambling to the oars, soaked in seconds and glancing over my shoulder in time to catch the next illuminating flash. The distance to shore had halved. In that same flash, I caught sight of something more sinister – less than 100 metres downriver lay a graveyard of semi-submerged tree skeletons. They were some long-dead victims of the relentless bank erosion, now half buried in the river-floor mud. With the current pulling us along at ten kilometres an hour or more, the sure result of a collision with any sharp protrusion meant that this was an especially bad place to be.

I rowed furiously, keeping the bow angled towards the middle of the river. My neck craned over my shoulder, waiting for the next burst of lightning that would light the way. Near-horizontal raindrops peppered the back of my head and beat a harsh rhythm against my earlobes. The air was filled with the alternating low grumble and peal of thunder. Gaining purchase on the choppy water with the oar blades was a struggle. The strobe effect of the lightning reminded me of a technique used in the movies to rapidly portray the passage of time; my very existence seemed fragmented into a succession of independent images. In each one, the world looked different. This apparent sleep–wake–sleep–wake cycle contrasted with my state of hyper-consciousness to make the whole situation seem utterly surreal.

Another flash. From the corner of my eye, I caught sight of a stake-like branch, jutting out of the surface at a low angle behind me. I had not seen it until then. The branch wavered in the choppiness and wind like a duellist's sword. Its point faced directly upriver, levelling off at chest height. At the speed we were travelling, it could easily have impaled any one of us. If one or two of my strokes had been . . . I let the rest of that thought go.

I sagged with relief, half of me overwhelmed, the other half believing we had now passed beyond this eerie garden of dead trees. And then we were all but on top of it – the granddaddy of all snags. Like an enormous gnarled and bony hand, it seemed to be reaching for us out of the frothing, murky water. My heart sprang to my mouth. Simultaneously, I clenched my teeth, sunk the oar blades deep beneath the waves, and heaved. My feet wedged, my head flicked back, I rose from my seat, loosening a drawn-out grunt. Every muscle in my body constricted in the bid to keep us out of the dead tree's frozen grasp.

Crack!

The sound erupted from one of the straining oar shafts. The blood froze in my veins. My grunting transformed into a cry of dread.

'Aaaaarrgh!'

'What the hell are you doing!' screamed Scott and Colin in near unison.

I was not the only one aware of how ugly things could have gotten with a broken oar. In the seeming eternity of the milliseconds that followed, my eyes riveted themselves to the shaft. Nothing more happened. The oar held, perhaps guilty of nothing more than its very own shriek of effort. The giant bony hand, having delivered only a few glancing scrapes, quickly fell behind. Yet another burst of lightning showed the path ahead clear.

With my back now to the still driving rain, I returned all my concentration to battling the wind.

Existence on board *Los Labios* was all about routine. Away from oar duty, we read books, wrote in our journals, dozed or simply watched the shore sliding by.

When the rhythmic sloshing of oar blades in water began to grate on our ears, one of us would switch on the shortwave radio and fiddle with the knobs again. It was a cheap and shoddy model that rarely managed to give us good, clear reception. For reasons that we guessed must have something to do with atmospheric activity, the more appealing stations like the BBC World Service and Radio Australia could only be picked up after the sun went down. Daytime belonged to the American evangelical broadcasters.

One of the more satisfying pastimes was the systematic execution of march flies. Several species plagued us but the worst of them was a certain jet-black variety. Dubbed 'the stealth bomber', it was discreet and quick enough to evade a slap. The needle-jab bites had us jumping, grimacing and cursing so often that bringing one down was almost worthy of celebration.

Above all else, though, our attention revolved around a small magnetic chess set, so much so that we'd launched a competition to see who could win the most games by journey's end. After each game, the reigning champion played alternating challengers and added to his tally with every subsequent win until he was defeated. The victorious challenger then became the reigning champion. Colin and I were old chess sparring partners and keen to decide once and for all who was the better tactician. Scott had made the claim before we left Canada that his mates back in the UK had rarely beaten him.

So routine reigned supreme, and came from within and was imposed from without. There was routine, say, in the way we battened down the hatches in the face of foul weather; and there was routine in the magnificent sunsets, in the arrival of afternoon headwinds, and in our daily encounters with the pink and grey dolphins. Then at times a voice inside one of us would scream '*Time out!*'

'Guys, we gotta stop. I need a bit of shore leave.' Scott's plea came abruptly and with unusual firmness.

Over the past few hours I'd noticed his mood darkening. He had been quieter than usual, grim-faced, and simply unable to sit still for more than a few minutes. I understood the feeling. We had not touched land for three full days. It could have been called 'cabin fever', if only the raft had a cabin.

'Mate, it's not the best place to do it,' I shrugged, gazing up at the steep clay bank sliding by only a dozen paces away. The dense forest perched some five metres above the river surface. As an arc, the bank curved far into the distance. To the eye, it was as if the outside bend of the river had been engineered from an architect's grand geometric plans.

I could almost hear Scott's teeth grinding as he scanned the bank downriver for a place to pull in. 'There! How about there?' he cried.

A section of clay wall had slipped into the flow. It created both an eddy for us to stop in, and a place where we might easily clamber up into the jungle. I spun the boat to face land, pulled hard on the oars and broke through the eddy-line.

As we nudged land, Scott let loose a satisfied 'aaah' and leapt ashore. He stretched long and loudly, then quickly scrambled up the loose earth ramp and over the top. Less excited about our first soil visit in over 70 hours, Colin and I unhurriedly secured the boat. We loaded film into our cameras and slowly picked our way up to the jungle.

Tree trunks and branches stuck out at all angles from the collapsed chunk of riverbank. A tangle of vines trailed back up to the forest. Some of these drooped like power lines, others were strung taut like steel cables. They were probably the only thing that prevented the bank here from completely toppling over and being washed away.

At the lip, Colin and I stood on a thick carpet of leaf litter and twigs, peering into virgin forest. Tree trunks, vines and foliage quickly swallowed all the sunlight coming in from its edge. The place looked mysterious and foreboding, as if unwilling to accept humans through its borders. We were just metres from the river, but I felt we'd stepped onto another planet. It was as though the river and the vast jungles existed on separate planes, as if they had no relation to one another whatsoever.

This made no sense. Maybe I'd spent too long on the boat, or perhaps the silty brownness of the Amazon now coloured my veins so strongly that going ashore was like going cold turkey.

'Ow!' The sting sliced through my introspection. I whacked my ankle.

'What the hell?' came a startled shout from Colin. He too began frantically slapping at his bare feet and shins.

Then I saw them, swarming all through the dead leaves and mulch – bloody ants, millions of them. I hopped swiftly up onto a rotting log but now my ear was suddenly on fire. One ant sank its pincers into my neck. How on earth were they getting up there?

I surveyed the forest immediately surrounding me. Every tree trunk and plant stem was a highway for the shiny black beasts. They scurried along branches overhead and, like kamikaze fighters, dropped into my hair. The pungency of formic acid was strong in the air.

Our intrusion had incensed them, either that or we were being pencilled in on the evening menu. South American rainforest is infamous for its army ants – a vicious species that moves through the jungle as a nomadic colony devouring all other animal life in its path, without exception and without mercy. Those terrorising us may or may not have been the dreaded army ants but, regardless, it was time to get out of the way.

Scott came into view, jogging through the undergrowth. 'If you run, the buggers can't hang on,' he said with a grin.

Meanwhile, several battalions had laid siege to my log and were in the act of storming over its mossy buttresses. We made a break for the river.

I edged *Los Labios* away from the bank, looking over my shoulder for the eddy-line where slow water met fast. From the stern, panic erupted.

'Oh, my God,' Scott spluttered. 'Row hard, Ben! Row fucking hard!'

My head snapped forward. 'What? What's ha –'

'*Row!*' bellowed Colin.

Not knowing why, I gave it everything I had for five strokes. I was confused and afraid, but recent past experience had taught me the valuable technique of doing first and thinking later.

Then Colin and Scott relaxed. 'Okay. We're good.'

They were both still staring back towards the place where the raft had been docked moments before. I peeked beneath the bimini that had blocked my view. My eyes grew wide at the scene unfolding behind us. Every tree on a ten-metre length of riverbank was toppling; beneath them, the lower half of sheer earthen wall had already disintegrated and been claimed by the water. Now seven proud old men of the jungle – trees perhaps centuries old – were making their parting bow, and in dramatic style. Overstretched lianas snapped one by one with a sound like whipcracks. The remaining vines reacted in slow motion, until an almighty sloosh swallowed 200 tonnes of riverbank in a single gulp.

Half-metre swells, like a detonation aftershock, sped out from shore to rock the raft. The starboard balsa wing rose up, then slammed the water heavily. Everything on the table crashed to the floor. The book I was reading got soaked for a third time. Better this than getting caught under 100 tonnes of dirt and wood, I thought.

The fact is, although the Amazon forever nibbles away at its banks with an erosive elegance, it also doesn't mind sinking its teeth in every now and then. Come to think of it, destruction on the scale we'd just witnessed probably takes place every second of every day, somewhere along the length of the river. Maybe such chomping happened twice every second, maybe ten times. The high-cut banks of the river reminded me of crumbling chocolate cake. For the first time they seemed like potential agents of doom. Death by chocolate, indeed. The idea of being pulverised by a ten-metre-high coconut palm as I coasted down the Amazon was not something I'd factored in previously.

Half an hour passed. Still at the oars, I was giving wide berth to another cliff-like section of bank. Then all chaos broke loose again.

'Yeeow!'

A dozing Colin sat bolt upright and slapped his shoulder in a lightning-fast reflex that shook the whole boat. He reached under his T-shirt to extract the half-squashed culprit – a big black ant. Despite having all six legs broken and abdomen flattened, still it tried to keep biting.

'Where'd that bastard come from?' Scott asked sleepily.

'Probably hitchhiked from back there,' I offered, with equally vague interest. As I said it, three ants scurried over the raft tube next to my leg. Out of the corner of my eye, I noticed another prowling around one of the dry bags. More climbed the tent-pole frame of our bimini.

Colin was on hands and knees, eyes darting everywhere. 'Shit, there's quite a few of them back here,' he said, looking like a man waiting for the bullet from a sniper. Scott was hit next. He swore loudly, and swatted the tender skin on the back of his thigh. The ant numbers increased. An invasion was under way. Five of them marched along one of the balsa logs; one by one, I sent them overboard. Seconds later, a dozen more appeared to take their place.

I was getting nervous. Where were they coming from? Had they swarmed our boat during our brief shore excursion and laid in wait until now? Or were they in the river and rushing us, like navy frogmen? I envisioned us being forced to abandon ship if things got too much worse.

We battled to stave off the tiny hijackers and scrambled all over the raft to flick them off, all the while recoiling from their parrying bites to our limbs. One especially brazen ant stole its way into my underwear, then launched an assault that brought tears to my eyes. 'Bastard!'

As I leant across to dispatch another ant from the stern, my gaze followed the long yellow rope tethering our dugout. A trail of moving black specks stretched back to a clod of branches, which had become entangled in the rope. It was now clear what had happened. When the forest fell, all sorts of debris had been thrown into the river. Every piece would have been teeming with ants.

I reeled the towrope in up to the clod. Colin and Scott, each armed with an oar, tried dislodging it. The ants were beside themselves with rage. Finally, the clod came loose. As it drifted away, we witnessed the grim spectacle of a fate that might easily have been our own: a sodden rat huddled on one of the branches, its twitching body slowly being eaten alive. No doubt the poor creature had been forced to swim after its riverbank home gave way. The lifebuoy it had found, in tragic irony, had simply supplied a slower, agonising death.

The more I thought about it, the clearer it seemed that of all the living dangers in the Amazon, ants were worthy of the highest respect. As with the fragile riverbanks, I'd never once considered them a threat to us. Now, part of me couldn't help but wonder if perhaps those ants had orchestrated the entire bank collapse as a means of foiling our retreat.

The blazing sun on my cheek and ear woke me up. I peeled the other side of my face from my red rubber pillow. I watched the bank for a minute and listened to Scott hauling on the oars. We were moving very slowly. I propped myself up on my elbows and looked around, reality dawning fast.

'Slow in here,' Scott declared, reading my thoughts.

'Where'd the current go?' murmured Colin from beneath his plastic blanket.

'Dunno.'

'What do you mean you don't know?' I challenged. 'You've rowed up one of those fucking side channels!'

Potentially, we could meander about for many kilometres before meeting up with the main river again.

'Ah, shit!'

Scott bristled. 'Calm down. It's not hard to do when its pitch-fucking-black!'

I softened my tone instantly, realising the injustice I had committed. There was no cause for me to be mad with Scott. I knew full well that the Amazon at night gave few clues as to what it would do next.

'Sorry, mate.'

I was grumpy with tiredness and frustrated by our bad

luck. The date was 29 December, and by our rough estimates, Manaus was still about 250 kilometres away. I had visions of us greeting the new millennium while floating downstream through a rainstorm, shivering miserably under the plastic sheets. Our chances of celebrating New Year in a jungle city were looking progressively slimmer.

SIXTEEN
MANAUS

30 December 1999 (day 109):
1800 kilometres to the Atlantic

What would a city of one million Amazonians look like? Until 1866 and the rubber boom, Manaus was merely an isolated and insignificant jungle village. The settlement quickly became a hub of distribution and export of natural rubber. When the boom ended almost 50 years later, the city was left as a virtual ghost town. Economic recovery only came in 1967, with the decision to make the port a duty-free zone. Modern Manaus exists as the Amazon's nucleus for commerce and tourism. Its opera house, the Teatro Amazonas, is world-famous, and the city boasts the only Harley Davidson motorcycle assembly plant outside of the United States.

By late afternoon on 30 December, there was still little to indicate that a big city was close. The waterfront of Manacapuru crept into view as the raft traced the outside of another seemingly endless bend. This was the biggest town we'd seen since entering Brazil ten days earlier, and at first we took it for Manaus. It was promising, nonetheless.

Workers at one of the floating fuel stations there gave us a range of distances to the big smoke. We tried a new approach.

'How long does it take the *lanchas*?'

But none of them, it seemed, had ever taken a passenger boat to Manaus.

'Do you have a map?'

More shakes of the head, although one worker claimed to have seen a map of South America several years before. This lack of maps made sense. What was the point of them when just two routes out of town existed – upriver and downriver?

'How long do you think it will take to row *this* boat?' I was clutching at straws. It was a futile question for two reasons. Firstly, most people had never seen an inflatable boat, and secondly, the act of rowing was unheard of.

Naturally, that didn't stop each man from offering an estimate with unwavering confidence. 'Two days, maybe three,' said one.

Since our arrival in South America, we had asked 'How far?' or 'How long?' countless times and, amazingly, we were yet to hear the reply '*No se*' – I don't know. It is as though South Americans can't bear the idea of being considered ignorant.

'Tomorrow morning,' stated the fellow at the cash register, before continuing his junk-food sales pitch. As usual, it seemed logical to him that, as westerners, we would not be able to resist Coke and Mars Bars dangled right under our noses.

That night, each of us rowed at a steady pace for our entire three-hour shift. The river was flat and glassy. On the morning of new millennium's eve, the weather turned foul. Headwinds slowed us to a crawl and heavy rain slapped the rower's back. Our hopes lifted as the *lancha* traffic increased. By midday, the weather had calmed and we again put the raft into top gear.

The city of Manaus does not border the Amazon. It is situated fifteen kilometres up its largest tributary – the Negro River. For a dozen kilometres, the Solimões and the Negro are divided by a narrow strip of land. We could not see a city, but the roar made by thousands of city vehicles carried on the wind.

At 2 p.m. we rounded a final sand spit separating the two rivers. Though much slower in flow compared with the Solimões, the Negro was a struggle to row against. We gained only a kilometre in the first hour, the same distance in the second. Manaus droned so close but seemed out of reach. By foot we could get there in a couple of hours but our problem was where to leave the boat. 'Where's the army or the police when you really need them for a tow?' puffed Scott.

It was a team of harbour divers who came to our rescue. They towed us the remaining distance and helped deposit *Los Labios* in a special marina for small boats, comfortingly known as a *vigil.* By 6 p.m., we were toasting our efforts in reaching Manaus.

Hustle and bustle surrounded a part of the inner city noted for its plethora of outdoor cafes and beer bars. The scene looked set for a truly massive street party. Yet as evening progressed, the throng steadily diminished. We patrolled the streets, surveying nightspots for their 'vibe'. Few offered anything more exciting than a rowdy table of drunks.

Eventually, we found somewhere that, from the

outside, looked and sounded lively. A neon sign reading, in English, 'The Dancing Pussy' supplied a clue as to what was happening within. Entry was cheap and included a free beer.

Despite the dim lighting inside, we had little chance of blending in with the crowd. Within moments, a leather-clad stripper was at our table and proceeded to sit on each of our laps in turn. However, instead of talking dirty, she was interested in hearing what had brought us to Manaus. Our journey enthralled her and she revealed a knowledge of geography leaps ahead of most other Brazilians we had talked to.

The club was closing at 10.30 p.m., and then she and her fellow strippers were all heading to a place called Ponte Negra, a 45-minute bus ride away, to party in the New Year. She insisted that we join them. Scott, Colin and I conferred in English.

'You know what will happen, don't you?' said Colin. 'We'll get all the way out to this place then a couple of thug pimps will grab us and demand cash for all the time we've spent with their "girls".'

It seemed a likely scenario, and one we simply could not afford. We left with the excuse of needing to meet friends.

The streets continued to empty of people. We found a *discoteca* playing techno music and there we made our last stand. There was nothing special about the music or the atmosphere. Drugs had turned everyone into stone-faced introspectives. And the DJ didn't even stop to make a midnight announcement. I only found out the hour had struck fifteen minutes later when I tracked down Colin and asked him.

We greeted the dawn of the new millennium asleep on a row of concrete park benches.

We needed a break from the river, especially the 24-hour rowing. Manaus might have failed to supply the party we wanted, but it would allow us to recharge and focus our energies on reaching the Atlantic. We checked into cheap accommodation, known in Brazil as a *pension*.

On 2 January we were wandering by a magazine stand when Scott noticed the front page of a newspaper. It showed a sea of people, an enormous stage and fireworks in the sky.

'Must be a picture from Rio de Janeiro,' I said.

Colin read the caption beneath, then made a face. 'Shit!'

'What?'

'This was in Manaus!' he cried. 'At Ponte Negra!'

At a cafe across the street from the *pension*, we met a schoolteacher named Elsio. He had moved to Manaus from the southern Brazilian city of Belo Horizonte. As in Peru, teachers earnt little money and Elsio supplemented his income by working part-time as a guide for a rainforest tour company. While we chatted, Elsio's girlfriend arrived to meet him. She was middle-aged, at least ten years his senior, and a divorced housewife. It seemed clear that Iacy was trying to recapture her youth, with a younger man and tight-fitting clothes that did not flatter her robust figure.

When Elsio heard about our New Year's Eve debacle, he promised to show us the best nightlife in Manaus. Scott and I took him up on the offer, but Colin was pre-booked. He had arranged a date with a girl he'd met at the techno club. It was his second attempt, after she had stood him up the previous night. The girl, Flavia, had come to the *pension* earlier that day to apologise, citing the reason for her no-show as her having had second thoughts. In the meantime, she had changed her mind again and was now keen to arrange another date. Colin's success in finding Amazon romance made Scott and I keen not to miss out. For the first time in a month, we shaved our beards off. We had deduced that facial hair was generally not well received by Brazilian women.

Elsio and Iacy took us to a trendy Parisian-style street bar. We sat down and soon drew interest from a table of four attractive girls. Their smiles and giggling led to an invitation to join them. Two of the girls excused themselves and left. Scott and I paired off with the remaining two.

Elsio and Iacy scowled. They were unhappy at having to sit with the girls. The teacher caught my attention and beckoned me closer. 'These are girls you will have to pay for,' he said.

'No, they're not,' I laughed, waving away this notion as ridiculous.

Scott had no doubts either. 'These are good girls,' he insisted.

Both girls said they were at university studying economics. Both wore denim jeans, not the typical clothing choice of harlots. I suspected it was a case of Elsio and Iacy feeling jealous that they had lost our attention.

Nevertheless, Elsio maintained his stance and repeatedly urged us to leave. Eventually he confronted the girls.

'Tell them what you are!' he demanded.

The girls knew full well what was being insinuated, but neither made any attempt to deny it. They told Elsio to mind his own business. The one sitting beside me linked her arm in mine and I decided that there was nothing to lose by asking her myself. She nodded. I shook my head to say it wasn't my thing. With barely an '*adios*', she got up and walked away.

We got back to the *pension*, where Colin was already in bed, having been stood up again by Flavia.

Our acquaintance with Elsio and Iacy didn't end there, however, for two days later Iacy came to the *pension* looking for me. She was wearing an excessive amount of make-up and a blouse that accentuated her cleavage. At her insistence, we walked to the nearby beer garden for a drink.

'Where is Elsio?' I asked, hoping he was about to meet us there.

'He is working on a rainforest tour.'

I smiled innocently and made awkward small talk but it was clear where Iacy's attentions were focused. Strangely, though, she seemed to be expecting *me* to make an announcement. I ignored every seductive gesture she made. Finally, Iacy cut to the chase.

'Before he left, Elsio told me that you were very interested in me.' Her eyes flashed with desire. 'I also like you very much,' she added. With that she reached over, grabbed my hand and squeezed it tightly. The look on her face belonged to someone who had just found the new love of her life.

Why Elsio had told her what he had I could only imagine. It was a cruel lie. The poor woman had spent an hour on the bus from her lonely house in the outer suburbs. In me she probably saw an escape from her life as a divorced housewife whose children had all grown up and moved away. Elsio spent more time getting drunk than being a good companion. I cleared up the 'misunderstanding' as honourably as I could and rescued an ounce of her pride by saying that I would write and send greetings when I got back to Australia.

For something a little less complicated, I visited the Manaus fish market. It occupied an enormous warehouse near the waterfront. The size of the place was testament to the abundance of fish in the Amazon and demonstrated the locals' reliance on fish as a source of food and livelihood. I spent hours ogling the scores of strange varieties we'd shared the river with but had never seen. The fish market was a porthole into another world, a sort of putrid-smelling natural history exhibit. Indeed, some of the species I saw were clearly from the era of dinosaurs.

The largest fish for sale was the pirarucu, which measured over two metres in length and looked like giant-sized carp. Many species had evolved huge, bulging eyes as compensation for turbidity. Others had given up on being able to see, their eyes tiny and obviously useless, while a few types had progressed to the point of having no eyes whatsoever. Every kind of fish seemed to assume a different mask of death – surprise, indifference, pain or, in some cases, horror.

In life, though, all had swum beneath us in the river sea, silently, invisibly. Yet Amazon fish did not always do so with absolute caution; occasionally, their paths crossed with ours. For a while during the rowing stage of our journey, I'd go for a swim every day, either to cool off or to cleanse my skin of sweat and dirt. On one occasion, something large and very slimy brushed against my leg. I clambered back onboard in record time. From that moment on, I preferred to endure the heat and go several days without a bath.

Amazon biologists are a long way from documenting every species of fish in the river's murky depths, such is the immensity of this river. The chance of encountering a carnivorous monster unknown to science is disturbingly realistic therefore. And, although most people we met played down the threat from piranhas, there is no shortage of known terrors. For instance, one of the smallest fish in the river is also one of the most dangerous.

The 'candiru' had achieved almost legendary status among the three of us. Villagers backed up what the few snippets of recorded information claimed this creature was capable of. The candiru is a catfish small enough to enter the gills of other fish, whereupon it sticks out barbs and feeds on their blood. It finds its prey by instinctively swimming against the flow of water coming from the gills. If humans urinate while they are in the water, a nearby candiru assumes this flow to be no different. It will swim a good way up the victim's urethra then stick out its spines. If the poor person can avoid bleeding to death, he or she must have the fish surgically removed.

In its own right, the Negro River ranks as the world's fourth most voluminous river. Its water is free of sediment, dyed by tannins and thus appears black. Due to both the tannins and an overall lack of nutrient input, life in the Negro is much less abundant than in the Solimões.

The junction of the Amazon and Negro rivers is a truly bizarre sight. A diagonal line extends from the headland as the interface between two mighty flows of water. They are different in so many ways and the marriage begins tentatively. Deep down, they exchange globs of themselves. On the surface, black boils erupt through the milky brown. Conversely, plumes of brown upwell to stain the black. The display has a definite yin and yang feel to it.

For about ten kilometres downstream of the confluence, water from the two rivers is separated by this distinct interface. The left half of the river is black, the right half, brown. Gradually, the left-hand side becomes cloudier, but it is not for at least 100 kilometres that the two rivers are said to have mixed completely.

Meanwhile, the river has shed its working title of 'Solimões' and for the first time is indisputably known as the Amazon River.

SEVENTEEN
THE TRUE AMAZON

9 January 2000 (day 119):
1400 kilometres to the Atlantic

The sun beat down hard. The air was still and heavily laden with moisture. At the oars I wore nothing but a pair of satin boxer shorts emblazoned with the cheerful mugs of Bert and Ernie from *Sesame Street*. Sweat ran in rivulets down my back, saturating the fabric so that it slipped against the shiny red rubber of the raft. With every oar stroke, the two puppets distorted into hideous ogres.

I quickened my pace. If the air didn't want to move, then I would try creating the illusion of wind. Not surprisingly, all this did was make me even hotter. I wished for some cool relief. I probably wished a little too hard. The vanguard of a breeze prodded the sweltering skin on my back. Above the downstream horizon, a sliver of grey–black cloud materialised. The river's glassy surface shattered into faint ripples.

The wind rose steadily in force, as if a control knob was being tweaked further and further around. I watched as the clouds progressively displaced more blue sky. And as with every tropical squall before it, I marvelled at the Amazon's rapid transformation, from placid colossus to raging brute. The ripples became erratic swells and very soon, my harmonic rowing degenerated into a display of two oars slapping water. It was like levering concrete poles through honey.

The stiffening wind grabbed and pushed at our non-streamlined bulk and, despite the strong current, we began to lose ground. No big deal. There had been enough of these conditions in recent times for us to have devised a countering strategy. It was one that worked amazingly well.

Colin got things started. He reeled in the dugout that trailed obediently behind our stern. Next, he rearranged the tethering rope so that it was connected to both tips of the dugout to form a Y-shaped configuration. Then, with a firm shove, he capsized the little wooden boat.

Instantly, the dugout surged forwards, disappearing beneath the stern, re-emerging beyond our bow and continuing downriver. It floated just below the surface, immune to the wind, harnessing the stronger current found there. Slack on the rope was quickly sucked up. In one practised, fluid motion, I shipped oars just as the sunken canoe began to pull. The rope went taut. We stopped moving upriver, spun around, and with a comforting jerk, resumed our forward progress at good speed. The tow rope's Y shape ensured that the dugout was aligned at right angles to the river flow and therefore maximised the amount of current we could exploit.

A wall of rain advanced as part of the main body of the squall. Bursts of near-horizontal droplets pelted our plastic shields like machine-gun fire. Through the slit created by a crease in the plastic, I saw the river swells effervesce under millions of tiny impacts. Ahead of us, the little wooden canoe steamed onwards like some lion-hearted tugboat hauling a stricken freighter.

Then the wind changed direction. Instead of hitting my forehead, the watery barrage now pressed plastic cold against my cheek and ear. I grimaced. My eardrum hurt from a flurry of loud slaps. Within minutes, wind was whipping across the river from the faraway left bank.

Such crosswinds made things tricky. Now, instead of dealing simply with directly opposing forces of current and headwind, more complex vectors came into play. If we did nothing, then as sure as anything, that wind would drive us to the right-hand shore. And given the river's three-kilometre width, there was enough fetch to guarantee that fairly sizeable breakers were pounding that shore.

For this scenario, too, we had an answer. Braving the downpour, Colin again reeled in the canoe (in fact, he pulled us to it). This time he shortened the left arm of the Y rope, angling almost 45 degrees to the Amazon's flow. Doing this inclined the dugout's course towards the left bank. And in turn, the red raft fought crosswind to maintain a respectable distance between the treacherous right-hand bank and us. At least for a time.

Squalls had become a part of daily life on the lower Amazon. They could hit at any time during the day or night. They ranged in size, too. Some were relatively small, like diffuse versions of a tornado. Others were big enough to have a distinct 'eye'. Like their tornado and cyclone cousins, a squall's behaviour was not dictated by prevailing winds. To us, they seemed almost conscious entities. Often it was possible to see two at once, one behind, one ahead, clear blue sky in between, with each squall moving in a different direction. At times, we would watch them up ahead of us, whipping across the river, out of harm's way, and we'd laugh aloud at this, saying that the squall had ill timed its charge and missed us. Then there were times when the squall had the last laugh. Abruptly, it would change course, cut back across the river, and belt us. On more than one occasion, a squall had battered us with wind, rain and chop, passed overhead, given us half an hour of respite, then turned around to slam us again.

Close encounters with a squall at night always made for a heady mix of anxiety and awe. Deafening thunderclaps would erupt from directly overhead. Out in the middle of the bucking river, I would brace myself for the crack of lightning that could blow us to smithereens at any moment.

One evening, a strange-looking atmospheric entity had transfixed us for over an hour. Off to the side of the river, far in the distance, there was an oddly stationary cloud mass. Shaped like a mushroom, its form had been illuminated every few seconds by internal bolts of lightning, much of which was unlike anything from our previous experience. The lightning moved horizontally, and instead of an instantaneous flash, it had wriggled through the mushroom in slow motion. We'd dubbed this 'worm lightning'.

With every squall before now, we'd negotiated similar terms, argued, tussled, then always found common ground. The one currently molesting us, however, meant to derail all discussions, seemed bent on humbling us.

A sudden gust almost ripped away my plastic shelter. Carefully, I tucked the edges in beneath clammy skin. I hunched my lanky frame down as low as possible, squeezing every ounce of protection from the raft tubing. The wind upped the tempo even more. It shrieked across the river and battered the rainforest on the near bank. That near bank was getting nearer. Despite the grittiest efforts of our sunken tugboat, we were fast heading for a rendezvous with mud.

Full of mistaken optimism, we waited for the squall to die down. In the end we almost waited too long.

I switched places with Scott. Arms fresh, he dug in both oar blades and worked, barely countering the wind. Once within 30 metres of land, the current naturally slackened. At this critical point, the push of the swells gained ascendency. The bucking chop made it impossible for us to bail out the canoe and get it floating in time. It was irrevocably shore-bound. Suddenly, our trusted ally became a lead weight that would drag us into the fearful embrace of the breakers.

Scott's muscles bunched. Each stroke lasted four or five arduous seconds. The cigarette he'd somehow managed to light one minute earlier was about to be bitten in half. Like the seasoned seaman that he was, Colin sprang into action once more. He wrestled with the binding knot of the towrope. There were no sharp knives to hand. Each charging white cap swept the canoe and us several metres closer to the verge of no return. Thank goodness it wasn't one of my stubborn knots being undone.

The rope came free. Moments later, the dugout caught a particularly large swell and surfed into the shallows. There it was pummelled into the vertically cut bank. We'd been just seconds away from the same fate.

Scott could do little more than keep us at a safe distance from the shore. Dark clouds carpeted the sky, offering no hint of a silver lining. One hundred metres downstream, however, the highcut bank was broken by an inflowing tributary. It was the respite we needed. Grunting and cursing, the South African steered us to the entrance. Then he relaxed, letting the waves carry *Los Labios* into sheltered waters. As we nudged dirt, a sense of relief passed through us all.

We tumbled out of the raft. I squished my toes into the mud, savouring the feel of having at least semi-solid ground underfoot. Grubby feet, I could handle. A shiver passed through me from head to toe. My skin swarmed with goose-bumps. In less than half an hour, the squall had successfully washed and blown away all evidence of that hot, steamy day. Only the palm trees insisted that we were still in the tropics.

As we set off to retrieve the dugout, there came a shout above the howling wind. 'Watch where you step!' Two boys, one a teenager, the other a toddler, stood watching from higher ground. Further up the tributary, a row of long, narrow motorboats bobbed gently to a melody of ripples. Perched above them was a village.

The teenage boy ran down to meet us, half leading, half dragging the toddler by his hand. Given the bedraggled barbarian look of us, it was a bold move. What he said next made it seem even braver.

'Señors, I saw a snake there just a few minutes ago.' He pointed to a patch of knee-high grass two metres from where I stood.

'What sort of snake?'

'A very bad one. It can kill you,' he warned. 'My brother went too close, so I hit it with a stick. Now I think it is angry.'

Our lack of proximity to a dose of antivenom (if, indeed, there was one for this species) did not inspire much peace of mind. For a local person, getting bitten might only allow enough time to say goodbye to family and friends before the poison did its deadly work.

'Do you see many poisonous snakes here?' asked Colin as he tiptoed back to the raft and stepped aboard.

'No, it is not a big problem. Last year, only three people in my whole village were killed by them.'

I glanced over at about 30 wooden huts. 'How many people live in your village?' I ventured.

'About 150.'

And so there it was, a fact frightening in its blasé observation. To a great extent, survival in the jungle from year to year (if not day to day) was a lottery.

Eating dominated the typical day from the moment the sun rose. Preparation of food followed a schedule as strict as that for rowing.

Whoever rowed the last nightshift swapped the oars for a place next to the stove. Usually, at breakfast the frying pan was wielded. The menu rotated between oatcakes, pancakes and our own style of crumpets, all cooked in palm oil. Occasionally, we'd substitute wheat flour for manioc, the popular carbohydrate staple in Brazil's jungle regions. Manioc flour is a coarse grit that comes from the root of an endemic rainforest tree. This same species is also the source of tapioca, another one of our breakfast options.

Lunch rarely deviated from sandwiches. If we were out of regular loaves of bread, we had the stove cranked again by midmorning to churn out flat breads. Every effort was made to ensure we always had a variety of interesting and tasty ingredients to put on them.

But it was the evening meal that we awaited most expectantly. A friendly competition had existed from the very beginning of the journey. Each of us prided ourselves on our flair for camp cooking. Whether consciously or otherwise, we strove to outdo the meal of the previous evening. Understandably, the stakes fluctuated in accordance with the ease of resupplying ingredients and the available cookware. Yet, once the kerosene stove was installed, culinary standards worthy of a plush hotel were quickly established. And woe betide the man who dished up mediocrity. His labours would count for little in the eyes of his companions, whose utterances of 'Thanks, mate' would have an unmistakable edge of scorn about them. Only in the case of inclement weather could he expect any sort of leniency.

The cook trod a fine line, feeling the watchful eyes of his companions on his every move. He had to interpret the mood on board on the particular evening and pick the right staple – potatoes, rice, pasta, beans, or perhaps a combination of two of them. And he knew that he was teetering on that line if one of his companions should offer to lend him a hand. Failure or success was judged in regard to the amount of food as well. No one ever refused seconds. And by some unspoken decree, the amount served up a second time needed to be at least equal to what had been served up the first time around. Thirds was optional, but viewed favourably.

Our appetites grew as the journey progressed. In opposition to the constant discomfort of being wet, cold and stinky, stuffing our faces became one of the chief pleasures of the day. And small wonder. Coping with eight hours of rowing a day demanded a generous input of fuel. Our muscles were continuing to bulk up. I had never in my life been as big in the arms and across my shoulders. Usually my physique was a slim one. I'd expected to make it home looking like a rake. Consistent with all my previously incorrect suppositions about the Amazon River, six months earlier I had visualised us relying on latent hunting instincts to get food during certain stages of the journey. The reality had proven much more palatable!

The disease threat was less of a myth. Fortunately, however, there had been no repeat of the dysentery episode of Corire. In fact, we had enjoyed sterling digestinal health ever since. We attributed this to our isolation in a boat floating down such a wide river. For the most part, diseases were a land issue. The ritual of bleaching everything we drank had continued, but at this stage, any nasties in the water were probably diluted by the sheer volume of the river.

Not by any stretch of the imagination did we rely solely on avoiding exposure to stomach bugs. We also employed a certain drug to avoid getting sick. It was no performance enhancer, but it did supply peace of mind. Experience had told us that 'rotten egg burps' were the surest early-warning sign that all was not well down below. The gas brought up was so putrid as to make the belcher feel like bringing up his last meal.

When the burps hit, we immediately popped a type of antibiotic tablet known as 'Flagyll'. Its effect on the gut was like intestinal carpet bombing: it killed everything without discrimination; all the good bacteria died as well as all the bad. Not surprisingly, a dose of Flagyll temporarily wrecked the gut's ability to digest efficiently, as there are many organisms in the human intestine that assist in breaking down food.

Colin had some advice on how to counter their loss: 'I remember my outdoor education teacher at high school saying that the quickest way to get back the good bacteria is to eat a mouthful of dirt.'

I looked at the colour of the river. We probably got a mouthful of dirt with every glass of Amazon water anyway.

Ultimately, we didn't care. Healthy digestion was something we could happily put on hold for a while. For now, the most important thing was not to be in a constant state of needing to empty our bowels. I became more 'regular' than I'd ever been. I could just about tell the time by my bowel movements. Much of the reason for this no doubt lay in the rigid scheduling of our existence. And although we put a lot of effort into making new and interesting meals, our systems were dealing with a limited selection of raw ingredients.

When the urge came, there was little time to react. From the moment I felt that first push, I was lucky if I could hold it in for more than a minute. Intriguingly, this was the case for all three of us (truly the Amazon had moulded our bodies in some peculiar ways). There was never enough time for us to reach land and at least be semi-civilised in our management of bodily waste. Because of the curve of the raft's pontoon, performing the act while onboard could only be done through taking up an awkward position. Trial and error had taught us the most economic contortion, but keeping one's balance still required a fair amount of concentration. We eliminated the need for toilet paper – in choppy conditions, the river essentially performed the role of a bidet.

On the fourth morning out of Manaus, Colin was in the river having his morning swim when the urge to evacuate struck Scott and me simultaneously.

'Colin, you're about to have some company!' Scott called out.

The Canadian didn't have enough time to climb back aboard the raft before we were forced to let nature take its course. Fully aware of the threat of rogue faeces, Colin maintained a safe distance.

Having so much spare time on our hands, it was inevitable that we would take a cursory interest in the fate of our turds. Sometimes they sank. Sometimes they floated. Sometimes they disappeared only to reappear a short while later. Depending on the influence of the wind on the raft, they either drifted ahead of us or lagged behind. Swirls and micro-currents, which had no effect on the raft, could carry them off in any one of a multitude of directions.

Colin waited about 20 metres away from *Los Labios.*

'Is the coast clear?' he asked after a few minutes had passed.

Scott and I surveyed the water. 'Yep, all clear,' we said.

Colin swam to the side of the boat, grabbed hold of the perimeter rope and bobbed there while he caught his breath. Suddenly, Scott was pointing to the water a couple of metres behind Colin's head.

'Look out – behind you!'

Two mischievous turds had resurfaced and – cue *Jaws* attack theme – were rapidly moving straight for him.

'Aaargh!'

Colin let go of the rope and ducked underwater as Scott and I erupted with laughter. Although I am loath to admit it, toilet humour played a prominent role in maintaining our sanity during the long, cramped days aboard *Los Labios.*

However, serious conversations also functioned as a pressure-release valve. Colin and I took pleasure in locking horns in intellectual debate. While neither of us could profess to be a specialist in any particular field of knowledge, we fancied we had excellent general knowledge. It was rare that one of us lacked an opinion on some contentious topic, and even rarer that we shared that same opinion. Neither of us would ever budge from our point of view, even if something the other one said appealed to our sense of logic. Rather than concede a point, we would cling even more fiercely to our original argument.

'I read it in a book' was a favourite line of mine if I wanted to dig in my heels or cast a seed of doubt in Colin's mind. More often than not, though, the opinions we defended were based on anything but what we had read. For his part, Scott would look on quietly, finding contentedness simply in smoking the tobacco pipe he had bought in Iquitos.

Inevitably, our stubbornness during some of these debates caused periods of tension between us. But it could only ever reach a threshold level of snide remarks, rebuttals and vicious sarcasm before attitudes softened. Then both of us would grasp the opportunity to defuse the tension. In this way, I think, we avoided the more serious confrontations that might have occurred if the frustrations created by our constant close proximity to each other had been stifled.

We found opportunities to release the pressures of cabin fever without needing to go to shore. As described earlier, the Amazon claims many prizes from the jungle that lines its banks. Combine this with all the forest debris washed into it from countless tributaries and the river rates alongside the Ganges as a carrier of the dead.

For the motorboats, speeding upstream and downstream at night was an exercise fraught with risk. Tree trunks up to a few metres in diameter, floating just below the surface like icebergs, could make a mess of their hulls. We, on the other hand, never shied from an interlude with a floating tree trunk. Some were so broad that you could run the length of them without them moving in the slightest. They were a great opportunity to stretch the legs. They also offered a chance to take time out from rowing and keep moving at a good pace. Because so much of its mass floated below the river surface, a tree trunk caught the fastest currents. Especially in blowy or choppy conditions, tying up to a massive hunk of dead wood saved us the hassle of preparing the dugout for action.

The Amazon is a carrier of life also. Interestingly, even

land organisms can find a place to live in the middle of the world's largest river. The Amazon is noted for its 'floating islands', aggregates of dead organic matter that create a foundation for blady grasses to grow tall and thick. Floating islands develop as tiny ecosystems in their own right, homes to a variety of insects and even small mammals.

The largest island we saw was about 30 metres in diameter. Most had a semi-solid surface, although we discovered the hard way that they could not support the weight of a human. Standing in the same spot for more than a moment was not a good idea.

It wasn't just vegetation that the river collected. Ever since our disastrous flip on the Apurimac, it had claimed a constant trickle of our belongings too. Rough conditions occasionally ripped something loose from where it had been hastily strapped onto the balsa wings together with the big dry bags. My greatest fear was that during a night-time storm, the constant bashing would snap off a wing altogether.

As cautious as we were, items still seemed to vanish, as though snatched away from under our noses while we weren't looking. We were down to one life jacket, two of our makeshift cushions/pillows having slipped over the side undetected a few weeks earlier. Clothes, washed and carefully laid out to dry, would invariably slide into the water. Sometimes these, too, exited our lives unnoticed. At other times, we would see a piece of clothing fall overboard, only to watch helplessly as it sank before we could row back to retrieve it.

Hardest of all to keep in our possession were eating utensils. But the fate of these was never a mystery. They went to the muddy bottom of the Amazon directly from our fingertips. It always happened post-meal. To avoid leftovers festering (a process accelerated by the tropical climate), each man was expected to rinse off his plate and cutlery when he'd finished eating. 'Ah, shit!' or 'Bloody hell!' announced immediately after a meal, and followed by a sheepish grin from the utterer, indicated that another bowl, plate, mug, fork, spoon, or even a saucepan, had gone to the river bottom.

The first few occasions were blamed on good old-fashioned carelessness. The culprit received pointed glares from his companions and condemned himself to an inferior substitute for that utensil until a replacement could be bought in the next town. Pretty soon, though, all three of us had notched up a tally of losses. Even being aware of the emerging trend failed to bring down the rate of loss. It became laughable. No one understood how it could possibly happen. However, because there seemed no reasonable explanation for it, we persisted with this method of rinsing. And we kept losing our utensils.

As with the many other bits and pieces that were gone forever, it seemed the river took them consciously, as though it collected a tax or toll for our passage.

The Negro River is one of several tributaries of the Amazon that individually would dwarf the largest rivers on several continents. Some 800 kilometres from Manaus, the Tapajós River flows in from the south, having done its bit to drain the immense tract of jungle that makes up central Brazil. Just before it meets the Amazon, the width of the Tapajós is an incredible seven kilometres.

At the confluence, we hit the city of Santarém. Even though there were still another 800 kilometres to the ocean, the harbour of Santarém looked like that of a respectable sea port. In 1682, Jesuit missionaries founded a monastery there and the Portuguese built a fort. Both powers were seeking, each in its own fashion, to gain control of the same area. The three cities – Belém, Santarém and Manaus – are still the key points of life on the Amazon, all marker flags that civilised man has placed at strategic points in that scarcely inhabited green expanse.

There is a chapter in the history of Santarém that gives it a special position in the Amazon story. When the American Civil War ended, it left 200 inhabitants of a small Dixie town feeling disappointed and bitter. With their slaves and implements they sailed to Santarém and settled there. These colonists have been absorbed into the local population, although traces of their influence can still be seen. Their descendants speak Portuguese and do not understand English. It is, in fact, the only case of an Anglo-Saxon colony letting itself be absorbed into a community into which it has settled. We spent a day in Santarém, kicking back on a sandy beach akin to some of Queensland's finest. There were beer bars with palm-thatched roofs, deck chairs, banana lounges, sun umbrellas and plenty of bikini-clad women. The Amazon was starting to live up to her nickname of 'inland sea'.

We catapulted out of Santarém on the back of a tailwind. None of us could believe it. It was the first we had encountered since our rafting voyage had begun. Headwinds had plagued us on an almost daily basis since the lower Apurimac. The tailwind set the tone of travel for the next few days. We covered up to 150 kilometres in a 24-hour period, the best rate of travel we had known to date.

But to think even for a moment that we had finally cracked this Amazon thing was a case of wishful thinking on our part. A day of sitting and relaxing on a beach in Santarém had done little to cleanse us of the discomfort and hardship that had aggregated every day we spent rowing around the clock. The cramped conditions and the steadily worsening weather were sucking the spirit out of us. Each of us suffered from niggling muscle strains and aching ligaments. The patch of skin behind our genitals was chafed red raw because of the prolonged friction between shiny rubber and the rower's sweaty underwear. We had already rowed a boat specifically designed for whitewater some 5500 kilometres. There seemed more than a touch of the eccentric in our ambition.

After everything else that had happened, we should have known better than to think the Amazon was going to let us finish quickly and easily. One last barrier separated us from the Atlantic.

EIGHTEEN
THE DELTA

19 January 2000 (day 129):
420 kilometres to the Atlantic

The Amazon delta begins some 400 kilometres from the ocean. It flanges out into a complex network of channels and islands. Biggest of these islands is one called Marajó, which is greater in area than the Netherlands. The mouth of the river straddles the Equator, overhanging it by more than 100 kilometres on either side.

One particular channel, known as the Gurupá Canal, slips between Marajó and the southern mainland shore. It carries one-eighth of the Amazon's flow south to join with the Tocantins River and several other rivers. This merging creates a river named the Pará, which flows west to the Atlantic.

There is heated debate as to whether the Gurupá–Pará system may be regarded as a branch of the Amazon. If so, then the Amazon is 80 kilometres longer than the Nile and therefore becomes the longest river on Earth. Hydrographers remain divided on the issue.

We decided to follow in the paddle strokes of Kane and Chmielinski, and go south. Amazon or not, we wanted to see those water molecules on Mismi and Quehishua through their longest course to the sea. Heading via the northern route didn't seem to be a good idea, in any case. We knew that twice a day, big waves swept upriver from the Atlantic. These *pororocas* can be up to two metres in height and are created by the bottlenecking effect of the delta. Water rushing in with the flooding tide gets funnelled by the steadily narrowing channels. Typically, the Amazon delta region is noted for having some of the most powerful tides on the planet.

By all accounts, a *pororoca* could easily flip us over. Thankfully, the southern side of the delta was free of them. Still, we were not prepared for the confusion caused by the Amazon delta.

As I squinted hard against the sun, glare coming off the glossy tourist map we'd bought in Manaus hurt my eyes nearly as much as its apparent uselessness had tried our patience.

'That's an island,' I said, gesturing with an impatient nod towards the right-hand shore.

Colin dismissed the notion.

'How can it be?' he scoffed. 'This passage here can't be anything but that one there.' As he tapped hard at a spot of blue print, then pointed towards a gap in the left-hand shore, I felt my own colour rising.

'Come on! Check the bloody compass.'

A few hours earlier, Colin had dropped my only pair of sunglasses over the side of the boat. I'd had them with me the entire journey to that point, and had treasured them much more than any other piece of equipment. In the same amount of time, the Canadian had managed to lose a total of *seven* pairs. It was an honest accident that had seen mine lost, but I was not about to lose this argument as well.

As usual, neither of us backed down. Soon, however, it became clear that winning this argument was irrelevant. We were lost in a maze; even the water seemed unsure of how to reach the ocean.

Twisting and turning uncertainly around islands that should not have been there, I dwelt on how naive we'd been to believe that a $5 map would do the job. Up to this point, we had travelled 5000 kilometres using nothing more detailed than a sketch diagram in Kane's book and the above-mentioned tourist map. At no point, except for at the major towns, had we known our positioning. 'Somewhere on the Amazon' had always been the adequate summation.

Saying we were 'somewhere in the delta' didn't quite have the same ring of inconsequence about it, namely because if we found ourselves in the wrong spot, we could end up getting steamrolled by a *pororoca*. But our situation was far from hopeless. All we needed to do was trust our compass and take the channels running south or south-west. In other words, we just had to take the right-hand option every time. Ultimately, this strategy would bring us to the Gurupá Canal.

The feeling of disorientation was offset by the jungle crowding in from both sides of these narrow channels. Never had it looked so untouched. Never had the birdsong sounded so passionate. Stilted houses clung to the shore, nestled into attractive palm groves. A colourful fleet of wooden boats chugged happily up and down the waterways, each with its own personality. Suddenly, I was back in the bathtub of my childhood, playing with goofy-faced toy boats. It seemed that in this place, frustration could dissolve entirely into captivation.

Every twelve hours, we were stopped by the flooding tide and forced to wait for six hours until the ebbing tide returned. Baffled delta folk descended on us and tried to make sense of what they were seeing. Often this meant hours of unashamed staring.

With my background in conservation, I had taken more than a passing interest in the scope of deforestation along the banks of the Amazon. From Atalaya, the vegetation had alternated between obvious regrowth and patches of what might have been the original jungle. More likely, though, such patches were actually second-, third-, perhaps up to tenth-growth forest. The Amazon's timber has been harvested for over four centuries and, understandably, the trees along the bank were easiest to get at and no doubt were first to bow to the axes and saws.

It seemed odd then that the only visible signs of active tree felling and lumber processing were to be seen in the delta, where the jungle appeared barely touched. We passed timber mills at regular intervals. Many supported tiny settlements of just ten people. The little wooden tugboats delivered a few logs at a time, usually ones with a wide girth.

The machinery used for processing was old, decades old. Long belts clattered unguarded between drivewheels. I wondered how many limbs they had claimed over the years. Overexploiting the local jungle was simply impossible, given the level of technology on display. Indeed, it looked as though the communities had not even made a dent in the jungle. At these modest mills, it took a lot of manual labour and time to convert each log into planks.

On most evenings, a bigger picture was revealed. The sky told the story of what was happening in Brazil's forests on a much larger scale. We had enjoyed magnificent sunsets all the way down the flat Amazon. The blaze of colours at dusk had often moved us to silent awe. That they were an almost nightly occurrence was not a natural wonder but a product of man. A haze of smoke hangs over much of the Amazon basin and emanates from the fires that burn what is left of the jungle after clear-cut logging operators have stripped away all the useable timber.

Fire clears the way for pasture, on which beef cattle are fattened. But the tragedy doesn't end there. Grazing is possible for one or perhaps two seasons, then, even the grass dies. Typically, rainforest soils are poor in nutrients. It is the recycling of dead plant and animal matter, the decaying layers of humus, that sustains the abundance of life. After the forest is gone, the humus is not replenished. When it is used up, the earth has nothing left to offer plants. Exposed to the sun, these clay soils are baked into hardened wastelands.

As we advanced on the Atlantic, the wet season advanced too. The narrow channels offered us protection from the wild weather. The fetch was too small for anything but very gentle swells to form, and often, the forest blocked the wind out altogether.

When the Gurupá Canal emptied into the Pará River, that protection came to an end. The Pará was immense. It looked not like a river, but like a lake. Interestingly, the few islands scattered through its upper reaches were not low-lying alluvial. They were dome-shaped or plateaus rimmed by sheer rock faces.

Tidal action now presented us with twelve hours of motionless time to kill every day. The sense of feeling restricted remained a fact of life. We were boxed in by the often inpenetrable rainforest.

The chess matches continued. Despite Scott's initial confidence, he had won just a handful of games. Colin and I were vying for the crown – only a few victories separated us. The intensity with which we played each other grew; as time went on, we hated defeat more and more. Soon we were taking up to ten minutes to make one move and sweating as hard as we did at the oars.

The intellectual stoushes in which we had engaged each other down much of the river seldom saw a victor so, instead, both of us viewed winning the subsequent chess game as validation of the theory we had championed during the last debate. In the heat of mental struggle, supremacy on the chessboard could seem as important as getting to the end of the river.

Maybe the intensity with which I entered into both a debate and a game of chess was all about exercising mental grit, determination and toughness. It wasn't about vanity or proving I was smarter than Colin, but about demonstrating a strength of resolve that would spur me on to the conclusion of this journey.

Our third night on the Pará was thankfully dry but intermittently gusty, and the boat had alternately rocked and glided through the water. As per usual, it was not the sort of rocking that soothed one to sleep. Balancing on the pontoon was a hard thing at the best of times. On *Los Labios*, falling out of bed meant a rude dip, and perhaps coming face to face with all the beasts that rose from the depths every night to peer at us through evil eyes.

Groaning, I sat up and let the breeze swirl under my heavy eyelids. A light beacon on the near shore marked dangerous sand bars for the large freight vessels. Probably for economic reasons, it had been set to flash just once every 30 seconds. It illuminated how only sluggish forward movement was possible against the wind that caught our very non-aerodynamic bulk. From behind, the busy surface water of the ebbing tide caught up, overtook us and sped onwards without sympathy.

Colin was battling with the oars and I could see he was glad of company. It got like that during an early-morning rowing shift. The other two men were so close by, but their slumber invited an air of loneliness. I think it stemmed from an obligation to stave off weariness and be awake, if not alert, during those three hours. The states of waking and sleeping are so far removed from each other.

In the morning we knew it was time to make a 'row for it', across the widening immensity of the Pará. Soon we'd be rounding the last almighty bend and the Amazon's water could then scurry in a straight line towards the Atlantic. That also meant unimpeded headwinds, direct from the Atlantic. Thoughts of the enormous swells driven by them scared the hell out of me.

As it was, crossing at this stage of the Pará made me nervous also. We guessed the distance to the land we could see at about six or seven kilometres. The tide would turn in two hours. Recent mornings had been calm but the wind was rarely absent for very long. A lot could go wrong out in the middle of a seven-kilometre-wide river. During the fight to gain purchase on the water, an oar might break, and threading the spare into the oar-lock as the raft propped and dipped violently would be nearly impossible. What if the broken oar sheared clean in half and the crucial paddle got swept away? Would whoever dived after it be able to swim back against the rushing tide, back to a raft that was out of control and held up by the wind? And if that scenario wasn't grim enough, there was also the possibility that if we were angled badly, a particularly large swell might tip us right over.

We crossed just in time. No sooner had we reached the other side than the wind began to howl upriver. We pulled the raft up on the shore to wait out the tide, keeping ourselves entertained by bodysurfing the incoming breakers.

A hut perched on the higher ground 50 metres back from the riverbank. The potbellied owner came to investigate. He lived alone and caught freshwater shrimp. He was a man of few words and didn't stay long before wandering off to check his pots.

We dozed, read or wrote in our diaries. Several hours passed, then an old man came to sit at the end of the raft. A raised scar cut the length of his face. I put down my book and said hello. The man only nodded. He did not smile, he just looked at us and around the raft. It was a style of interaction not unknown to us. After a few minutes he spoke.

'Do not go on the river at night.' Seeing a fire blazing in his rheumy dark eyes, I knew I wasn't going to like the reason why. '*Peeraches com heeflez*,' he said in a hushed tone.

They were new words to us. 'Something' *with* 'something'. We shrugged our shoulders and asked him to repeat the statement. Instead, the old man raised both hands to make the motion of shooting a rifle. Then we understood. 'Pirates with rifles.'

'It is a problem here,' he added.

It triggered an instant discussion between Colin, Scott and myself. Colin had once heard that the north-west coast of South America was a hotspot for boat piracy. We were not too far away from the Caribbean, the past haunt of men such as Blackbeard. As we talked, the old man quietly got up and left.

There was no improvement in the weather when the

tide turned in our favour. Going anywhere that evening was out of the question, in any case. We didn't see the old man again. I wondered if he was the ghost of someone killed by the pirates, if not a dead buccaneer himself.

The shrimp catcher invited us to watch television with him. For bedding, he could only offer his wooden floor. There was just one hammock, in which he slept himself. I didn't mind at all. After weeks of trying to sleep on a rocking, rain-soaked raft, the dry, warm and motionless wooden floor of the hut felt like a four-poster bed.

Rowing conditions were marginal next morning. It took two hours to fight our way a few kilometres. Then the oar shaft broke.

Since the days of our first bamboo creations on the lower Apurimac, we had broken a total of five oar shafts. Bamboo stems were naturally a little crooked, causing the oar handle to skew in the hand. In terms of durability, they had also been found wanting. Each of those original shafts had lasted only a couple of days. The next set had proven themselves both the hardest-wearing and the straightest. They had been made from a long narrow balsa trunk Scott found washed up on the beach. After a month of faithful service, the constant friction had worn them down to a critical breaking point. Beyond the balsa, we'd turned to harvesting saplings from the forest. With no shortage of species to select from, finding ones with a rigid stem never took long. Our policy with a broken oar shaft was to effect immediate repairs and avoid being caught without a spare. The nearest beach for our pitstop was littered with driftwood. The forest behind appeared uninhabited. We quickly located a replacement shaft and began the refit.

Two young men appeared. They sat down on a fallen tree to watch the bizarre spectacle. When we asked where they lived, one pointed through the trees to a hut. I was surprised. It had been invisible until now. A teenage girl arrived, followed by an elderly, yet lithe, woman. More and more people arrived, until there was a group of ten on the beach. They represented two families. One family, the la Rochas, lived in the hut. The de Silvas were their old neighbours who had moved to Belém some years back. They were back visiting for the weekend.

There was no hint of wariness or suspicion towards us; the mood was jovial and very welcoming. Fruit was hastily gathered from the jungle for an impromptu beach party. Anna la Rocha, a seventeen-year-old beauty, showed us how to eat the fruit of the cocoa tree. She split open the yellow fist-sized pod. The cocoa beans inside were covered in a gluttinous white slime. She put one in her mouth, sucked off the slime then spat out the bean. Ever the adventurer, Colin tried chewing his bean. He quickly spat it out.

'Yuck! How do they make a Sublime out of that?'

I tried some out of curiosity and wondered the same thing. Whoever discovered that you could make something as tasty as chocolate from the cocoa bean must have been a very patient and determined person.

As relaxed as these people made me feel, I still had the scar-faced man's warning playing over and over in my mind. I asked about pirates. The smiling faces suddenly turned grim.

'Oh, yes, yes, there are pirates on the river at night.'

'They come from Belém,' added someone else.

Gus de Silva told the story of two foreigners who were recent victims of the pirates. One of them was an Australian. 'They were lucky,' Gus said. 'The pirates took their boat and told them to jump overboard. They lost everything but they are alive.'

We spent the rest of the day and that night with the two families, during which time every aspect of riverside life was on display. We had spent up to a week in several of the Amazon's cities, towns and villages. But never had we stayed more than a few hours with the isolated residents of the river, the lonely huts home to families and individuals who led a life of relative seclusion. These were the people closest to the natural essence of the Amazon. For the most part, they were self-sufficient and wise in the ways of reaping the abundance from all around them.

Despite having a foam mattress to sleep on, I tossed and turned most of the night. Tides and inclement weather had already slowed our progress to a crawl. The addition of pirates into the equation set back our estimated finishing date even further and could well mean we didn't finish at all.

Every day, the natural sequence of the tides got shifted forwards by about an hour with the progression of the lunar cycle. Currently, one of the two daily flooding tides happened between 8 p.m. and 2 a.m. This was also the prime tide because night usually brought much gentler headwinds than the day did.

How things had changed. We'd gone from covering up to 150 kilometres per day pre-delta to now barely managing 20 a day. Our passage down the last 5000 kilometres had been relatively carefree. Now, anxieties similar to those caused by the Apurimac's rapids and the cloud forest's guerrillas were breeding. But there was a vital difference between then and now: here in the delta, the threats posed by man and nature were operating in sync.

The Barcarena Canal disgorged us into the Capim River, 20 kilometres from where it met the Pará. On the far side, the hazy skyline of Belém resembled Manhattan.

Closer inspection revealed the poverty in this city of

2,000,000 people. The waterfront district we saw first was a succession of poorly maintained piers and rundown warehouses. None of the vessels moored in the area could boast a better state of repair.

As we rowed past one of the most neglected industrial properties, I noticed a man wandering among the concrete rubble and scrap metal. He was completely naked, with a nest of hair and a long beard. The yard was clearly his domain. While I looked on, the man walked to the water's edge, put one foot up on a wooden post and defecated. All in all, it didn't require much imagination to see this place as home to river pirates.

We needed to find a safe haven for the raft. Colin suggested we try our luck at the Belém yacht club. Given our proximity to the sea and the city's size, he predicted a good representation of international sailboats. From his own sailing experiences, he knew wealthy yacht owners were partial to lavishing interest and hospitality on young adventure seekers. It didn't take long to find the club. And even less time to discover that Colin's hunch was right.

Our benefactors were Spaniards on board a 50-foot ketch, a veritable Rolls-Royce compared with almost every other boat we'd laid eyes on over the past two months. The crew of four was part of a millennium project commissioned by the Spanish Government. The skipper of the ketch, a veteran mariner named Eugenio, invited us to dinner and to sleep in comfortable beds. Also on board were two men named José and one called Marc. The two Josés were both professional divers from Málaga. Marc was a journalist and radio personality from Barcelona. We drank wine and shared stories well into the evening.

The Spanish project involved humanitarian visits to several destinations in the Caribbean and South America. They had just returned from a cultural exchange with indigenous tribes along the Xingu River, a major Amazon tributary draining the little-known region of Mato Grosso in central Brazil. One of the Josés had a passion for the customs of Xingu Indians. He believed the theory that there are tribes living in the remotest and most inaccessible valleys of Mato Grosso that are yet to have contact with the outside world.

Belém represented a last chance to run errands. We booked tickets for a bus to Rio de Janeiro and warned the few media outlets who were tracking our progress that the end was just a few days away. Hearts beat quickly, breaths were held when Scott and I went to withdraw cash from an ATM. We didn't know how much credit remained on our Visa cards, only that if 'insufficient funds' had flashed on the screen, it would have not been a shock. But the transactions went through and we could pay for the bus tickets.

The Spaniards were staying put in Belém for two more weeks and happily agreed to mind three of the four big dry bags until we returned to the town. To cut down on weight even further and reduce wind resistance, we cut the wings off the rowing frame. We took with us just one tent and a single set of clothes.

Before leaving Belém we studied Eugenio's navigational charts of the Pará River's final 100 kilometres. We drew a mud map of the canals which threaded their way like worm tunnels through a strip of land bordering the main river. The less we exposed ourselves to the main river, the better. Unfortunately, the canals were the ideal haunt for pirates. They were within easy striking distance of the city and provided the opportunity to ambush and then make a discreet getaway from any authorities patrolling the area.

At low tide that evening, we sought a place to camp. It was no easy task finding a clear patch of ground unlikely to be submerged when the water level reached its highest.

Eventually, we came to a concrete boat ramp. The higher ground above it was occupied by a resort of some description. An expanse of well-manicured lawn stretched in front of modern eco-designed apartments.

Scott offered to go up and ask for permission to pitch our tent on the grass. A few minutes later, he called back down: 'Can one of you blokes come up here? I can't understand what this guy's saying.'

I walked up the ramp to stand beside Scott. A man, probably the caretaker, was standing in the middle of the lawn brandishing a shotgun.

'I think the message is pretty clear,' I said. 'He doesn't want us to stay.'

The caretaker looked nervous. Anything Scott or I said only incited a waving of the shotgun barrel.

'Okay. We're going.'

As we rowed away, Scott interpreted the situation correctly: 'Everyone's scared shitless of the pirates.'

By some strange meandering effect of the canals, the flooding tide was actually pushing us in the direction we wanted to go. With no option but to tie up to shore and sit in the boat, we reasoned that the risk in continuing to row was equal to that of staying put. We decided to go all night, or at least as long as the current was in our favour.

A gentle breeze rustled the canopy foliage, which in turn muffled the sound of oars breaking the water's surface. There was no moon. With the lantern killed, *Los Labios* blended into the darkness. The loudest noises came from someone slapping a mosquito.

The next day passed without incident. The day following that one brought us to the town of Vigia. Vigia was a reminder of just how long ago the Portuguese settled what is now Brazil. A stone church dated to the middle of the sixteenth century. In a place where rock is in short supply, the church stood out as very unusual. The rock was volcanic, far from ideal for a mason to work with, but was no doubt the material that had been nearest to hand. I imagined the church had brought comfort to the first settlers, who probably regarded the jungle of the Amazon delta as hell compared with the 'civilised' world of Europe.

Being in Vigia confirmed to us just how close we were to the sea. Its economy was based on fishing. The trawler hulls were made of iron, not wood, their bows high and pointed, designed to cut through the big swells on both the lower Pará and the ocean itself.

A man beckoned to us from one of the fishing boats. Rico and his three brothers operated the vessel and split the profit according to their ages. In his early twenties, Rico was the youngest. He asked for our saucepan and filled it with half-a-dozen chunks of raw fish. Then he gestured that we should boil them. I was about to scoop up water from over the side, as usual, when Rico stopped me. 'Cholera,' he said.

At low tide, Vigia's harbour was a cesspit. The mud below the harbour wall was littered with broken bottles, rusty oil drums and sludge. Vultures fought for the guts and heads tossed there by fishermen cleaning their catch.

It was Friday evening, and Rico wanted to show us the Vigia nightlife. He arranged for some other fishermen to watch the raft, then shepherded us through a maze of streets and sodden walkways to his stilted cottage. There he outfitted us in clothing more suitable for partying than the set of festering rags each of us had worn since Belém.

It was obvious that, in Brazil, if you couldn't dance, you were at risk of being a social outcast. Being westerners, we had an excuse. Everybody knew that westerners couldn't dance, it wasn't our fault.

A style called Brega was most popular during our time in the country. It was straight from the ranks of the lambada style that had created such uproar in the west during the 1980s. And yet, I could be forgiven for thinking that, here in Brazil, sex and dancing were considered mutually exclusive. On countless occasions, I had watched two complete strangers come together, lock hips, clutch buttocks, and grind their loins into each other for the duration of a song. At the end of it, they thanked each other and parted ways.

Things were no different in Vigia. Also no different was the way that we westerners went about mutilating the sensual art form that is the Brega. Executed properly, the dancers writhed and slithered as one. We, however, trod on toes, moved our hips without any shred of rhythm and usually got embarrassingly aroused before the song was even half over.

Vigia's waterfront precinct bustled with revellers. Outside the cities especially, nightlife wasn't confined to bars, discos and other venues. Wherever possible, Brazilians drank and danced in the open air. Whether you bought your beer in a bar or from one of numerous stalls selling it on the street, you were free to drink it anywhere you pleased. Partying in the street didn't just happen at New Year and during the national three-week-long Carnivale extravaganza, it was a *nightly* event.

The weather next day mirrored our hangovers. Conditions even in the sheltered Vigia Canal were rough. The wide-open Pará must have been horrendous. We decided, unanimously, to stay put. Impatience could bring us undone. We rowed *Los Labios* from the harbour up a narrow waterway servicing Rico's neighbourhood and moored her at the back of his house. After all, 148 days had passed since the beginning of our journey. We could wait one more.

NINETEEN
THE ATLANTIC

8 February 2000 (day 148):
20 kilometres to the Atlantic

On the morning of our third day in Vigia, the sky was still overcast and a light drizzle fell. The wind seemed to be dying down, however. At the harbour, I asked a recently returned fishing crew what the conditions were like. They said there was only a low swell on the main river.

The wind died further, but we had to wait another two hours for the tide to reach its highest point. I ground my teeth impatiently. From experience, calm weather was typically short-lived. Our window of opportunity might only be a matter of hours. Rico was adamant that the weather would soon get worse; however, we suspected he did not say this from an innate ability to read local weather patterns as much as from a desire for us to stay longer. For all his generosity and kindness, I had sensed that Rico regarded our staying in his house as a means of his gaining community respect.

We set off before the water level had peaked, rowing against a flooding tide that grew steadily weaker. We stroked the oars with a real sense of urgency. The two non-rowers were unable to relax. They were frustrated by their helplessness and excited by the nearness of journey's end. According to Eugenio's charts, there were no other side channels or inlets between the outflow of the Vigia Canal and the mouth of the river. Over the last 20 kilometres to Ponte Taipu we would be completely exposed. I felt like Jack trying to snatch the golden egg–laying goose before the giant woke up.

After half an hour of rowing, we exchanged the flat waters of the Vigia Canal for the undulating expanse of the main river. It seemed that the latter was incapable of ever being completely at peace. Its far shore, the island of Marajó, lay over the horizon. The only thing to indicate that we were still on a river was the absence of salt in the water.

The conversation was given over to speculating on what could go wrong at this stage. So many times in the past, it had seemed that the river was capable of conscious action. Was the Amazon plotting to undo us right at the very last? I think we hoped that by verbalising our fears in great detail, we made them less likely to come true.

One fear in particular had occupied a corner of my mind for a number of weeks. I couldn't recall whether it stemmed from a rumour I'd heard or was a scenario I'd conjured up myself. It involved a combination of strong current, a ferocious ebbing tide and irresistible tailwind sweeping *Los Labios* far out to sea. The rushing water would make the rips on an Australian beach appear tame. It was well known to us that the Amazon discharges a fan of freshwater up to 200 kilometres into the Atlantic. I pictured crazy ocean currents coming into play and hindering our most frenzied efforts to get back to the coast. I envisaged us dead of thirst before we managed to do so. There was a diabolical irony in such a scenario.

Colin claimed that it was very unlikely to happen, but, let's face it, getting shot at by guerrillas had been unlikely too.

'We could try for the west coast of Africa,' joked Scott. 'Bet no one's tried rowing a rubber boat that far.'

A story from Colin's repertoire of famous sailing mishaps and subsequent feats of survival certainly didn't put my mind at rest.

'Ever heard of Steven Callahan?'

I said I hadn't.

'When his yacht sank, he floated around the Atlantic for 76 days in an inflatable life raft until he got rescued.'

'He must have looked like shit,' Scott observed.

'He caught seagulls and ate them raw.'

Colin seemed almost inspired. I was horrified. The ocean spooked me. Our voyage along an inland sea was more than enough.

Light rain fell throughout the afternoon. The wind gusted, creating patchy swells. Conditions seemed precariously balanced and capable of falling apart completely at a moment's notice. The outgoing tide remained sluggish. My fear of being swept out to sea was partially laid to rest.

We maintained a distance of at least a couple of hundred metres from shore. Any closer and the current slackened off too much. There was another good reason to stay so far out. If we got into the zone where the swells became breakers, things could get messy. Even if we managed to ride them in without getting flipped, there was no way we could row back out into the open river. At this stage of the game, the banks of the Amazon were like an exposed seashore.

At dusk, the tide turned on us. Through a miserable twilight, we pulled hard on the oars until we could fight it no more. A beach extended out from the edge of the mangroves. Landing there was pointless because it would soon be inundated by the rising water. We had no anchor, and nothing heavy enough to function as one. Fortunately, a scattering of fishing stakes gave us something even more secure. These sturdy wooden poles, driven into the river bottom, were used by locals throughout the delta as a means of setting nets and for tying up their dugouts while they fished.

As night fell, a strong easterly came, bringing with it rain and swell. Initially, the waves did not reach us. A sand bar, 100 metres further out, acted as a buffer, sheltering our position. But as the water level rose, the bar became less and less effective as a shield. Soon *Los Labios* was being rocked from bow to stern, as metre-high swells charged at her directly from the Atlantic. As luck would have it, we were just beyond the point at which they started breaking. The strain on the stake must have been much greater than normal. If it snapped, our fate didn't bear thinking about. We would be carried swiftly to the mangroves and thereupon pummelled by every wave that came.

Together, the rain, wind and pitching of the boat made it impossible to do anything except wait for morning. Even huddling under the plastic was a useless exercise. We had been drenched for most of the afternoon. As I shivered and shook, it seemed outrageous to think that the Equator was only 150 kilometres away. All the struggle and hardship of five months seemed epitomised by this moment. Eventually, I fell into exhausted sleep, oblivious to the raindrops splattering against the side of my face and in my ear.

'Wake up, guys! Check this out.'

It was Scott.

I opened my eyes. It was still dark, but the moon and stars had replaced the covering of clouds. Without moving, I gazed up at them. Almost a week had passed since I'd last seen a clear night sky. At first I thought this was the cause of Scott's excitement.

'Oh, my God!' This was Colin.

'Ben, do you see them?'

'The stars?'

'Hell, no.'

Then I looked down and did see them. The water was glowing green. Billions of phosphorescent algae had transformed the swells into something otherworldly. The swells sparkled with a clarity not seen since the Amazon's upper tributaries. I gasped. This was not the murky river we had spent the better part of three months rowing down.

Scott leant over, scooped up some water and put it to his lips. In the moonlight, I could see the South African beaming.

'It's salty,' he said.

EPILOGUE

When dawn came on 9 February 2000, we saw the light-house that had been marked on the sailing charts at Ponte Taipu. The structure was nothing more intricate than a steel pylon and barely poked above the mangrove tops. As a beacon for shipping, the lighthouse was out of service. For us, it signalled the end of a long voyage.

There was none of the imagined romance in this moment. I was not standing on a golden beach, squinting into a rising sun. And no salty breeze ruffled the curls of my hair.

Instead, the coffee-coloured water had returned with the ebbing tide. So, too, had the drizzle, as though only the briefest hint of a clear sky had been set aside for our midnight revelation. Muddy sand swallowed my feet to the ankles and the grit trapped beneath soggy clothes scraped against my skin. I had nothing dry to wear. I was cold. I was wet. And there was absolutely nothing I could do about it.

But none of this mattered. All I knew was triumph; everything else was numbed by this sensation, cast into irrelevance.

Several weeks earlier, in anticipation of this moment, we had bought cheap fabric and glue, then each of us had gone to work making our nation's flag. Now we tied one on each oar, just below the blade, and jammed the oars into the mud. We opened $2 bottles of champagne and sprayed each other like racing-car drivers on a victory podium.

We had expected it to feel like a moon landing (the bleakness of the grey mud flats at Ponte Taipu certainly helped foster that illusion). In any case, hoisting flags and guzzling champagne was the thing that explorers did. Because that was how I felt – an explorer. No, I had not gone anywhere uncharted in a geographical sense, but five months on the Amazon River had stirred emotions and senses in me that had previously been dormant.

I had surprised myself. If I could have known beforehand about several of the episodes that would come to pass, I would have expected myself to show far less resistance in the face of them. Well and truly, the borders of my comfort zone had been redrawn. For the first time in months, I felt safe when I looked to the future. Two-buck champagne was going straight to our heads, but it was the elixir of life that truly made us feel giddy. We had survived the Amazon. We were out of harm's way, and the rest of our lives from this moment onwards seemed like a wonderful gift.

As we watched our flags cracking in the wind and slapped one another on the back, each of us was caught up in our own retrospection. Yet on each man's lips there was a common thought: if we had known at the very beginning what we knew now, would we still have undertaken the journey we had? The answer was the same for all three of us

– *no*. Who in their right mind would willingly subject themselves to a succession of situations that had each tempted disaster and death? It was a strange feeling. Ignorance had made this journey possible for me. And, ultimately, it was igorance that had spawned so many revelations about myself.

Not for a moment did we neglect the role of good luck in our achievement. It was something we referred to many times as we reflected on the journey as a whole. Despite no shortage of pain and discomfort throughout, including the miserable conditions here at the end, we were very aware of how much worse it could easily have been.

There was one thing that luck could not take credit for: the natural accord that had existed between the three of us. Having said that, we knew that the camaraderie and good spirit we had enjoyed right to the very end was a rare thing. We felt privileged to have made a journey of this nature in each other's company. Conspicuous through its relative absence was the conflict that so readily goes hand in hand with the type of circumstances that prevail on such journeys. To any outsider, it must seem like a miracle. How could three men live together for three months, 24 hours a day, on a boat just four metres long and one-and-a-half metres wide without killing each other? We realised how much of an anomaly this was, and we were grateful for being atypical.

Arguments, standoffs, backstabbing and all round dummy-spitting had been an integral aspect of the 1986 Chmielinski–Kane expedition. Throughout history, in fact, few expeditions ever reached their conclusion without a good dose of animosity and hatred. Many have failed because of a fundamental difference of tactics or an acute clash of personalities. Often the disputes claim more limelight than the feat itself.

The significance of the harmony that still reigned

aboard *Los Labios* was not lost on us. We realised how much tougher, if not impossible, our voyage would have been otherwise. Internal conflict might have brought us unstuck as surely as any Senderista bullet, Amazonian predator or deadly jungle illness. As determined as a team is to maintain good relations and goodwill, adverse conditions are always likely to bring out the rawest edges in human interaction. For us to have avoided these was something of which we felt very proud.

The flying of three flags reminded me that I had grown up so far away from where these two companions of mine came from. Indeed, to look at our respective birthplaces on a globe, it would be hard to find three points spaced further apart. And then there were the gaps that separated us as individuals, the disparities in the lives we had led before coming together for the Amazon. There were few similarities in our upbringing or childhood interests. We were three men with vastly different backgrounds, characters, demeanours and careers.

In the final wash-up, all of this seemed nothing more than a curiosity. If anything, parading the individual flags of Australia, Canada and South Africa appeared to contradict the unity we had known.

'We're a Commonwealth team,' mused Scott aloud.

'Yes, we are,' Colin and I agreed.

I had greater pride in this than in my newfound status as the first Australian to trace the Amazon from source to sea.

Commonwealth – the literal meaning of the word could be used to describe us. (At the very least, it was a fitting irony given the everpresent precariousness of our finances.) Common fear, common pain, common wonder, common glory. With few exceptions, everything had been shared. Just how close-knit we were would become apparent a couple of weeks later. Each of us would comment on vague feelings of anxiety when it finally came time to part ways.

We rowed around Ponte Taipu and several kilometres up an estuary to reach the settlement of Saõ Caetano de Odivelas. There, we chose a spot on the bank of the estuary to disassemble our rowing set-up and deflate *Los Labios*. She had seen better days. Slime encrusted her underbelly. The pontoons sported several cigarette burns and a gaping hole in the outer layer of the floor bladder denoted where a mosquito coil had nearly caused a major breach. Kerosene spills had eaten away at the hypalon in several places but an overall dulling of *Los Labios*'s once bright, shiny red colour was the result of straight-out sun bleaching. The paddle blades were bent, the bimini fabric faded and brittle, and the waterlogged balsa had begun to disintegrate. Feeling both relieved and sentimental, I went for one last row. While the raft itself was bound to be used again, I knew we would never be able to replicate the bizarre additions we had made to her.

In more than one respect, Saõ Caetano was a dead-end town. The bored locals were far more impressed by all the bits and pieces of equipment we gave them than by the story we had to tell. The only things we took back with us on the bus to Belém were the raft and paddles.

We had to wait until we arrived back at the Belém yacht club to hear our first words of congratulations; the Spaniards lavished us with praise. That triumphant day ended with us sipping fine wine, then laying our heads on real pillows.

The bus trip from Belém to Rio de Janeiro lasted two whole days. It soon became clear that we had some readjusting ahead of us. Watching the forest zip by behind a wall of glass was so alien that it made me feel uneasy. On the river, our speed had barely eclipsed eight kilometres an hour. All of a sudden, we were travelling at over 100. At one point, we passed the mangled wreckage of another coach. An unmistakable hint of bile returned with the realisation that the wreck had been a bus from the same company. More than once on the way to Rio, I yearnt to be back aboard *Los Labios*, rowing into a squall.

Our arrival in Canada happened without any fanfare whatsoever. The face of the customs official at Calgary Airport lit up when he heard that we'd been in South America for six months. Given the red-eyed and grotty state we and our bags were in, he must have fancied his chances of busting three traffickers with a cache of illegal substances. He reached into the first dry bag and pulled out a handful of Colin's filthiest, most putrid-smelling underwear.

Word spread of our return. The three men whose plans the media had revealed six months earlier on the likely assumption that they would fail spectacularly, had survived. Articles ran in all the major newspapers across Canada. We made the front page in Colin's home city of Victoria and were interviewed on TV and radio. Colin and I even spent three days with a journalist from *Reader's Digest* who had been commissioned to tell our story. In Australia, feature articles appeared in several newspapers, and *60 Minutes* asked to see our footage with a view to airing a report.

And yet, despite all of this media attention and public back-slapping, the sobering reality was that we had little more than a few bucks between us. Within a week, Scott had returned to London and begged for his old job back.

For a brief moment, I reflected on the fateful neatness of it all, the way the exhaustion of our funds had coincided so perfectly with journey's end. But now my poverty was all-consuming. There was no time for me to sit down and start digesting all that had happened from a distant perspective. I landed a job as a waiter in a fancy restaurant on a ski hill near

Banff, earning $5.75 per hour plus tips. My torn and mouldy rags were exchanged for a suit and tie. Three months passed before I raised the cash to fly home to Adelaide.

Strangely enough, despite my mind retaining images and sensations as vivid as when I first knew them, the Amazon journey was for me fast relegated to another era. Consciously I looked for but found little relevance in it to my life back home in Australia. Everything about the journey had no parallel in the rest of my existence. Also, the 150 days and their countless incidents were inextricably tied together. The Amazon experience as a whole stood alone.

This seemed fitting but at the same time a great shame. I had gone to South America expecting to come back feeling changed in some way, able to apply some new attitude in the way I went about my day-to-day life. Yet, apart from the memories, several scars and a tan, I couldn't say that I looked or felt much different. I still saw myself as one of three ordinary blokes, straight off the street, who had decided to have a crack at something unusual.

That said, my perspective on that original self-evaluation *had* changed. In retrospect, I no longer considered myself as having been unqualified for the journey, and that was not because I had quickly mastered survival skills (I hadn't). I knew more about my tolerance for physical and mental strain. I knew, for example, that I had the lungs of a mountain goat. I knew I could absorb body blows in thrashing whitewater. And I knew that if someone pointed a gun at my head, I wouldn't curl up into a ball and start screaming. The realisation hit home that I had *always* been qualified.

And it was this realisation that didn't fade, remaining prominent in my everyday thoughts because it was so different from what I had anticipated. This went hand in hand with the sum of everything I had witnessed, smelt, tasted and touched during those five months. The impression of the Amazon River I now had bore such a vague resemblance to the one I'd taken with me to South America. The scale of that discrepancy, too, stayed fresh as the months went by. It made me sceptical of what I read or heard about other parts of the world that were noted for being wild, untamed. Nothing could substitute for personal field experience. My sense of curiosity became more acute. Nowhere on earth seemed out of reach.

Halfway down the Amazon, we had speculated on the kinds of questions the media (if any of them cared) would ask us on our return. There was one that we had no doubt would be asked: 'Where are you going next?'

We knew 'I don't know' or 'Nowhere' would be unacceptable answers, even though either might well be the truth. In any case, why close the door on opportunity? Indeed, every interviewer did ask the question. And we were ready for it: 'Siberia.'

One Sunday afternoon, about a month after my return to Australia, I had a heavy old atlas in my lap, opened up to the 'Soviet Union'. Unaware (or perhaps acutely aware) of my thoughts, Colin emailed me the very next day.

'Let's do another one,' he wrote.